Evidences for GOD and His Creations: Nature, the Flood, and the Bible

EVIDENCES FOR GOD AND HIS CREATIONS: NATURE, THE FLOOD, AND THE BIBLE

A Summary Apologetics Book Assembling a Puzzle

Dr. T. J. Tofflemire

authorHOUSE®

AuthorHouse™
1663 Liberty Drive
Bloomington, IN 47403
www.authorhouse.com
Phone: 1-800-839-8640

Published by AuthorHouse   08/21/2012 revision

ISBN: 978-1-4634-2701-6 (sc)
ISBN: 978-1-4634-2700-9 (hc)
ISBN: 978-1-4634-2699-6 (e)

Library of Congress Control Number: 2011911033

Contents

Introduction and the Problems

This book provides summary apologetics from many references. Apologetics has to do with defense and proofs of Christianity. 1Pet. 3:15 states "but set apart the Messiah as Lord in your hearts, and always be ready to give a defense to anyone who asks you for a reason for the hope that is in you." Some people ignore apologetics because it seems too abstract, intellectual and rational. Reason is a friend and not an enemy to faith states Kreeft 94(p.20). God loves truth and is truth. Truth is not as important as love, but it is important. There are four **reasons for studying Apologetics: 1. to convince and prepare minds for winning unbelievers, 2. to sow seeds of truth in the culture, 3. to instruct and build up believers in knowing God and 4. To protect the faith of youth who can easily be lost from the church.** Mr. Ham stated that most Christians can't give adequate defense of their faith especially with respect to Bible accuracy and truthfulness(Lisle09, p.8).

A recent Barna survey showed that **only 30% of the 20-29 yr. age group attend church.** Ham09 (p.25) notes in his book *Already Gone*, that 61% of those 20-29 not attending church, attended church as a teen, but then disengaged. **Of that group 91% believes in moral relativism.** One of the reasons they disengaged appears to be due to the atheistic-evolutionary teaching they received in schools and colleges, which challenges their faith in the Bible as truthful. This prompts the apologetics approach to counter the naturalistic evolutionary teachings which contain falsehoods and deceptions which are accepted or not questioned by the common man. New findings of science and clear logic disprove much of the naturalistic evolutionary teachings and relativism, but are not well known. Schools and churches that teach apologetics are **able to reduce this loss of youth from 70% down to about 26%** (web2a). Still many churches favor entertainment, devotions, and activities for youth, with no apologetics(Craig p. 20). The youth are then left with no good arguments to give for their faith. This can allow the world and their worldly argument to beat down and erode their faith. Jude 3 says to contend for the faith while 2Cor. 10:5 tells us to bring down strongholds and everything that exalts itself against the knowledge of God. Titus 1:9 tells us to exhort and convince. The early disciples and Paul used arguments to win belief: Acts 17:2-3,17; 19:8; 28:23-4; 14:15-18. Downs(p.12) noted that some sow seeds and others reap. Apologetics sows seeds in minds, so that one is more open to the gospel. Craig (p12) noted the **primary way we know Christianity is true, is by the self-authenticating witness of God's Holy Spirit(HS).** Thus apologetics prepares the mind, but the HS is the convicting agent, and a personal relationship with Jesus maintains our faith as in 1Pet. 3:15 "but set apart the Messiah as Lord in your hearts." Also Mat. 13 and the parable of the sower relates here, in that weeds can choke out the plant of the spirit.

Recent surveys indicate that 74% of Americans believe we are in a state of moral decline(Web1). In addition **only 34% of American adults believe that moral truths are absolute and only 9% of the adults hold a biblical world view**. For the purposes of the survey, a "biblical worldview" was defined as believing that absolute moral truth exists; the Bible is totally accurate in all of the principles it teaches (Web2). **This shows the high percentage of belief in moral relativism which fits with believing the Bible is not true.** The Bible is the inspired word of God and its historical truth will be shown. Some effective arguments to affirm the truth of the Bible and to counter moral relativism will be presented herein.

A survey of Christian college views and their negative effects was given in the book *Already Compromised* by Ham 2011. Wheaton in *University of Destruction*, 2005 also noted the great testing and loss of student faith in college due the perils of sex, alcohol, and ungodly teachings that lead to rebellion. He tells of how to be an overcomer in the process.

Meister (p.12) stated that we live in an age of social and moral changes. Pluralism is promoted and absolutism rejected. Society is moving towards legalization of gay marriage, and acceptance of abortion. Public schools teach molecules-to-man evolution as truth and reject most prayer. Alternate religions to Christianity are more common and must be openly accepted and accommodated. Islam and new age religions are growing. President Obama is quoted as saying "Given the increasing diversity of the American population, the dangers of sectarianism have never been greater. Whatever we once were we are no longer just a Christian nation: we are also a Jewish nation, a Buddhist nation, a Hindu nation and a nation of nonbelievers."(Web3). Pluralism is taken too far when we can no longer assert what we believe, because it contains exclusive truths. A recent article (Newsweek, April 13, 2009, page 34) indicated **a 10% decline in Christians in America for 1990—2009. At the same time there was a fourfold increase in the number of atheists and agnostics.** There is also a large decline in Christianity in Great Britain and growth in Islam (Ham09 p.10-15). Great Britain represents a large part of our roots and the trend there may repeat in America. Atheism and Agnosticism are widespread in Europe and have become influential in the U. S, particularly in the universities (Craig p.16,78). What is the rub with pluralism of views and relativism then? People are entitled to their views, but all views cannot be simultaneously true. There is the basic law of noncontradiction. All differing views can't be true. Moral relativism can lead to almost no morals and to following whatever the 'in group' thinks is right, as occurred in Nazi Germany. Absolute beliefs and truth are regarded by many as being narrow, arrogant and rigid. As a research scientist, engineer and active Christian, these trends are very troubling to me. My viewpoint is also colored by being an engineer: Often engineers read and study from various scientific disciplines, synthesize knowledge and put it to practical use. This has an advantage to a lay reader of not being too complex to understand, but a weakness of being too brief and not having sufficient depth for specific scientists.

This Book's Scope and General Purpose

The book's purpose is to give an overview of the problems and big picture first, and then provide some summary details and references to allow the interested reader to dig deeper. As a summary book it is written very concisely. At times a sentence or two in this book will be described by 10-50 pages in another author's detailed book. So this book is a summary of the book summaries with some discussion and integration added. Key points are bolded to aid the reader in remembering and noting the main points. The book is also designed to allow the reader to give big picture talks on various topics where there is consensus from the scriptures or from logic. See Appendix 8 and web site: http://creationapologetics.net which has book summaries in keeping with **the summary apologetics theme**. The book summaries are somewhat unique in that a 1100 pg. book is summarized in 18 pgs. It also aids the Christian in having ready apologetic answers to common questions and differing world views. Lastly it is hoped this will strengthen one's faith in the truth of the Bible and God's presence in the world. My faith has been strengthened by the study of apologetics and also by prayer and God's answers to prayers and by putting my faith into action. In talking with friends, their faith was also strengthened by brief study of apologetics and answering questions skeptics might ask. The task was driven by several problems, as noted above: 1. The decline of the % of Christians and Christian beliefs in Bible authenticity. 2. The increase in moral relativism, humanism and the lack of recognition of absolute truths. The book will start with a discussion of what is truth and then proceed to world views which shape our initial thinking. It will then explore philosophy and other related topics in more depth. Web site papers are available on various topics for the interested reader to fill some gaps. In addition some summary talk scripts are available that briefly summarize and condense many pages in various books to one or two pages that are useful for a talk. See Appendix 8 and the web site. Chapter summaries from various books are given when they provide key information. The reader can follow tangents of interest as desired. Geisler(p.20) points out that we need a box top picture to the puzzle of life and its questions. This book attempts to view different parts of the **puzzle** so they fit together. Do you like putting a puzzle together? The table of contents with pg. numbers should help in fitting pieces together. Some open minded weighing of views is needed in assembling the puzzle.

After fitting the puzzle together, it fit best with a Christian conservative view, so this is contrasted with other world views and liberal Christian world views. Almost everyone has a world view or opinion on things. I will be taking the role of **a literature reviewer, providing brief summaries giving the original authors' views.** The book also attempts to be objective and offer logical justifications for the views and truths presented. Where authors' views differ, some brief summary integrations and discussions are provided and I pray for God's help with this. Error is possible on integration of some complex topics. Here the reader should check the original references. As Geisler (p.32) notes, it takes more faith to be an atheist than a theist. This book has noted creations of God in the title, as there is more that one and He is still creating. That is, He still performs miracles and transforms people. After the initial days of creation, and the fall and cursing of the world, there was the world flood, which all Christians do not hold to. Some say the days were periods of longer time or ages. There was the confusion at the tower of Babel and the dispersion of peoples, which all Christians do not hold to. The section on World Views delves into to this further, as there are differing Christian world views also, including young earth and old earth views. We have the birth of Christ and his death on the cross and resurrection. Then we have the God-guided end times or consummation with a new heaven and world. These events are termed the Thelein framework or the 7 C's of creation: Creation, Corruption, Catastrophe, Confusion, Christ, the Cross and Consummation. They constitute a core of Christian history. In addition we have the old and new testaments of the Holy Bible which is termed the special revelation along with Christ's life. Nature is often termed God's general revelation. (see Thelein in the *Theological Dictionary of the New Testament,* and in AIG-web4). **One's view of Bible inerrancy also affects their theology** and world view as will be noted in those sections.

A few introductory references and disciplines will be cited first. It is suggested that one read a basic book on philosophy, if one has not had a course in this. Philosophy deals with how we view truth, reason and morals and can shape our world view. There are book summaries of a number of philosophy books on a web site. It is assumed the reader has some knowledge of basic science disciplines as it is difficult to provide primers on them in this work. Three good references relating to logic and world views are—Lisle, J. *The Ultimate Proof of Creation;* Meister, C. *Building Belief,* and Strobel, L. *The Case for a Creator.* Tofflemire, T. *Defending Biblical Creation by Logic* provides a detailed summary integration of the 3 references. Wikipedia on the internet is a good reference for defining and researching terms, but it has a naturalistic bias. The book *I Don't Have Enough Faith to be an Atheist* by Geisler is also very good. One can grow by integrating references that give differing views. The day age theory with a local flood and progressive creation Christian views have some scientific support but tend to invalidate the Bible and many Old and New Testament verses. Then the question boils down to this: Do you really believe God's word or do you believe Man's word (the majority scientific view, which is for the most part based on naturalism that allows no miracles)? The minority scientific view, which has some very good arguments and logic, is often discounted, and unknown by the common man. Many authors have stated that the Bible was never intended to be a scientific textbook, covering every detail. Some details are not stated but what is stated is true. Our life is a continuing journey of growth in knowing more about God. We should never stop learning, because if we do, we stop growing. You may have heard of the three-legged stool of Christian growth: **Spirituality** which deals with prayer, devotion and worship; **Discovery by study** which is the topic of this book; and **Christian Action.** We need to grow and spend time in all three areas.

A. Truth, World Views, Philosophy and Logic, Apologetics, the Bible, a Historical Jesus, History and Language

What is truth? How would you define it? Is it related to knowledge? The answers have been debated by philosophers for a long time. The most widely favored theory of truth is the correspondence theory which states that **truth corresponds to reality** and the way things are (Kreeft04, Lisle09, Popkin93, Meister, Geisler p37, Web5,6). This was first developed by Plato and refined by Aristotle. A second choice is the coherence theory of truth. This states that ones beliefs must be internally consistent and agree with all facts in a oneness. This has one exception—that fairy tales can be internally consistent and logical but not true(Kreeft94, Lisle09, Meister). Truth is closely related to knowledge and the theory of knowledge (epistemology). Several authors state that knowledge is a subset of truth and belief and is **justified true belief** (Lilse09 p.41,Web5,6). Kreeft94 (p.33) gave a similar classification of possible truths held by **faith**(belief), **reason**, or a **combination of both** where there is **overlap(FR).** See Kreeft94 or the **Appendix 1.** As we will see later **a considerable portion of the Christian faith can be supported by reason** and logic which makes it somewhat unique. Lisle10 stated (p.28) God wants us to use reason and He is the source of the laws of logic. Also Isa. 1:18 states "come let us reason together." Lisle09 (25) stated that we all have presuppositions, like the beliefs in the general validity of our minds to reason and in our memory to operate. Without these how could we know anything? Kreeft94 (p.32) cited Aristotle in the notion that all truths can be understood by reason, discovered by reason or proved by logic. Like Lisle, Kreeft also noted that Pascal held that trusting our reason is an act of faith. In the circles below it appears logically possible to have beliefs that may not be true and truths may exist that we do not know. "Truth is discovered, not invented. It exists independent of anyone's knowledge of it. (Gravity existed prior to Newton)" (Geisler p37). Truth is unchanging and absolute, although our beliefs about it may change. However if one can't give a logical or supporting reason for a truth, it becomes a belief and not knowledge. Cornish(p. 21) noted that ideas and beliefs shape our actions and have consequences. These ideas shape our worldview and philosophy of life(p.75).

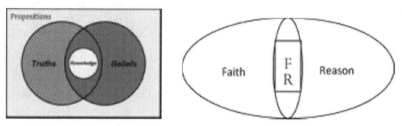

From Wikipedia.org

Plato held that some universal truths are Forms or ideals that are lasting and not dependent on our limited minds (Popkin p.196). Magee (p.15) and Tofflemire09b noted that the **great philosophers who were also mathematicians or had great respect for mathematics, believed in God or abstract universal realities**(Plato, Aristotle, Isaac Newton, Francis Bacon, Descartes, Leibniz, Kant, Frege, Russell, Einstein). Thus the laws of mathematics and of logic are held as universally true by many philosophers. Descartes held that innate ideas are clear and distinct like a specific circle (Popkin p.200). **Other questions:** Are the laws of logic and mathematics true on other planets where there is no human life? Can we trust the scientific laws like gravity, and of physics to be true? An atheistic naturalist might say the laws are just human constructs and are not universal. One could then say there may be differing laws on other planets that came from differing minds. If another galaxy had no minds, would that mean it had no scientific laws? Just because laws have some exceptions to them doesn't make them untrue, they just need conditions and exceptions.

In summary **truth is** best described as a **justified true belief. The law of noncontradiction** is a basic law of logic that says that A can't equal-A or the opposite of A. For example, I can't be eating out in a restaurant and at home not eating at the same time (Burch p.47). In other words the opposite of true is false. Other less justifiable views of truth include pragmatic and relative truth. The pragmatic view is what is true for me, works for me. The relative view could say what is true for you is OK, and what is true for me is OK, even if they differ. This does not fit well with the law of noncontradiction or with the favored correspondence view of truth.(Meister p.28). Examples of some contradictory views follow: One can be saved only by believing in Islam. One can only be saved by believing in Jesus. One can't be saved, but can only transcend by believing in Buddhism. Some versions of Hinduism believe that we have past lives in animals and are evolving and that there is no personal God who created and sustains the universe. Obviously these contradicting views can't all be true. There is also the basic **law of the excluded middle**, which applies in many areas. For example God exists or He does not (Geisler p.62). The law of identity says A=A. Sproul (p.281) states that babies and even dogs recognize these basic laws.

Logic and Arguments

There are two basic kinds of logic: **inductive and deductive**(Lisle09 p.107, Geisler p.62). The inductive method draws a general conclusion from specific observations. The law of gravity is an example: If you drop enough objects that fall, you draw a general conclusion that most or all objects will fall. Induction is used extensively in science (Geisler p.64). Inductive arguments are likely to be true if its premises are true and are thus classified as strong or weak.(Lisle09,p108). For example: I just phoned Dr. Tofflemire and he did not answer. Therefore it is likely he is not at the phone location. This is a moderately strong inductive argument. It could be affected by other facts like, does he often let calls go into recordings and then answer? Deductive arguments follow rules and are classified as valid or invalid if they follows proper rules. An example follows: 1.All mammals have kidneys 2. All dogs are mammals, 3. Therefore all dogs have kidneys. If the premises are true, the conclusion is automatically true. It follows proper rules so it is also valid. If one of the premises is untrue, then the argument will be untrue, but still may follow valid rules. (Lisle09 p.108). Textbooks divide logic into formal and informal logic. Formal logic and deductions can look a lot like algebra. Informal logic is often used by the common man and can have many errors according to accepted classifications. Lisle09(p.109) and Burch(p.6) cover this in detail and more detail is in **appendix 2.** Inductive and deductive arguments can be made about the existence of God. One might ask how this can be, as God can't be observed and is invisible. Gravity is also invisible and can only be indirectly observed by noting effects.

Lisle would add that **one who believes in a view or theory without basic logic or internal consistency is a fool**, and the Bible points this out in Prov. 26:4-5. Prov.1:7 indicated that knowledge begins with respectful submission to the biblical God and that rejection of wisdom and biblical instructions lead to irrationality—to foolishness (p.40). Proverbs 26 also gave instruction on how to answer a fool. This is a two step process of don't answer, and answer in which you reflect back the foolishness of his extended argument. For example consider this argument of a relativist. "I don't believe in absolutes. We can talk about the Bible if you like, but you can't use any absolute statements." We should respond as follows: "I don't accept your claim that there are no absolutes. But for the sake of argument, if there were no absolutes, you couldn't even say that there are no absolutes, since that is an absolute statement. Your standard is self refuting."(p.71-74) Rom. 1: "[20] From the creation of the world His invisible attributes, that is, His eternal power and divine nature, have been clearly seen, being understood through what He has made. As a result, people are without excuse. [21] For though they knew God, they did not glorify Him as God or show gratitude. Instead, their thinking became nonsense, and their senseless minds were darkened. [22] Claiming to be wise, they became fools [23] and exchanged the glory of the immortal God for images resembling mortal man, birds, four-footed animals, and reptiles." Everyone believes in a series of presuppositions which together make up his world view. Belief in the laws of logic and the uniformity of nature are common presuppositions that both creationists and evolutionists believe in. Often the evolutionist is not aware of his presuppositions and the reasoning for them.

A **witnessing dialog** adapted from Evangelism Explosion (EE-Kennedy) and Geisler p.41 is also instructive: "Can I ask you a spiritual question?" Most people are curious enough to say OK. "If you died do you think you would go to Heaven?" "If you were to die today and stand before God, and He was to ask you, Why should I let you into my heaven, what would you say?" The respondent might say I don't believe in God or I am an atheist. Then we could ask are you absolutely sure there is no God? If he says no; Then we would say then you are an agnostic, right? If he says yes, we would point out the two circles argument and that our knowledge is only a very small part of total knowledge.(See Common Arguments p. 36 and Appendix 2). We could also point out the inconsistencies in the atheistic naturalistic arguments. If he acknowledges he is an agnostic, then we can ask if he is an ordinary or ornery agnostic. An ordinary agnostic says he doesn't know anything for sure, while the ornery one says he can't know anything for sure. If we can't know anything for sure, we can point out that it(general skepticism) is self-refuting. Then we can ask if he is willing to look at some evidence to better answer his questions. If he is, we can share more evidence or give him a book to read. We can ask him to read the book of John asking the question—God, if you are real show yourself to me as I read? EE answers could also be used (Kennedy).

Pascal stated (Geisler p 51) "People almost invariably **arrive at their beliefs** not on the basis of proof, but **on the basis of what they find attractive**." Often beliefs come from what society (parents, friends, culture) tells you. They sometimes come from psychological reasons (comfort, pleasure, desires, and needs). Religions and world views can also contribute to our beliefs. However in the final analysis, the best reasons for our basic beliefs can come from logic, reason and philosophy(Geisler p.51-5). Some may say, what difference does all this make? They may be apathetic or uninformed about truth, and morals and religion. However when it comes to money, health, sex and marriage, and general living they take positions. They may believe in relative morals, but don't like to be swindled out of money, or lied to. Choices in life are based on morals with some leading to a fruitful life and others to ruin and unhappiness. Religious views can lead to heaven or to hell. In Hitler's time it was socially acceptable to kill Jews and the mentally ill. In Saudi Arabia, some school children are taught that Jews are pigs and non-Muslims(infidels) should be killed.(Geisler p.68). So our beliefs do make quite a difference in our lives. Sample arguments, errors in reasoning, and the ultimate proof argument are unpacked further in Appendix 2.

Other World Views and Christian Views

Meister (p.39) stated that our world view is a collection of beliefs and ideas about the central issues of life. As we see later it is closely related to philosophy. Lisle09 (p.26) stated "**Our world view is a bit like mental glasses.** It affects the way we view things" For example, when I observe a magician cut a person in half, I conclude it was trick, regardless of what I saw(my actual observations). When your neighbor, tells you he saw a UFO, your world view on this may affect what you conclude. The debate over origins and God ultimately boils down to a debate over competing world views (Lisle09 p.25). It is clear that creationists and evolutionists have different world views, and as a result they interpret the same evidence and facts differently. Any evidence not fitting a world view can always be explained by a **rescuing argument** or device (27-28). For example, secular scientists say diamonds are millions of yrs old. However, radiocarbon dates them as being only a few thousand yrs old. To rescue this discrepancy, secular scientists may then say the many diamonds were contaminated by recent organic deposits, accounting for the misleading young age. Thus, if one is committed to their world view, rather than being open minded, they discard contrary evidence. One should be objective and careful not to discard too much contrary evidence that really tips the balance of the position. We all have limited knowledge and can not fully know the answer to every question. There is a difference in being open minded and opting for no opinion, like the agnostics do. The ordinary agnostic says he doesn't know anything about a certain topic for sure. The ornery agnostic says he can't know anything about a certain topic for sure. He has made a philosophical decision not to know or to take a position. We use only a small part of our total mental capacity and can't know everything. Drawing circles of **all knowledge** (Boa) and **our knowledge** will illustrate this(big vs. tiny circle), and make the belief of no God more difficult to support(see apologetic section). Also note the kinds of proof and knowledge: Historical, philosophical, moral, personal, religious in addition to scientific knowledge. The verdicts of most courts are based on legal historical proof, not just scientific proof.

Scientists say most knowledge is probable and not 100% certain(even the law of gravity). This should stop us from walking off a high building however, as we are quite certain we would fall. We live and act with probable knowledge daily. In addition, our views can be related to the measurement or observation techniques used and what one searches for. An example is the duality of light, between a particle and a wave. Depending on the focus of the measuring technique, one can find one answer or the other, but not both simultaneously (Wikipedia-light). The same is also true of the electron. Satinover states (p.231) "Ever since the scientific revolution, the world has looked more and more like a giant machine—a spiritual wasteland." The Bible code and quantum physics may offer a way out (p.235). William James interweaves the spiritual and scientific. Many forces are deterministic but there is the mysterious aspect of free will. In quantum physics there is an aspect of randomness and of the decision of an experimenter influencing the outcome. There are quanta where a particle jumps from one level to the next and back. This happens in coordinated-opposing ways with groups of particles, and in a probabilistic way for individuals. In the quantum universe, outcomes are emerging from innumerable quantum uncertainties possibly influenced by God by finely tweaking certain parameters for certain outcomes (p.243). As James hinted, this ordered randomness is closer to action by free will, rather than to predetermination. James's description of the mind-world connection was in terms of a "stream of consciousness (psychology)" (web 82). Schaeffer(1979) also discussed world views and determinism.

History is full of scientists that believed in God, had a biblical world view and made great discoveries for science. Examples from Schaeffer(p.131-41) are noted: Galileo, Isaac Newton, Michael Faraday, Robert Boyle, Johannes Kepler, Louis Pasteur, Blaise Pascal, James Maxwell and Francis Bacon(who developed the scientific method). Many of them did their work in a time when the church promoted learning and biblical creation of the world was an acceptable world view. Logic flows naturally from a biblical worldview. We were created by a very intelligent and logical God, and thus could be expected to also have logic and intelligence (Ham2006 p. 206). Alfred Whitehead and Robert Oppenheimer, both non-Christians, stated that modern science was born out of a Christian world view (Schaeffer p.132). Many early universities were founded by the church (Williams 2005 p. 34). Schaeffer noted(p.138) that the universe is orderly with laws coming out of it. **Einstein stated "I cannot believe that God plays dice with the universe"**. Science springs from looking for underlying causes and laws. **It is logical that laws come from a law giver.** What has changed in science then? Schaeffer states that the renaissance scientists believed in an open system universe with God giving the laws. Now the common belief is in a closed system universe with the laws just being. God and man were formerly outside of the uniformity of natural causes and there were miracles. Now the view is that everything is one big cosmic machine, including man(p.142). This was influenced by Darwinism which progressed to social Darwinism and naturalism or humanism(p.150). This trend will be discussed further in the philosophy section and in Schaeffer's book summaries under the theology section.

Lisle09 (p.100) states we should do an internal critique on our world view using the AIP (arbitrariness, inconsistency and preconditions) test. A number of world views and philosophies fail this test and are internally inconsistent, including skepticism, empiricism, naturalism and pantheism. An example follows: All truth is relative. This is an absolute statement and refutes itself. How can one know for sure all truth is relative when the statement refutes itself? Lisle09 (p38). The same applies for the skeptical statement—we can not know anything(so how then can we know this is true?). This will be discussed later in the philosophy section.

Morris89(p.43) notes the **pervading influence of evolution and humanism**. The departments of philosophy and religion in secular universities are humanistic, atheistic or pantheistic. The great universities that started to promote biblical Christianity in their original charters have changed to promote humanism. Christian colleges and seminaries teach theistic evolution and the early chapters of Genesis are treated as allegory and fables(p.44). Some teach the day-age theory or the gap theory. This is largely because they accept macroevolution as a fact from science. An organization called the American Scientific Affiliation (ASA) has been promoting theistic evolution and progressive creation(p.105-6). Humanism is considered a philosophy or a religion that does not include the idea of God(p.45)(Amer. Humin. Assn). Morain is quoted from the Humanists: "Humanism does not include the idea of a God and as such is considered a philosophy rather than a religion. In a way, it is an alternate to all religions . . . a way of life." This is often repeated in humanist literature(p.113). Law has also turned to humanist side as Oliver Wendell Homes and Brennan and others voted to favor an evolved view of the constitution rather than a founding fathers view(p.50). This pervading evolutionary view has affected politics, social life and morals in a negative way. (p.52). **Social Darwinism was promoted as racism, militarism and imperialism**. A subtitle for Darwin's book was "The Preservation of the favored Races in the Struggle for life(p. 60). There is a long list of main line evolutionists who were racists: Osborn, Hooton, Hrdlicka, Huxley, Darwin, and Haeckel; they believed blacks and Australian natives were inferior races. Nietzsche was a follower of Darwin and extended his racial theory to include God is Dead and the promotion of a super race(p.72). Nietzsche's philosophy was followed by Hitler. E. Haeckel also built on

Darwin's theory and influenced Hitler in racism and imperialism(p.73). With Hitler, evolutionary philosophy reached its full power in action. His writing repeated phrases of the theory "He who does not wish to fight in the world where permanent struggle is the law of life, has not the right to exist." Mussolini also repeated such phrases in Fascism(p.79). Dr. Edward Simon, professor of biology at Purdue Univ., an evolutionist, stated "I don't claim that Darwin and his theory brought on the holocaust; but I can't deny that the theory of evolution, and the atheism it engendered, led to the moral climate that made a holocaust possible"(p. 78). The philosophies of socialism and communism are also based on evolution. Marxism in its imperial form, as Russian Communism, was every bit as militaristic, totalitarian, and xenophobic as Hitler with Class substituted for Race. The competing units are social classes. Lenin, Trotsky and Stalin were all atheistic evolutionists. The following is quoted from the communist party journal: "The explanation of the origins of the humankind and of mind by purely natural forces was, and remains, as welcome to Marxists as to any other secularists. S.J. Gould, a Prof. Harvard Univ. and N. Eldredge of the Amer. Museum of Nat. History wrote: "Hegel's dialectical laws, translated into a materialistic context, have become the official state philosophy of many socialist nations. These laws of change are explicitly punctuational, as befits a theory of revolutionary transformation in human society . . . It may also not be irrelevant to our personal preferences that one of us learned his Marxism, literally at his fathers knee." Gould and R. Lewontin both favor Marxism(p.88). So here we have University Professors injecting their religious-political beliefs into science, which is "OK" as long as it is not Christian. Lewontin and Levins have coauthored a **book on Marxist biology**(The Dialectical Biologist). Here the data are selected and interpreted in accord with one's preconceived beliefs(p.89).

Branch (Areopagus Journal 2010) is quoted: "In 1985 Neil Postman wrote a somewhat "prophetic" book, *Amusing Ourselves to Death*. In it he argued that the shift from print media to television affected the entire public discourse with a result that the American mind was made shallower, and that Americans were "on the verge of amusing ourselves to death." "Postman claimed that the **entertainment and marketing model**, where **"image is everything"** had so affected our epistemology (i.e., theory of knowledge) that a cultural shift had taken place—from modernity to postmodernity. Culture is defined by image and emotion rather than deliberative content. Postman recognized that to restrict or ban commercials or emotional images in programs was not possible but that "the solution must be found in how we watch". "Sadly the Christian community, by and large, looks much like the secular society. Surveys often indicate an erosion of a biblical worldview in the Church, and therefore, little difference between those who call themselves Christians and those who do not. Often what is termed "progress" in the culture is a "progression" toward harm or destruction. This is largely due to a decline in the percentage of Christians in the world, a lack of evangelism, and the accommodation of the Church in general to a fallen culture. This "conforming to the world" is in large part due to a lack of worldview teaching, ministry, and discernment in the Church. Christian pollster George Barna released a research report in March of 2009 which focused on "changes in worldview among Christians over the past thirteen years." It may be shocking for you to hear that **only 9% of all American adults believe in a biblical worldview** (inerrancy of Scripture, absolute moral truths exist, salvation comes only through faith in Christ, Jesus was sinless, etc.). A 2005 Barna study demonstrated that only 16% of Americans claim to make moral decisions based on the content of the Bible. Another study revealed that only one-half of Protestant pastors have a Biblical worldview. This is because of the liberalism which permeates many churches in the U.S."

Meister (p.48) compared **three world views** (Theism, Atheism and Pantheism) relative to five categories of items including acquiring knowledge. Theism believes that knowledge is derived primarily through the senses; But God can also inform us in other non-empirical ways. Atheism holds that knowledge is acquired only through the senses. Taoism, Buddhism and the New Age Movement have some association with Pantheism. Pantheism believes that true knowledge is acquired through meditation and empirical knowledge can be illusionary. Theism maintains morals are grounded in God and are objective and absolute. Atheism holds morals are human constructs emerging through societal agreement, and thus relative. This is a major problem for atheism, as it provides no true morals, or reason for living. Pantheism believes that morals are illusionary. Meister reasons that each of these world views differs in the five categories of beliefs and therefore all three world views cannot be true. After comparing the three world views on the basis of logic, Meister (p.65) found that **only Theism is logically consistent**. Lisle09 (p.45-66) agreed and provides some detailed logical arguments. Geisler (p.198) noted that only theism fits the cosmological, teleological and moral arguments: This rules out non—theistic religions including pantheism and polytheism. He also noted that theism does allow angels and demons, but they are created by God and under his control as limited finite beings. Non-theistic world views will be discussed again under the section on philosophy. Sire2004 also provided and excellent comparison of world views and held that Christianity is most consistent and logical.

Scott (p.64) compares six differing Christian views on creation including New Earth Creation and Old Earth Creation theories including the Gap Theory, the Day Age Theory, Progressive Creation and Theistic Evolution. The views differ widely and cannot all be true due to the law of non-contradiction. An additional theological view is the **Framework Hypothesis**(FM). J. Morris07 states (p.9) that in the FM view, only things in the Genesis account in the Bible relating to theology are assumed correct and statements relating to history and science not correct. J. Morris07 (p.26-32) and Tofflemire(2008c) discussed the history of these views and their weaknesses. New Earth Creation has the longest history and most internal biblical support. The Old Earth Creation theories are more recent and some compromise the validity of the Old and New Testament verses in the Bible which state the sins of Adam and Eve were the start of all sin, and of death and disease, and of the curse God placed on the earth. Some theologians stated that the later creation theories are an attempt to compromise the Bible to fit science. AIG (Ham06 p.94) has argued that the six days of creation in Gen.1 used an ordinal number and the words evening and morning, with the word day to emphasize the 24 hr day. The word day is accompanied by a singular ordinal number 359 times in the Bible and it always means a 24 hr. day. The day is accompanied by the phrases evening and morning 38 times and it always means a 24 hr day. Exodus 20:9-11 also states "for in six days the Lord made the heavens and the earth and sea and all that is in them, and rested on the seventh day." **This was written by God's own finger** (Ham p.27).

Presbyterian Church of America (PCA-web7) issued a large report on creation views in 1990 from which quotes are taken: "We believe that the Scriptures, and hence Genesis 1-3, are the inerrant word of God. We affirm that Genesis 1-3 is a coherent account from the hand of Moses. We believe that *history*, not *myth*, is the proper category for describing these chapters; and furthermore that their history is true. In these chapters we find the record of God's creation of the heavens and the earth *ex nihilo*; of the special creation of Adam and Eve as actual human beings, the parents of all humanity (hence they are not the products of evolution from lower forms of life). We further find the account of an historical fall that brought all humanity into an estate of sin and misery, and of God's sure promise of a Redeemer. Because the Bible is the word of the Creator and Governor of all there Is, It is right for us to find it speaking authoritatively to matters studied by historical and scientific research. We also believe that acceptance of, say, non-geocentric astronomy is consistent with full submission to Biblical authority. We recognize that a naturalistic worldview and true Christian faith are impossible to reconcile, and gladly take our stand with Biblical supernaturalism." "*A theology wed to the science of one age is a widow in the next.*"

"First, the *four most prominent views* of the creation days in the PCA are (in no particular order) the **24-hour view, the Day-Age view, the Framework view and the Analogical Day view**. The Framework view was not widely held at the founding of the PCA, although it does not seem to have become controversial until recently. The Analogical Day view in its most recent expression was not circulated broadly until the 1990s. Fourth, there is a conviction among many that Christians are engaged in "culture wars" for the very survival of the Christian heritage and worldview. Reformed Christians rightly agree that the doctrine of creation lies at the basis of the Christian worldview." In summary, the PCA accepts these four views, although the 6-24 hr day is favored by some. This report is unique in that it gives somewhat unbiased descriptions of the many different creation views and lists the pros and cons of each. The theistic evolution and progressive creation views were not favored by the PCA. **A cited weakness of the Day-Age view is that it would be hard for plants to exist for thousand of yrs. after the day 3 creation, without the sun on Day 4 or the pollinating insects and birds on days 5 and 6.** Arguments against the framework view and others are found in the AIG papers (web 52).

Ross04 noted(p.51-7) most of the early creeds do not state 6 days of creation, with the exception of the Westminster Confession. Several creeds note the creation of man and woman in God's image. Modern statement of faith by the PCA and by the Westminster Seminary allows various views including the day age theory. Ross Chap 22 gave details on the church councils.

St. Augustine believed in instantaneous creation but he did not have the benefit of **Galileo's views**1610-30(Web10): "After 1610, when he(Galileo) began publicly supporting the heliocentric view, which placed the Sun at the center of the universe, he met with bitter opposition from some philosophers and clerics. He was tried and forced to recant in 1632 by Catholic Church." J. Calvin died in 1564 and Luther in 1546. They and all the theologians before them including, Augustine and Origen may have believed in the geocentric view with the earth being the center of the universe. They also may have not been aware of the earth's once per day rotation. The AIG view is that all that was needed was for God to provide his continuous light in the vicinity of the sun and also set the earth in rotation, as His spirit was hovering over the earth on day 1. This would have produced 24 hr days with light and darkness, as it is the earth's rotation that causes this. This avoids the more tenuous idea of God putting forth and withdrawing his light as in the PCA write-up. If Augustine had known this he may not have been so strong in favoring the instantaneous creation view. His main stated problem was the Sun not being created until day 4. Ross04(p.42-49) noted that a number of early church leaders did not firmly hold the 6-24 hr—day view of creation. Most of the early creeds do not state 6 days of creation, with the exception of the Westminster Confession. Several creeds note the creation of man and woman in God's image(p.51-7)

Mortenson noted the following in Chap 14 of his book *Coming to Grips With Genesis*, "**Luther, Calvin and Wesley** on the Genesis of Natural Evil." by T. Ury: **The 3 founders above held Genesis 1-11 as real history and the flood as global and catastrophic(p.401).** Wesley wrote about the 6 day creation, and also affirmed the flood as 1656 yrs. from the creation. Also Anglican bishop Hugh Latimer held this view. This was based on careful exegesis of the scriptures. Hall claimed in Chap. 2 of Mortenson (D. Hall p.53) that the reformation church fathers held to a 6 day creation. Also Thomas Horn, an Anglican, did a lengthy three volumes titled "Introduction to the critical Study of the Holy Scriptures" in 1818. A condensed version published in 1827 that was widely used in seminaries and also held this view. It was only after the scientific opinion shifted in the late 19th century, that other long age positions developed to accommodate a scientific view. Hall's write up covers 25 pages and 116 references in tracing the history of creation from Luther to Lyell. Dr. Morris(2007 p.26-32) notes that most of the **other theological views of creation with long ages** became popular after the theories of uniformitarianism and evolution became dominant; they **are an attempt to make the Bible fit science**. Snelling(p.186,479), in the section on geology, traces the history of these theories and how Lyell had a prior agenda to be rid of biblical geology and flood catastrophes. Lyell issued a false report on the erosion rate of Niagara Falls, which when corrected, fits better with biblical timelines (web 58).

What view should one hold then when arguing for the historical truth of the Bible, and trying to counter the complete naturalistic and evolutionary philosophy which is so common in high schools and colleges? Historical occurrences of importance include the creation of all life and man, the fall, the global flood, and the dispersion of the peoples and languages at the tower at Babylon. **If one treats these as myths, fables** and allegory, **much of the history and some of the reasons to believe the Bible is true, are lost**. Some apologists suggest that to argue for only the 6-24hr day is too difficult in the college setting, because of the strong biases against this view from accepted science. It is agreed that there are strong biases against this view. There are many differing views of creation by theologians, and it is difficult to be very certain that the 24 hr day view is correct. One can and should make many apologetic arguments without reference to the days. However this 6-24hr day view appears most supported by exegesis of the scriptures and fits with the consistency of supporting Bible as true throughout. Some recent discoveries of creation scientists also support the view, although they are in the minority. If one accepts theistic evolution, this fits with the big bang theory, the evolution of all life from one cell, and the changing of chimp into man. Some say God started this all rolling or had his hand in it. However, this is so close to complete naturalistic evolution, that it is a small step to just take God out of it or suggest Deism where God is not personal or involved. The next step some liberal theologians take is to rule out all miracles, as they do not fit with popular science. An example of this is the **Jesus Seminar** (Web8) where 150 scholars and theologians did a study and report on Jesus' history and ruled out all miracles including the virgin birth and Christ's resurrection. "**A theology wed to the science of one age is a widow in the next**"(**PCA**). Many authors have stated that the Bible was never intended to be a scientific textbook, covering every detail. Many details are not stated and there are mysteries to be studied. John 21:25 notes "there are also many other things which Jesus did, the which if they should be written every one, I suppose that even the world itself would not contain the books that should be written."

An example of liberal theology not far from the Jesus Seminar above is taken from Wikipedia(web 44). **"Liberal Christianity**, sometimes called **liberal theology**, is an umbrella term covering diverse, philosophically informed religious movements and ideas within Christianity from the late 18th century and onwards. The word "liberal" in liberal Christianity does not refer to a progressive political agenda or set of beliefs, but rather to the manner of thought and belief associated with the philosophical and religious paradigms developed during the Age of Enlightenment. The theology of liberal Christianity was prominent in the biblical criticism of the 19th and 20th centuries. The style of scriptural hermeneutics within liberal theology is often characterized as non-propositional. This means that the Bible is not considered a collection of factual statements but instead documents the human authors' beliefs and feelings about God *at the time of its writing.*" "Thus, liberal Christian theologians do not claim to discover truth propositions but rather create religious models and concepts that reflect the class, gender, social, and political contexts from which they emerge. Liberal Christianity looks upon the Bible as a collection of narratives that explain, epitomize, or symbolize the essence and significance of Christian understanding." BioLogos (web 46) teaches progressive creation. The Discovery Institute (web 47) favors intelligent design. Also see the ASA (web 48). These sites favor liberal views and that scripture has errors.

Mayhue, R.(Chap. 4 of Mortenson) argues against adding a new book or view to the Bible based on science. Ross, Hugh *The Fingerprints of God*, Promise Publ. 1989, described an old age creation of 16 billion yrs. H. Ross in *Creation and Time*, Nav. Press 1994, p.56 stated "The facts of nature may be likened to a 67th book of the Bible." Do we really need to revise how we interpret the Bible due to the recent findings of science? Mayhue refutes Ross and asserts the truthfulness of the Bible. He cites an International Council on Bible Inerrancy (ICBI-web9), 1986, which included 300 biblical scholars and affirms his position in their concluding documents(p.122-4). Statham (web66) agrees that **general revelation should not take priority equal to or greater than special revelation** and be a 67th book of the Bible. Also see the Bible Authenticity section.

To give alternate views on scriptural interpretation **Ross's views** from *Creation and Time* are given below. This contrasts with the AIG view on pg 15. A number of early Christians did not hold to literal 24 hr. days of creation: (Ross p.17-20) Irenaeus, Hippolytus, Clement of Alexandria,

Origen, and Augustine. The first two held a day is a 1000 yrs. All had a problem with the sun not being created until day 4. He cites one example where an ordinal number is used for longer time periods than 24 hr days: Hosea 6:2; The 7th day in Gen. 2:1-3 has a different format than the days 1-6, as evening and morning is omitted. Citing Ps. 95 and Heb. 4 this implies the 7th days is ongoing(p.49). For Gen. 2:23 he notes Adam says on seeing Eve "at last or at length". He says this implies a length of time. For Gen 2:4 "These are the generations of the heavens and of the earth when they were created, in the day that Jehovah God made earth and heaven." He notes 'generations' is used with 'day' and it implies a longer period than a day. Some Bible translations don't use the word day here however. Some Bible passages imply an old earth: Ps. 90:2-6, Prov. 8:22-31, Ecc. 1:3-11, Micah 6:2, Hab. 3:6 and 2 Peter 3:5.

Ross also noted the following: **1.** Death through sin is not equivalent to physical death(p. 60). In Rom. 5:12 he claims the death referred to is spiritual death, and that Christ brings spiritual life. He suggests the verse is referring to soulish life of birds and mammals. 1Corin. 15:12-23 As in Adam all die, in Christ all shall be made alive. Some plants and animals have short life cycles and could have died in a one day or brief time period before Adam's sin. **2.** Bloodshed before Adam's sin does not alter the doctrine of atonement. Heb. 9:22: Not all animal's death is for atonement, only those sacrificed. Heb.10:1-4 indicated that animal sacrifice will not take away sin, but is a sign of things to come—Christ's sacrifice. **3.** Rom. 8:20-22: Some Bible versions say "bondage to **decay**" and some say to corruption. Ross reasons that decay must have occurred before Adam's sin. Food digestion requires decay or breakdown for useful energy. The decay statement addresses when decay will stop and not when it began (p.66). The process of energy usage and decay occurred after the days of creation, when the laws of physics were established. **4.** God's rest from creating will someday end and he will create the new heavens and new earth with new laws. Gravity would not allow a 1500 mile cube to stand as in Rev. 21. Ross also encourages open exchange of ideas and not accusing Christians believing in old earth creation as being unchristian. **See Appendix 5** for more of Ross's views from his book *The Genesis Question*.

An opposing view on this is given by Ham2010: Ham said that Rom. 5:6-11 also implies physical death, since Christ physically died for us and we will return to dust as in Gen. 3:17-19. We will also get new bodies in heaven. Man and animals were vegetarian before sin, and man was to be vegetarian until after the flood; Gen 1:29-30. God also declared everything very good. A problem is then animals eating other animals, and having cancer and tumors before sin, for millions of yrs. In Rom. 8:20-22 it is stated that all creation groans under sin. Acts 3:21 mentions that all things will be restored in heaven. It thus makes sense that the creation was good, then decayed under sin and then is restored in the new heavens and earth. Plant death and use as food is allowed as in Gen. 1:29-30. The Hebrew word for life here is **Nephesh which includes soul creatures** and some mammals and birds.

The Biblical Conservative Christian Young Earth World View

This view is favored by Answers in Genesis(AIG), Institute for Creation Research(ICR), and Creation Ministries International(CMI). AIG is one of the biggest apologetics organizations and ICR one of the oldest. However not all apologetic organizations favor this view(like the Apologetics Research Center and Reasons to Believe "RTB" and BioLogos) (Web 17,41,50). Some favor an old earth view with a local flood. See the previous discussion on the PCA beliefs under World Views. RTB view of progressive creation with ages has some scientific literature and support (web 41). The Gap theory would harmonize with cosmological portion, as it would allow billions of yrs. for formation of heavens(the universe) and earth. However, once the flood is reduced to a local flood and much death of animals with fossils is allowed before Adam, more scriptural twisting and invalidation occurs. There are many biblical indications that the flood was global (see section on geology and the flood). There are some indications Adam's sin and the fall was the start of death and disease (the animals were also cursed as in Gen 3:14). If there was much disease and cancer in animals before the fall, how could the creation be declared very good? Also if the history of man is described as 100,000 yrs, the genealogies of the Bible are invalidated. BioLogos believes Adam and Eve were one of many Neolithic couples, one of which God put his spirit in. This invalidates Paul's view of Adam and Eve as the start of the human race. Much of scripture is invalidated by this procedure. Kenton Sparks, for example, writing for BioLogos, suggests that any rendering of the Bible as inerrant makes the acceptance of theistic evolution impossible. He suggests that the Bible indeed should be recognized as containing historical, theological, and moral error (Web 51). **Once one invalidates much of the Bible on a pick and chose basis, it becomes difficult to argue the Bible is true and should be followed**.

The young earth view of AIG is based on the Bible and God as the ultimate standard (Lisle09 p.32). Morris2009 gives summary arguments for this view. There can be secondary standards like observation and science that add to truth. Wisdom starts from the Lord as in Jam. 1:5 "If any of you lacks wisdom, he should ask God"; Prov. 9:10 "The fear of the Lord is the beginning of wisdom, and knowledge of the Holy One is understanding." Lisle(p.146) pointed out that this world view is rational and internally consistent and is one of the few world views that is logically consistent. "As such the creationist believes that an all powerful (Matt. 19:29), all knowing (Col. 2:3) God created the universe in six ordinary days (Exod. 20:11) thousands of years ago (based on genealogies such as Gen. 5:4-32)". "Today God upholds the universe by his sustaining power (Heb.1:3) in a logical and consistent way that we call the laws of nature or the laws of science (Jer. 33:25)". "The world was a paradise when it was first created (Gen. 1:31). The first Man (Adam was given charge over all creation (Gen. 128, 2:15)" (32). "God had created the original animals and plants after their kind (Gen.1:11, 21,25), indicating that there are discrete barriers between basic animal and plant kinds," but that there can be variation within kinds. Natural selection happens and animals and plants can adapt to their environment. However, the processes involved never substantially increased the information in the DNA (p.33). Adam rebelled against God (Gen 1:16, 3:6). As a result God cursed the creation (Gen. 3:14-19) which is why we now see death and suffering and thorns and thistles in the world (Gen. 3:17-19, Rom. 5:12, 8:21-22). All humans are descended from Adam and Eve and have some nature to seek and be close to God (Acts 26-27), but also have a sin nature and tendency to rebel against God. For all have sinned and fallen short of the glory of God (Rom. 3:23). The wages of Sin is death(Rom. 6:23). This is why Christ became a man (John 1:1,14) and died on the cross for us if we believe in Him (32). God once flooded the entire earth in response to man's wickedness (Gen. 5:7-17) but sparred a few people and animals on the Ark (Gen. 5:9,18; 6:19). Creationists believe that most of the fossils found on the earth today are a result of the global flood. (p33) A more rigorous discussion of the truth of the Bible will be given in a later section. To maintain consistency, how can the first book of the Bible be invalid and full of myths while the rest of it is true? Theology provides another part of the Christian worldview as in the Apostles Creed as taken from the book of common worship as follows: **Some** of this is **based on faith** and not on reason and on the belief the Bible is true.(Web 11). The creation is logically supported, while Jesus' death and resurrection is historically supported.

> I believe in God, the Father almighty, creator of heaven and earth.
> I believe in Jesus Christ, his only Son, our Lord, who was conceived by the Holy Spirit, born of the Virgin Mary, suffered under Pontius Pilate, was crucified, died, and was buried;
> He descended into hell. On the third day He rose again;
> He ascended into heaven; He is seated at the right hand of the Father, and He will come to judge the living and the dead.
> I believe in the Holy Spirit, the holy catholic Church, the communion of saints, the forgiveness of sins, the resurrection of the body, and the life everlasting.

The Evolution World View

The evolution world view generally includes the following: They reject the account of Genesis. Their ultimate standard is either **naturalism** (the belief that nature is all that there is) or **empiricism** (the idea that all knowledge is gained from observation). As a result evolutionists believe the universe is billions of years old and it originated from the big bang. This was a rapid expansion of space and energy from a point. The energy cooled and became matter, some of which condensed into stars and galaxies Lisle09(p.33). The stars made heavier elements, some of which condensed to become planets. Our solar system in particular, was formed 4.5 billion years ago from a collapsing gas cloud. On earth certain chemicals came together to form the first self-replicating cell. This cell reproduced others like it, but occasionally a mutation produced a variation. A few mutations benefited the organism and were passed on to the offspring resulting in more complex organisms over time. In this way all life evolved. Evolutionists believe that there was no global flood. Rather, the fossils were laid down over hundreds of millions of years of gradual processes. This is the process of uniformitarianism, that present rates and processes are representative of the past (p.34). The PCA reports cites two types of uniformitarianism: "Substantive uniformitarianism: the view that, over the course of the earth's history, the intensities and rates of the geological processes have remained the same. This position, associated with Charles Lyell's 1830 *Principles of Geology*, is not widely held by modern geologists. Methodological uniformitarianism: the view that, though the processes have always been the same, nevertheless their rates and intensities may have varied over the earth's history (and therefore the earth's history may in fact include catastrophic upheavals)."

The following questions are raised about **naturalism**: If atoms, matter and energy is all there is, how can we have the universal laws of mathematics and logic? How can we know that the laws of nature and physics will be the same tomorrow as today? Aren't matter, energy and atoms always changing and in flux? Do you assume our mental reasoning and memory is reliable? Why would that be true if our minds are random movements of molecules and charges? Why should there be any order in the universe? Why should there be any moral standards if we evolved from chimps? Lisle09(p.69) points out these are good arguments against naturalism who often argue from inconsistent positions. Lisle09(p.142) noted the importance of an **ultimate standard**. We all have presuppositions like the laws of logic, being consistent and non-arbitrary, rational, truthful and relying on our memory. These are descriptions of God in the Bible and we are to imitate Him (Eph. 5:1). We can't get started with any learning or argument without them. For any belief, a person can always ask "How do you know that is true?" This will form a long chain (p,q,r,s,t) until it gets to the ultimate standard. If a chain goes on for ever, it cannot be completed. An incomplete argument does not prove anything. If t is the ultimate standard it cannot refer back to r, and if t is false it calls into question p,q,r, s. However, **in relation to the ultimate standard some circular** and self-attesting **reasoning is necessary**. A way to show that a particular presupposition must be true is to show that even to argue against it one would have to use its component presuppositions to argue against it. This would be true for the laws of logic. This is also true for God and His book the Bible. Arguments from creation scientists are also useful to shoot holes in macroevolution and uniformitarianism on an academic or truth basis. This goes back to one's view of truth. **Is God or man the initial source of all wisdom?**

Introduction to Philosophy

Some terms were used common to philosophy (naturalism and empiricism) in the above paragraph, so it is time to discuss this subject more. **Philosophy** is defined from the Greek **as the love of wisdom**. It also provides a long ranged detached view, an analytical and rational world view(Popkin p. x). Magee(p.5-6) noted that in an attempt to be rational and nonbiased, philosophers attempt to exclude religion. However this attempt is not easy or complete as many philosophers were Christian and there are some strong arguments from philosophy for God and for an ultimate source of wisdom, morals, being and universally true principles (like the laws of logic and mathematics). Wikipedia notes "Philosophy is the study of general and fundamental problems concerning matters such as existence, knowledge, truth, beauty, law, justice, validity, mind, and language." Philosophy has a number of divisions like epistemology (the study of knowledge), metaphysics (including cosmology and ontology) where ontology is the study of being. Ethics and morality is also a branch of philosophy, as is logic and philosophy of religion.

Philosophers thus raise some of life's ultimate questions, and try to explain them with a rational framework. Most philosophers had great minds and were notable scholars in a number of disciplines. **A brief introduction to major philosophers** will be provided. Socrates' student Plato had many writings and is regarded by some, as the greatest philosopher of all time(Magee p.24). Plato also had a high regard for mathematics. "**The whole cosmos seems to exemplify order, harmony, proportion**—the whole of Physics can be described by mathematical equations" **Everything in this world of ours he regarded as being an ephemeral, decaying copy of something whose Ideal Form has permanent and indestructible existence outside space and time.**"(Magee p.27). His famous work, *Republic* describes the nature of justice and ideal government, while *Symposium* describes the nature of love. "These physical bodies of ours come into existence and pass away, always imperfect. But they are the merest and most fleeting glimpses of something that is also us and is non-material, timeless, and indestructible, something that we may refer to as the soul. These souls are our permanent forms and constitute ultimate reality" (Magee 29). **Plato, Socrates, and Aristotle** were all non-Christian yet **recognized some eternal principles**. Socrates offended the government and was sentenced to death. A later student of Plato was Plotinus who taught that since ultimate reality was Plato's Ideal Forms, what exists is ultimately mental. There he believed three levels of forms: The lowest is the human soul, the next level is the Ideal Forms, and the highest level is the good. Reflective human beings are engaged in an attempted ascent towards oneness with the good. "Christians translated this into their doctrines that the world has been created in the mind of God, and human beings are aspiring to oneness with God, who is perfect goodness."(p.29). Plato's gifted student was Aristotle; however he disagreed with Plato on the importance of abstract Ideal Forms. We need concrete objects and observations based on our existence to conclude things and he argues for materialism as being important (p.32-34). He developed the words for logic, physics, political science, metaphysics, meteorology, rhetoric, and ethics. He developed the laws of logic(p.34). Things can be identified by their apparent form and shape and by their purpose or what they do(Magee p.35).

You can see the importance of philosophy to life's eternal questions and to religion. Several papers give brief summaries of books of philosophy (Tofflemire09b,10). Some relevant items taken from philosophy books follow: **Descartes** (p.87) said I know myself to be a very imperfect being, perishable and finite, and yet I have in my mind the concept of an infinite being, eternal and immortal, perfect in every way, therefore this perfect being must exist and has implanted this awareness in me. **Rationalism** argues that self-evident propositions are deduced by reason and are the basis of knowledge. **Empiricism** argues that knowledge must be derived from the senses. However mathematics and the laws of logic are not of the senses. Descartes viewed the world as having two kinds of substances: mind and matter, the Cartesian dualism (Magee p.88). Two of his writings included *Discourse on Method* and *Meditations*. **Descartes famous quote is** "I think, therefore I am" "I am, I exist." In order to think about life's questions, I must exist(Popkin p.98). These are profound statements about **being and ontology. Innate** ideas are clear and distinct like a specific circle. Mathematical ideas are innate as is God and are implanted in us by God. The idea of a substance that is infinite, eternal, immutable, independent, all-knowing, all-powerful must be God, and he implanted that idea in me.(Popkin p 201) "The belief in an external world is a natural one, God would be deceiving us unless it were true. Since God cannot be a deceiver, there must be an external world" (Popkin p.202). Descartes was a Christian and some of his views were noted above. Pascal followed him.

Spinoza studied Descartes and was **a rationalist**, but rejected Cartesian dualism and asserted mind and matter are one under God and in humans. If God is infinite and everywhere then he must be in everything. One set of categories is abstract and mental and another material, but they encompass the same reality (Magee p.92-3). He wrote some biblical analyses and criticisms and *The Theological-Political Treatise*, and *Ethic*s. He started **Pantheism** and believed that all is God and He encompasses the universe. Some pantheists are mystical but he was not. He also argued that we are not completely free agents, as we are not aware of everything that conditions and motivates us. He was a Jew and **deist**. See p. 55, Other Religions.

Rationalist philosophy is criticized by the skeptics, empiricists: They say there is no absolutely certain knowledge. Popkin(p.205) questions whether we need absolutely certain knowledge. "All we seem to posses and employ is probable knowledge. If there really is certain knowledge, it does not appear to be required for the ordinary purpose of life"

Empiricists: John Locke, David Hume held that all knowledge is based on sense experience, observation, and mental organization of these. Our mind when born is like a blank paper(p.207). He denies **innate** ideas. Primary observation leads to secondary ideas, to demonstration and to organizing and testing ideas. "We really cannot know anything about what goes on outside of the ideas in our minds." "What we call knowledge is just one man's opinion" (Popkin p.212). Criticism: If all ideas are opinions in our mind, how can we tell which to take seriously, which to use as a basis for knowledge of our world? Which are imaginations or very personal opinions? **Berkeley's response:** The skeptic philosophy above leads to paradoxes and doubts, which leads to general skepticism (p.217). Then the so called wise philosophers deny the most basic things that ordinary people believe, they too become unbelievable. Do matter and energy really exist or are they only in our mind? The skeptics would question this (sensible things cannot exist other that in the mind). Berkeley argued that matter can crush us and heat can burn us. If we do not rely on our perceptions of these, we could die. Common sense would say that if I look at and touch a nearby tree that it does exist. **Berkley then states "The existence of things consists of their being perceived"** One way of accounting for how they(matter and energy) exist is to say **they exist**

in the mind of God and, whether one is there or not to observe them, they still exist. Berkeley gave the **theory of Immaterialism**: "All that we can perceive is an idea. Ideas belong only to the mind of the observer." Does that mean that matter and energy do not exist if I am not there to perceive them? "Therefore there must be some universal mind or God in whose mind these things are perceived" Most people do believe that the material things they perceive in front of them are real and this does not lead to any paradoxes (p.220). So Berkeley states it is logical to distinguish between things and ideas. Popkin noted (p.224) that even if impressions we get from our senses are uncertain and subject to psychology, it is the best information we have and what we act on. The theories of knowledge by the rationalists or by the skeptical empiricists do not appear completely consistent and satisfactory and are still being developed (Popkin p 235). Lock and Hume were atheistic, while Berkeley was a Christian who was also an empiricist and believed in God with and infinite mind who could communicate experiences to us. The city of Berkeley, Ca. is named for him (Magee p.111). He argued against abstract ideas, yet for spiritual substance. Hume was an empiricist and skeptic and questioned if we could know anything.

Kant stated that we gain knowledge through experience and understanding. He added our brains and nervous system to the five senses as way of comprehending things. He wrote *Critique of Pure Reason*. He argued that two types of things exist; those that we can sense and those that we cannot sense. Our appreciation of an entity is limited to what we can sense of it. Some things we have limited ability to sense like a rainbow. This noumenal world is transcendental because it cannot be registered in experience. We cannot conceive of anything as existing without it being something and having an identity (Magee p.132-3). Material objects exist only in a space-time framework. He argued that in addition to the world of material objects there is another level of reality that is outside of space and time, but human beings can experience only a small portion of it. God and a soul are part of this world. "It is thoroughly necessary to be convinced of God's existence, it is not quite so necessary that one should demonstrate it"(p.135). Humans are also material objects which obey physical laws, but go beyond this in having free will which cannot be predicted. He maintained morality was a possibility for rational creatures only, not for most animals. He stated that there are universal laws for the empirical world, so there must be universal laws for the human and moral world also. Here God provides an answer but not a proof. Schopenhauer extended Kant's theories and the differentiation of the phenomenal (objective) world and the noumenal world. He described the noumenal as will, and compassion as the foundation of ethics and love. Geisler (p.60) criticized Kant's view of the real world of objects being distorted and somewhat untrue. Rather real objects exist, but our view can be distorted. In other words, your mind doesn't mold the tree, the tree exists and molds your mind.

Frege showed that both mathematics and basic logic were related and true beyond the human mind; this is shown forth in a new theory of calculus called the *Concept Script*. (Magee195). A quote is taken from the Stanford Encyclopedia of Psychology-SEP (Web12) on Frege. "Friedrich L. G. Frege (b. 1848, d. 1925) was a German mathematician, logician, and philosopher who worked at the University of Jena. Frege essentially reconceived the discipline of logic by constructing a formal system which, in effect, constituted the first 'predicate calculus'. In this formal system, Frege developed an analysis of quantified statements and formalized the notion of a 'proof' in terms that are still accepted today. Frege then demonstrated that one could use his system to resolve theoretical mathematical statements in terms of simpler logical and mathematical notions. One of the axioms that Frege later added to his system, in the attempt to derive significant **parts of mathematics from logic**, proved to be inconsistent. **Nevertheless, his definitions** (of the predecessor relation and of the concept of natural number) and methods (for deriving the axioms of number theory) **constituted a significant advance**. To ground his views about the relationship of logic and mathematics, Frege conceived a comprehensive philosophy of language that many philosophers still find insightful."

Russell continued the mathematical view after Ferge, and turned his analysis to language. He independently confirmed that mathematics and logic are closely related in his book the *Principles of Mathematics*. This has been regarded by some as the greatest contribution to logic since Aristotle (Magee p.197). He then launched analytic philosophy which made close analysis of all propositions and terms. This developed into **logical positivism** that asks the question "What should we have to do to establish the truth or falsehood of this statement?" They noted that statements that purport to be about reality, but whose truth or falsehood makes no substantial sense or difference. An example of this is the gasoline advertisement statement—"Put a tiger in your tank"—which is not to be taken literally. Russell stated "The sense of reality is vital in logic."(p.201-2) Whitehead was a coauthor of *Principles of Mathematics* and went on to formulate Process Philosophy and Theology.

Kierkegaard developed the philosophy of **existentialism** and that the individual hopes to uncover meaning in life through investigating the mystery of his own existence. "Life can only be understood backwards, but it must be lived forwards"(Magee p.208). "It is the individual himself that is the supreme moral entity; therefore it is the personal subjective aspects of human life that are the most important." It is through decision making that we create our lives and become ourselves. Our existence from the beginning is a shared social one. He believed in Christianity and the relationship of the individual soul to God. Others like Barth, Tillich and Bultmann developed this theme. Barth developed the Barmen Declaration which became the doctrinal basis of the anti-Nazi confessing church. Other existentialists like Heidegger have split off without God. He developed the great work *Being and Time* which points out our existence is in time and in the world environment that we relate to. Our being and experience relate to the world and to our history (time). We long for our lives to have some meaning or basis in reality; yet if we have no assurance of meaning, our lives are ultimately meaningless and absurd. It becomes difficult to find meaning without God. Schaeffer (p.166) noted how existentialism separates reason from spirituality in God and puts this in the area of non-reason. See the Theology Section. The drug culture expanded on this escape to non-reason. Husserl developed the philosophy of Phenomenology that concentrates on what is consciously experienced. Gestalt (212) psychology takes off on this principle and understanding the whole of our experiences. Bergson states we have persistent drive or life force to experience and grow. He also maintained that we have **intuition** that provides an additional source of knowledge. Our life develops a flow like a river with choices. He was an evolutionist and his critics agree that we have the above characteristics, but there is no good logical argument that they come from evolution (Magee p214-217).

Magee stated that Einstein's theories disproved Newton's and caused a revolution in science. His view is that scientific theories are only true for a while until a better theory comes along (p.225). Einstein did state "Only daring speculation can lead us further and not accumulation of facts"(p.221). Others do not agree with this view of Einstein disproving

Newton. "**Einstein did not disprove Newton**. The Newtonian equations are still embodied in Relativity as the special case of low velocity/low mass. All Einstein did was model the case of where Newton is not applicable. Einstein didn't disprove Newton's laws. He just showed that they were not complete and needed to be adjusted in some extreme cases: For instance, if you have objects moving close to the speed of light, or if you have objects in strong gravitational fields." "When this is not the case Einstein's relativity theory can be approximated with Newton's laws. So Newton's laws can give a very good approximation to the planetary motions in our solar system for example, but they cannot explain the slow decay in the orbits caused by gravitational radiation, here we need to use relativity theory." (Web13)

Popper stated that scientific theories were not incorrigible truths; they were theories and products of the human mind. They approximate truth and can be changed. He also held that physical reality exists independent of the human mind, and may not be fully apprehended (Magee p.220-2). No general theory can be fully proved, but it can be disproved. We can test general statements by searching for contrary instances. "This being so, **criticism** becomes the chief **means by which we do** in fact **make progress**."(p.225). Popper wrote several books including—*The Logic of Scientific Discovery* and *The Open Society and Its Enemies*. In the 2nd book, he makes the point that in open societies there is free press and criticism can be expressed. In society as in science, this is where the most progress is made. He also wrote a strong criticism of Marxism, and noted the social failure of Nazism in this regard.

Nietzsche assaults the prior values and morals based on Greek philosophy and the Judeo-Christian traditions. He says society has changed in1880 and must formulate new values based on man's thoughts. He says societies develop best when the strong eliminate the weak and the clever eliminate the stupid. He also maintained that this life of ours is largely a meaningless business of suffering and striving, driven along by an irrational force we call will. We are free to choose whatever values are most in our interests and these are surely the values that have lead us out of the animal kingdom. He did say live life to the fullest and dare to become what you are(p.174). He stated "The bite of conscience is indecent" and "Man is a rope, tied between beast and superman, a rope over an abyss."(Magee p.175-7) Mussolini, the founder of Fascism and Hitler of Nazism both read and valued Nietzsche's writings. **The Nazis' made repeated use of Nietzsche's** words in their propaganda(p.177). Some comments on some result of following Nietzsche's beliefs(he was an atheist) follow from Wikipedia:(Web14) "Nazi ideology stressed the failure of both laissez-faire capitalism and communism, the failure of democracy, and "racial purity of the German people", as well as Northwestern Europeans and persecuted those it perceived either as race enemies or *Lebensunwertes Leben*, that is "life unworthy of living". This included Jews, Slavs, and Roma along with homosexuals, the mentally and physically disabled, Communists and others. To carry out these beliefs, the party and the German state which it controlled organized the systematic murder of approximately six million Jews and six million other people from the aforementioned and other groups, in what has become known as the Holocaust. Hitler's desire to build a Germanic empire through expansionist policies led to the outbreak of World War II in Europe. Hitler discovered that he had talent as an orator, and his ability to draw new members, combined with his characteristic ruthlessness, soon made him the dominant figure. The Nazi Party might never have come to power had it not been for the Great Depression and its effects on Germany. A further decisive step in the Nazi seizure of power (*Gleichschaltung*) was the "Enabling Act", which granted the cabinet (and therefore Hitler) legislative powers. The Enabling Act effectively abolished the separation of powers, a principle enshrined in the German Constitution. The Enabling Act, termed for four years, gave the government the power to enact laws without parliamentary approval, to enact foreign treaties abroad and even to make changes to the Constitution. Germany had a policy instituted by Bismarck called "Kulturkampf". This policy was an attempt to "modernize" the German people by moving the culture away from Catholic values to Government inspired values. Paradoxically, the more completely the Nazi regime dominated German society, the less relevant the Nazi Party became as an organization within the regime's power structure. Hitler's rule was highly personalized, and the power of his subordinates such as Himmler and Goebbels depended on Hitler's favor and their success in interpreting his desires rather than on their nominal positions within the party. The party had no governing body or formal decision-making process—no Politburo, no Central Committee, no Party Congress. Real power in the regime was exercised by an axis of Hitler's office, Himmler's SS and Goebbels's Propaganda Ministry." The press was taken over and press criticism of Nazi activities was prohibited.

A few references from more recent as opposed to historical **philosophy** will now be cited. Green (1969) conducted a symposium on knowledge and authors Winger, Pols and Polanyi are cited. Winger (p.34 Epistemology of quantum Mechanics) noted that the limit of science is bounded by the limits of the human mind for assimilating knowledge, and forming increasingly subtle and sophisticated theories. Knowledge is built on prior knowledge and on recent observations of the senses in gathering data from experiments we have designed (p.31-36). Pols (p.287-313, Philosophical Knowledge of the Person) noted that **creative reflection** is something that **goes beyond the mind as a computer.** Looking back at our life and assessing it and then planning for a different future requires a higher level of consciousness. The awareness of many discrete life events and their fusion into a single entity is also advanced awareness of self and expanding rationality. Polanyi (The structure of Consciousness (p.315-327) uses the example of a person looking at a pair of stereoscopic photographs and integrating them into one. This act requires a higher level of consciousness than simply observing data. Writing a book or playing chess also suggests a stratified level of higher rationality and consciousness. There is also a difference between the structure of and the organizing field of an animal or person. The organizing field deals with their growth and behavior. He also points out that **creative retrospect suggests a consciousness of being**. Also see a separate summary write up on Popkin's book.(Tofflemire 2010).

Discussion of Philosophy Including Skepticism and Empiricism

Skepticism: The philosophy of skepticism asserts that no truth is knowable (Kreeft94 p.367) or only probable (Popkin p.205). It has similarities to empiricism. Some say the scientific method also asserts probable findings, because the number of cases tested is always limited (Popkin p. 211). "In fact, the scientific method doesn't even claim to deliver what we mean by certain knowledge." It is probable knowledge. (Kreeft94 P 19). The scientific method can't assess the basic laws of logic or morality or philosophy. One could ask a student—if no knowledge or truths are knowable why study at all? The basic premise "no truth is knowable" also refutes itself as how can one know this? (Kreeft94 p.373). Skepticism also goes against a common sense idea that we can know something and the belief that some truths are necessary to carry out ordinary life (Popkin p.220). The following arguments (A-D) were given by Kreeft94 (p.368-71):

A. We do err. We are fallible and even fallible about when we are fallible. Error does not prove skepticism; it refutes it, because we recognize error against a standard of truth.

B. Certainty comes by adding a reason, a proof, to an idea; many premises and proofs needed—ad infinitum. Aristotle refuted; it is not an endless chain, but there are first principles, self evident truths. Examples: Good ought to be done and evil avoided; A whole is greater than its parts; things that begin must have a cause for their beginning; A not = -A.(law of non contradiction).

C. Burden of proof should be on the believer not on the skeptic. No, the burden should be on anyone who believes any idea, even skepticism and upon the minority view. Scientific method is only truth: There is no scientific method proving the scientific method.

D. Freud says our reasoning depends on our desires and reasoning is rationalizing: This is self contradictory (Kreeft94 p. 371). It denies 2+2=4 and not-A=A. If we deny reason, we must use our reason to do so. Some reason insists on doubt, but our nature insists on assuming innate principles. (Kreeft96 p.112)

Empiricism: Some empiricists assume all knowledge is based on sense experiences and our mental organization of what we observe (Magee p.102;Popkin p.207). This basic assumption must be assumed a priori and is not self validating (Popkin p.217, Lisle09 p.37). There can't be a demonstration by empiricism that it is the only truth (Kreeft p.19). Is all knowledge man's opinion with no universal truths? What about 2+2=4 and A= not A? Hume also held that propositions can only be meaningful if they meet one of the following 2 conclusions: **1.** the truth claim is abstract reasoning such as a mathematical equation, or logical definition or **2.** the claim can be verified empirically through one or more of the 5 senses(Geisler p.57). Geisler stated that since the two points can't be obtained by the senses or by logical definition, the view is self-contradicting and by Hume's assertion meaningless. The view of Hume, denying that abstract truths are universal or that there any sources of knowledge other than experience, seems untrue to me. Animals and babies have born instincts, like a baby's instinct to suck the nipple and take its first breath. For a more in depth discussion of instincts see the quotes from Wikipedia and SEP on **innate** behavior, another name for instinct (see appendix **4**). Also there is some ability to gather information beyond the five common senses—as by mental telepathy and by intuition and by God's revelation. DNA and cell research have shown that we have programmed information on how to reproduce and maintain cells, maintain organs and our whole body. It is possible that we have programmed information in our mind on how to think logically and to speak. More details on information science and how it is also universal are given in Gitt's book. It is very unlikely that thinking logically, retrospective consciousness and our systems of memory evolved by random chance. The principals of logic and mathematics extend throughout the universe, even where there may be no brains or biological life. So if the five senses and brain experience are the only sources of logic, how can logic extend throughout the universe? Why should we expect mathematics and our logic to be true on a different planet? Perhaps there are different brains and senses and experience there that would invalidate our logic and mathematics. The **great philosophers** who were also **mathematicians** or had great respect for mathematics, **believed in God** or abstract universal realities.(Plato, Aristotle, Isaac Newton, Francis Bacon, Descartes, Leibniz, Kant, Frege, Russell, Einstein). The theories of Descartes and Kant were somewhat predictive of future discoveries in science.

Three arguments commonly used to prove God's existence are as follows: 1. **Teleological**—The universe exhibits design, order and purpose, 2. **Cosmological**—Someone of infinite wisdom and power created the universe; 3. **Ontological**: The most perfect nature of being must exist by definition. St. Anselm and Kant supported this last argument (Magee p57). The first two of these are developed further in a second paper on logic by Tofflemire. The third could be stated somewhat differently. It is my opinion and also Lisle's and Meister's that there are no objective and true bases for morals or ethics or meaning to life without God. The appendix of Tofflemire2009b gives a link on Meta-Ethics(web 15). If ethics are intuitive, where does our intuition come from? About 95% of all philosophers as noted in Magee's book delve into these topics. Without a basis for morals or ethics, this topic all becomes very relative—man can set whatever morals he wishes. Pantheism and Buddhism believe that morals are illusionary (Meister). Only a few major philosophers in Magee's book stated that morals and ethics are not important. Nietzsche is an example. Following his philosophy resulted in the atrocities under Mussolini and Hitler where there was no free press or criticism (alternate views) allowed. In addition, the large majority of those great philosophers who were mathematicians and valued the laws of logic believed in God. Those philosophers also thought the laws of logic and mathematics were universal abstract truths and not just experience. How can there be universal laws extending throughout the universe unless a universal mind created them? Magee (p.57) pointed out that the **Christian religion is a history with assertions and beliefs**, rather than a philosophy and that God cannot be proven. However much of the history of the Bible has been proven true and it is a good source book for archeologists. See the section in Bible authenticity. The theological assertions are taken on faith (Popkin p.152).

Schaeffer 1990(p. 7) noted that formerly absolutes were recognized in the areas of morals, truth and being. The line of despair began in Europe-Germany in 1890. It started in philosophy and spread to art, music, general culture and theology. **It was first called rationalism and like humanism began with man finding all knowledge, meaning and value, without God.** Philosophy began with drawing circles or systems to encompass thoughts and reality. The next philosopher would cross out that circle and draw a new one. Eventually they came to the place where no circle was adequate, and despair set in, as there were no good systems, absent God, to give meaning and purpose to life. Rationalism led to Positivism; that too was severely criticized by Polanyi(p.310). Thus Schaeffer said we are left with **two philosophies which do not answer the big questions of morals, truth and being: existentialism, and linguistic analysis.** With God the philosophical questions of the subject and object being real and a basis for knowing things becomes clear. Everything God made in nature is real, including a tree, even if no humans see it(p.325). With God and the Bible we have an objective basis for correct moral decisions, knowing right and wrong and loving other persons(p.330). A few more key insights on philosophy are given by Schaeffer in the Theology Section.

Information as Separate Entity

Because information and language relate to philosophy and appear relevant they will be discussed. Gitt (p.50-53) stated that **information is a third entity** in addition to matter and energy. The laws of nature govern matter and energy and are universally valid. Gitt includes laws and information as nonmaterial entities along with the laws of mathematics. He gives many theorems about the laws of nature and information. Information is related to will or volition. "Information only arises through an intentional volitional act."(p.53) Information comprises the nonmaterial foundation for all technological systems and works of art and for biological systems. **Information** as defined by Gitt involves **transmitting a coded message from a living sender to a living recipient.** It has five levels, the last four of which make it intelligible. The lowest level is a raw code signal like random numbers or letters. This has no intelligible meaning. The next four levels include: **1.** code that can be understood; **2**: syntax that has rules; **3.** the message gives an expected action or meaning; **4**: the message has an intended purpose. Examples of codes include—Morse code, a computer program, languages, hieroglyphics, musical notes, genetic codes, and figures made by gyrating bees. He states "There is no natural law through which matter can give rise to information, neither is there any physical process or material phenomenon known that can do this."(p.80) Information is not the thing itself, neither is it a condition, but it is a representation of material realities or conceptual relationships. The complete reality being represented by the information is not usually present at the time and place of the transfer of the information. Information plays a substitutionary role.

In 2006, a team of scientists of various disciplines met and came up with a Universal Definition of Information (**UDI**)(Ham08 p.197). **This includes 4 elements** above of—**code, syntax, meaning and purpose**. As defined the following do not represent information: A. a physical star—it lacks code and meaning, it is the physical object; B. a physical snowflake—it lacks code and meaning, C. a random sequence of numbers or letters—it lacks syntax rules and meaning **The DNA code** contains 4 letters ATCG arranged in 3 letter words. It **has syntax, meaning and purpose**. The information encoded in DNA is billions of more times more compact than a modern PC hard drive (Ham08-204). Both Gitt(p.80) and Yockey (Heeren p. 67) agree that **DNA is an information code**. Gitt stated (p.89) man is undoubtedly the most complex information processing system existing on earth. The total number of bits handled daily in all information processing events occurring in the human body is 3×10^{24}. This includes all deliberate as well as all involuntary activities. The number of bits being processed daily in the human body is more that a million times the total amount of human knowledge stored in all the libraries of the worlds, which is about 10^{18} bits." (Gitt p.89).

The flight of **migrating birds** is a navigational masterpiece, stated Gitt (p.253-4). Experiments have been conducted with pigeons that were tagged, anaesthetized, and transported to an unfamiliar, remote location. They invariably returned to their homes or usual migratory destination by taking the shortest and best route. The birds have the amazing ability to extract the required data from the environmental and then follow a set course to their destination. In doing this they correctly compensate for crosswinds, and can cover great distances over which they have not flown before. A man with a compass, an airplane, a sextant and map could not do this unless he also new his starting location on the map also and he made some mathematical calculations. We do not know how the birds do this. We use a special term to cover our ignorance and say the birds have **instinct** (p.254). Their mechanics of flying is also a masterpiece, as they conserve energy and ride on lifting updrafts also. The **Monarch butterfly** has a brain the size of a pinhead and yet can pinpoint a location 3,000 miles away and navigate there with an accuracy of 100 feet. This is a one time migration to a location they have never been before(Web 16). How does this fit with Locke's philosophy of **Empiricism**—that we only acquire knowledge by experience? The butterflies that are flying had no prior experience of their journey.

The chapter on the origin of **languages** by Gitt is interesting (p.116-8). There have been many evolutionary speculations about this. Perhaps we copied animal sounds; perhaps we developed various grunts and gestures and then language. These theories are not very convincing. At present there are about 5100 languages and dialects spoken on earth. Why would so many different languages develop from evolution of common ancestors, unless God confused and gave the languages? Some of these languages are very unique. The Comanche and Navaho languages were odd enough to be used as secret codes during the world wars. Gitt concludes "All languages are unique and perform their functions very well.

They comprise morphological, grammatical, and semantic complexities and structures which were not devised by any person. The members of aboriginal tribes do not even know the structure of their grammar. J.P. Submilch established that man could not have invented language without having the necessary intelligence, and also the intelligent thought in its turn depends on the previous existence of speech.(**Words and thoughts are related-as an exercise try to think an intelligent thought without using any words**). The only solution to the paradox is that God must have given human beings language as a gift." This would fit with giving the animals instincts at birth and birds and butterflies knowledge of how to navigate the world from any location. Written language is an important achievement. This allows the propagation of knowledge based on prior discoveries. History demonstrates that groups without writing do not go beyond a certain stage and do not become very advanced (aboriginal peoples for example)(p.218). The syntax and rules of organization of words and grammar would be difficult to assemble correctly by trial and error. One language has different syntax rules than another. There are of course commonalities in some languages, and dialects.

An extension of the reasoning on language, information theory and UDI occurs in the search for extra-terrestrial intelligence (SETI). UDI codes are used for the search, and no extraterrestrial intelligence has been found. The Fermi paradox (why there is no response back) remains after 37 yrs. and $60 million of searching; Heeren (p.74). See the **Appendix 3** for more details. Thus SETI uses UDI but has had no alien response.

Common Arguments from Apologetics and Philosophy.

Apologetics(Ap): A number of papers on Ap. are on the www. ARCapologetics.org(web17) and I have done summaries of a few. Another good reference is *I don't have enough Faith to be an Atheist* by Geisler (Web 35), which points out it takes more faith to be an atheist than a Christian. We know that our heart is our center, not our head. Apologetics gets at the heart through the head. The head is like the navigator and the heart is like the captain. Both are important. **Reasons for studying Ap. include:1. to convince unbelievers 2. and to instruct and build up believers.** Reason and faith are friends, companions, partners. **Ap.** It is to be used like a sword, not a bomb; the user's tone, sincerity, respect, in the context needed for the listener is also important. Today we are in an intellectual, moral and spiritual crisis and need good **Ap.**(Kreeft p.23,24). Intellectual achievement and pride, moral relativism and humanism, secularism and pluralism, accepting all life styles are popular. Boa(p.21)noted in answer to the question: Is there really a God? The possible answers are Yes, no, maybe. Try to 1st move no, to maybe, by asking them to draw **circles of their knowledge** and all knowledge as in the figure below. We use only a small part of our total mental capacity and can't know everything and the circles will illustrate this. 1st discuss the philosophy of life without God—No morals, meaning or purpose. Note the kinds of proof and knowledge: Historical, philosophical, moral, personal, religious in addition to science. The verdicts of most courts are based on legal historical proof, not just scientific proof. We can use cause and effect evidence.

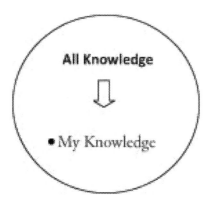

Why is there something rather than nothing at all? Boa (p.27) noted that **Leibniz** stated there must be an outside reason and cause. The cause cannot be found in any single thing in the universe because it must also have a prior cause and is part of the universe. The cause must then be out side of the universe, in a being for whom reason is self-contained and somewhat beyond time (Craig p.83, Meister p.105). **Four alternates** to examine follow: **1.** the universe is an illusion, **2. the universe is eternal**, **3.** the universe emerged from nothing (nothing produces nothing), and **4.** the universe was created by an eternal being. Premise **1.** Is like saying there are no objective facts. **2.** If the universe is eternal, **then it would have to be in equilibrium which is not supported by the facts or by 2nd law of thermo**; also goes against the big bang and the Omni-directional background radiation that indicates it was once small, hot and dense.; there is a large presence of Hydrogen(H) in the universe, but it is being converted to Helium thru fusion in a one way reaction and new H is not being formed(Boa p.28-34).

The argument for an eternal being was given; now **is he personal or impersonal**? Three reasons are given for a personal God: **1**. A personal God could make a choice to create at a certain time ago. An impersonal God may not interfere with the universe.**2**. The universe had order and complexity and symmetry and has many predictable and reliable laws. This is evidence for careful design by an intelligent being. There is also evidence of purpose and beauty, in living systems (teleological). Boa (p.35). Personality is also reflected in man's intellect, emotion and will so it is logical his creator would have these characteristics. **3**. Man's consciousness and moral sense of right and wrong argues for a personal creator of the highest morals. The only objective foundation for morals is a creator God. To achieve these, atheistic evolutionists can say that chaos and randomness produced order, lifeless matter produced all life, chance produced intelligence, and accidents produced purpose and beauty. Also people have trouble living a philosophy that rules out purpose, meaning and value in life(Boa p.35)

The cosmological argument is given by Craig in his book The *Kalam Cosmological Argument.* Both philosophical reasoning and scientific evidence show that the universe began to exist. 3 Steps: **1**. Whatever begins to exist has a cause, **2**. The universe began to exist, **3**. Therefore the universe has a cause. One atheistic defense is that the universe sprang into existence uncaused out of nothing(Craig p.93-4). They say it is only one step more—than God did it from nothing. This leaves out a cause however. God existed in undifferentiated time before the creation of the universe. An actual infinite number of things cannot exist; a beginningless series of events in time entails this. There can be a potentially large list approaching **infinity** as a limit. The actual mathematical infinity is a unique number. Inconsistencies in reasoning from the axiom "the whole is greater than the parts" occur when we tie an infinite series to a specific day, like the creation or big bang(p.97). This occurs when we say the universe existed for ever and never had a beginning. You cannot get an infinite number by adding one event at a time to a finite list.(P.98). The Big Bang model provides scientific confirmation of creation in time: The big bang is said to have occurred about 15 billion yrs. ago from a state of infinite density and creating space and time (p.100). Hubble discovered the red shifts which indicated all parts of the universe are growing apart and expanding. The theory is that it started from a singularity which is almost nothing (p.102). This is confirmed by Einstein's theory of general relativity in which space, matter and time all started from the singularity at one point in time(Geisler p.83). The spreading out of these three is also evidenced in the carefully measured ripples in the cosmic background radiation (Geisler p.81). This is confirmed by a director of NASA, R. Jastrow, in his book *God and the Astronomers* W.W. Norton & Co., NY 1992(p.84, 414 F. Heeren *Show me God.)*

The **alternate models** are also **not** very **convincing**: The steady state models say it never has a beginning and existed forever. They have little experimental justification. The evidence of cosmic background radiation indicates that the universe was once in a very hot and dense state(Wilson and Penzias). A second model is the oscillating one. It's like a spring expanding and contracting for ever. Many scientists believe this is physically impossible (Craig p.103). There is no known physics to reverse a collapse. As the universe contracted, black holes would suck everything up in a heat death. There are 2 possibilities: the universe will at some future time recontract, or it will continue expanding forever in a cold death. In order for it to recontract, 99% of the matter in the universe would have to be invisible, which is unlikely(p.105) There is not much evidential support of invisible dark mater. The COBE satellite measurements of Cosmic Background radiation argue against dark matter. Another class of models are the vacuum fluctuation ones that appeal to quantum effects. With this the whole universe is only an expansion of a part of it in a vacuum. There is not much support for these models(p.107). One model that has been more cited is the quantum gravitational model by S. Hawking, of Cambridge in his *Brief History of Time*. He eliminates the singularity at 10^{-43} sec. of time after the big bang by using imaginary and negative numbers. Then the distinction between time and space disappears. The model has been criticized as not depicting actual reality because of the use of imaginary terms and because of the philosophical problems of using imaginary time. It also defies elementary quadratic equation solutions with two answers: a real number and an imaginary one; the real one is always accepted. Hawking admits when you use real numbers the singularity reappears(p.112.) These quantum models have space-time originate in a quantum mechanical region which is a 4-dimensional space involving imaginary time (Craig p.113). These models defy what we know about space and time in the present. There are three forms of the cosmological argument(Craig p.98). Some details of cosmology are discussed further in the section on Cosmology.

Argument from the 2ⁿᵈ law of thermodynamics. A closed system tends toward equilibrium, where process will run down and quit in an expanding cold death. Dr. Tinsley stated that an expanding universe at 10^{30} yrs. would be 90% dead stars, 9% super massive black holes and 1% atomic matter manly hydrogen(Craig p.115). This argues against a universe with no beginning, as it would now be at equilibrium. Some scientists thus say the universe was started and wound up with energy and is decaying. Both the expansion of the universe and the 2ⁿᵈ law argue that the universe had a beginning. It follows that the universe had a cause. It is logical that an intelligent personal agent, God, created the universe and he is eternal. By definition he is eternal, changeless and all powerful.

The great fine tuning of the universe argues for an intelligent designer. Barrow and Tipler estimate that the odds against the assembly of the human genome are astronomical(Craig p.118). God must be immaterial, space-less and timeless, since matter changes with time. Methods of arguing: the arguments are mainly philosophical and the scientific evidence show the universe had a beginning and an intelligent designer. We can use world views also. Like physical laws there are spiritual laws. Kreeft94(p.51) adds to the **causal argument**: Many things cause other things to happen and to come into existence. If one follows this reasoning chain back to an original cause, what is the original cause if there is no God?(Kreeft p.52) <u>Question</u>: *Why do we need an uncaused cause? Why could there not simply be an endless series of things mutually keeping each other in being?* <u>Reply</u>: Things have got to exist in order to be mutually dependent; they cannot depend upon each other for their entire being, for then they would have to be, simultaneously, cause and effect of each other. A causes B, B causes C, and C causes A. That when extended is absurd.

Ontological Argument: If God is conceivable he must exist. This was formulated by Anselm and defended by Scotus, Descartes, Spinoza, and Leibniz. God is the greatest conceivable being, so nothing greater than God can be conceived. So he must exist(Craig p.79). A more detailed version is give by Kreeft94(p. 69). The Argument was devised by Anselm:

A. "It is greater for a thing to exist in the mind and in reality than in the mind alone.

B. God means that than which a greater cannot be thought.

C. Suppose God exists in the mind but not in reality.
D. Then a greater than God could be thought of (one that also has reality).
E. But this is impossible, for God is that than which a greater cannot be thought."

Challenge point 1. *Suppose I deny that god exists in the mind.* This commits you to the view that there is no concept of God. Few would go that far as very many have this concept. Challenge point 2. *Being is just one more concept like omniscience or omnipotence.* Being is a much greater quality than just another quality.

Teleological Argument: This argument is **from design** and means to an end; Plato and Aristotle used the argument; there is an order that pervades the cosmos, and the order of the stars and source of the soul. A design implies a designer. Aristotle mentions it in *On Philosophy*, and in *Metaphysics*. This argument was extended by Thomas Aquinas who noted: All things work towards a plan and goal. Acorns grow into Oaks(Craig p.85). **Wm. Paley wrote: *Natural Theology*:** He used the watch maker argument and continued it by a length catalog of things in nature and in comparative anatomy that show design. He also reasons that just because an error is found in the watch, does not prove there was not an intelligent designer. It is also not enough to say that the watch was produced from another watch and so on. Design is still involved. The many contrivances and unique design in nature did not occur by chance (Craig p.85). Kreeft gave additional details on the argument: The universe displays a large amount of order and beauty. In our experience this amount of beauty and order comes from intelligent design not random chance(Kreeft94 p.55). This argument has been extended to many scientific constants finely tuned by Meister in *Building Belief* and to information and information codes like DNA by Gitt *In The Beginning was Information*. The source of these must be an intelligent designer or mind. Complex information codes that transmit intelligent information from a sender to receiver cannot occur by randomness. (Gitt p.80.) This argument is of wide and strong appeal(Kreeft94 p.55). Some will challenge it by the theory of evolution. This theory is weak to oppose the argument (Kreeft p.57). The sun, earth and moon size and locations are carefully balanced for life. Small changes in these would result in destruction of all life. Meister (p.72) goes on to state that **about 50 scientific constants of physics that**

are finely tuned for life. Small changes in these would upset the balance and the universe would no longer exist. Some of these constants include the gravitational constant, the velocity of light, the strong nuclear force constant, the relative masses of elementary particles, and the cosmological constant. Geisler (p.105) stated there are more than 100 finely tuned constants and discusses 10 more including the speed of rotation and tilt degree of the earth. Astrophysicist Hugh Ross calculated the probability of all these constants being fine turned is one chance in 10^{138}. Astronomer Fred Hoyle had his atheism shaken by noting all the fine tuning and design and concluded that this required intelligent design(Geisler p.106). There is an argument from philosophy by Norris Clark of Fordham Univ. that the world is an interconnected, interlocking dynamic system cosmic wide order that is only explained by a cosmic design and mind (Kreeft p. 62).

Moral Argument: (Craig p. 88) There is a gradation in values; some things are more good and more noble. There must exist the best and most noble and that is God. Wm. Sorley in *The Ethics of Naturalism* refuted the historical evolutionary approach to ethics. There is a difference between subjective and objective morals. Our moral judgments are fallible. The objective and true moral must reside somewhere. Moral purpose is often confused with personal happiness which is elusive. Morals in action involve personal choice and free will. Bad morals involve bad choices(Craig p.89). Without God morals become relative. Hitler's morals of killing the weak and insane then become OK. Kreeft94(p.72) extended the argument:

A. Real moral obligation is a fact. We are really, truly, objectively obliged to do good and avoid evil.
B. Either the Atheistic view of reality is correct or the religious view.
C. The Atheistic view is incompatible with their being moral obligation.
D. So the religious view is correct.

Craig (p.172) presented a differing argument: 1. If God does not exist, objective moral values and duties do not exist. 2. Objective moral values do exist, 3. Therefore, God exists. Plato asserted objective morals do exist. There is still no reason or obligation to follow them from atheism(p.180). God provides divine commands and this establishes duties. They are an expression of his just and loving nature.

Challenge question 1. *The argument has not shown that ethical subjectivism is false. What if there are no objective moral values?* If ethical subjectivism is true then the argument does not work. However almost no one is a consistent subjectivist. Even remote tribes have a sense of right and wrong. Moral standards were held as universal forms by Plato and as noumenal truths by Kant. The Christian view is that God has given us a moral conscience and objective standards in the 10 commandments and in the two great commands(P.73). Also morality is based on God's eternal nature: Lev. 11:44 "sanctify yourselves therefore, and be holy, for I am holy." Kreeft94(p. 76).

There are many arguments for the existence of God. Kreeft94 gave **20** of them and stated that taken together they form a very strong case for God. A summary of the 20 is in Tofflemire 2010.

Argument from Change: Kreeft94 (p.50) "The material world we know is a world of change." The oak tree comes from an acorn. The result of the change cannot exist before the change. The changing thing has the potential for change but needs to be acted upon by other factors before the change can happen. Nothing changes itself(p.50). Even an animal is moved by desire, will, instinct, DNA programming or other factors(my notes). The universe is the sum total of all these changing things. If there is nothing outside the material universe, then there is nothing that can cause it to change. Therefore there must be something outside the material universe to cause it to change (God). This appears related to interacting argument.

Argument from the World as an Interacting Whole (by Norris Clarke of Fordham Univ.) "The world is a dynamic, ordered system of many active component elements. Their natures are ordered to interact with each other in stable, reciprocal relationships which we call physical laws."(Kreeft94 p.62). "In such an interconnected, interlocking dynamic system, the active nature of each component is defined by its relation with others, and so presupposes the others for its own intelligibility and ability to act." The world system is not merely an aggregate of many separate, unrelated laws, but rather a tightly interlocking whole, where relationship to the whole structure determines the parts"(p.63). In such a system no component part can be self sufficient. One part can't act unless other parts are there to interact reciprocally with it. He draws three conclusions from this:

A. Since the parts make sense only within the whole, and neither the whole nor the parts can explain their own existence, then such as system as our world requires a unifying efficient cause to posit it in existence."

B. "Any such cause must be an intelligent cause, one that brings the system into being according to a unifying idea.—Hence it must be somehow actually present as an effective organizing factor." "Since the actual parts are spread out over space and time, the only way they can be together at once as an intelligible unity is within an idea." "A cosmic-wide order requires a cosmic-wide Orderer" and mind (p.64).

C. "Such an ordering mind must be independent of the system itself, that is transcendental, and not dependent on the system."

Argument from Consciousness

A. We experience the universe as intelligible, but we have finite minds. This means the universe is graspable by our intelligence. (Kreeft94 p.66-7)
B. Either this intelligible universe and the finite minds so well suited to grasp it are products of intelligence, or both are product of chance.
C. Not blind chance.

C. S. Lewis in *Miracles* extended the argument to our thinking and judging. **Naturalism** cannot explain correct thinking and judgments and is **void of any rational plan or guiding** purpose. Also thought called knowledge and thought called error are states of the brain and can occur by chance equally. Therefore there must be some guiding programming to assess truth from error. Lisle stated we must trust our senses, memory and reason or we can't know things. 1 Cor. 1:20-25 "Where is the wise one?—God's foolishness is wiser that human wisdom"

Argument from Religious Experience: It is a fact that very many people over the earth have had religious experiences that confirm divine reality to them. It is hard to believe that they were all wrong. It is probable that they were correct in that a divine being exists(Kreeft p. 81-2).

The Common Consent Argument: This is similar to experience argument above.(Kreeft p. 83-4)

A. Belief in God-that being to whom reverence and worship are properly due-is common to almost all peoples of every era.
B. Either they were correct about there being a divine being or not.
C. It is most likely that they were correct.

World statistics (Web18) show that about 16% of the world's population is classified as secular/atheistic/agnostic, with the rest being religious. About 50% of the world is either Christian or Islamic. Everyone admits that religious belief is widespread throughout history. Either people have a collective psychosis about God or he exists. It is more reasonable to believe that those who refuse to believe are in denial and rebellion. If there is no God, one can do anything he wants to satisfy his selfish desires. "I am reminded of a statement in McGrath's book (30) that comments on the *God Delusion* by Dawkins who is an atheist. The question is raised by Dawkins—why do so many people believe in God?—Even well respected scientists and natives in remote tribes, throughout the ages. Dawkins alleged that there is something in our genes leading us to look for and believe in God, and he calls it the Meme error. Perhaps there is something in the genes or the soul and spirit that draws us to God. Erickson(p.46-47) states that this is the natural theory of God's Revelation—that God does implant some knowledge of Him in us."

Pascal was described by **Kreeft**1996 as a very concise and insightful apologist in his Pensees: "Christianity is not a hypothesis, it is a proposal of marriage"(p. 31). "Our intellect lives off our will and emotions, as a plant lives off the earth"(p.32). The Christian spy's mission is talking like an ordinary person, although he has deeper motives(p.34). A direct attack may embitter the person; humor, humility, gentleness aid. Thus look for a person's point of view and point out consequences of it. An indirect approach is better, asking simple humble empathetic questions. "Man is neither angel nor beast, and it is unfortunately the case that anyone trying to act the angel acts the beast." Man's dualism is so obvious that some people have thought we had two souls"(p.51-2). "Man must not be allowed to believe that he is equal to animals or to angels, nor to be unaware of either, but he must know both."(p.52) Angel like: Pantheism, new age humanism; Animal like: Marxism, Freudianism, Behaviorism, Darwinism. Possible question: Who is more beautiful—Madonna with her blasphemies or Mother Teresa with her wrinkles? He described **Man's Problems as wretchedness** (animal of desires, selfish, unhappy), vanity, injustice, irrationality, alienation, death, sin, selfishness(p.19-21). He goes from problem to solution: Man is happy with God and wretched without God. Today people are not convinced of sin and resent being told they are sinners as guilt-ridden and judgmental. "The world thinks men are good and saints better. Pascal knew men are sinners, and saints are miracles"(p.43). Pascal uses wretchedness and happiness in their deep, ancient meanings (objective state) rather than in their shallow modern meanings(subjective feeling). To get to the objective state, point out the big picture: From the view of long time and the universe we are but a speck in time and make little difference; isn't that true? Freud's view was that we operate on the **pleasure principle.** The pleasure principle states that people seek pleasure and avoid pain, i.e., people seek to satisfy biological and psychological needs. Babies want what they want when they want it(Kreeft1996 p.161).

The two most popular Pseudo solutions: Diversion and Indifference(Kreeft p.161) A child's question: Why doesn't anyone have any time, when we have many time saving devices? In silence we can seek God and see the gap between Him and us(p.168). "If our condition were truly happy we should not need to divert ourselves from thinking about it"(p. 169#70). Often the person or society who has the most diversions and amusements is not the happiest but the unhappiest. Our society, the USA has high rates of depression, divorce, suicide, drugs, violence. We don't want to divert ourselves from happiness, only unhappiness. Some diversions don't really satisfy and make us happy; for example: alcohol, drugs, pornography, gambling, riches etc. They leave with an unhealthy desire for more. **Indifference:**(p.98#427) You can love and hate a person at the same time but not be indifferent to a person and love him. The devil's allies are darkness, fog, sleep and death. The Lord's is passion and light. Rome's attitude—indifferent, decadent, sophisticated, skeptical, relativistic, jaded, bored, promiscuous-resulted in its decline(p.188). If you are lukewarm I will spit you out of my mouth. **Why God Hides:**(p. 245). He came to give light as a gift, not to force light on us. A gift must appeal to freedom. "He gives exactly the right amount of light. If He gave less, even the righteous would be unable to find him. If he gave more, even the wicked would find him, against their will"(p.250). "God wishes to move the will rather than the mind. Perfect clarity would help the mind and harm the will."(p.248)

Summary Arguments from *I Don't Have Enough Faith to be an Atheist* (Geisler): Some arguments not fully given before will be noted here.

Some arguments not fully given before will be noted here. **DNA is very complex and ordered information.** The DNA information in a one-celled amoeba would fill more than 1000 volumes of a standard encyclopedia(Geisler p.116). In addition to the ordered complexity, the origin of the DNA is also a problem for Darwinist's. It is a difficult chicken-egg dilemma, because DNA relies on proteins for its production, while the proteins rely on the DNA for their production. The probability of getting one protein molecule by chance(with about 100 amino acids) is virtually zero noted Michael Behe(p.125). The 1960 movie *Inherit the Wind* depicted the 1925 Scopes trial as crazy religious fundamentalists versus objective science. The debate now is not about the Bible and religion versus science, it's about good science versus bad science or about reasonable faith versus unreasonable faith(p.120). The evolutionist Fred Hoyle suggested the evidence is so strong for design in creation that he proposed the Panspermia theory, which involves aliens seeding our earth with life. This simply puts the problem off a step; as who made the aliens? Hubert Yockey stated that "the belief that life on earth arose spontaneously from nonliving mater, is simply a matter of faith in strict reductionism and is based entirely on ideology"(p.122). Both he and Richard Lewontin agree that Darwinists accept absurd "just so" stories that are against common sense because of their prior commitment to materialism as a philosophy. Lewontin stated "materialism is absolute for we cannot allow a divine foot in the door." The philosophy of materialism or naturalism (M-N) is often coupled with science but there are many things it cannot explain: 1. The laws of mathematics and logic; 2. metaphysical truths like human consciousness and reason; 3. ethical judgments; 4. aesthetic judgments like beauty; 5. internal or self proof of the philosophy(p.127). Science doesn't really say anything, but scientists with philosophies do. The philosophy of M-N must be assumed and is not self proving.

Geisler (p.140-2) noted the process of **microevolution** involves small changes in species that are known to occur and differs from **macroevolution** which involves the whole tree of life from molecules to man. Creationists agree micro changes are true. Evolutionists commonly use micro changes as proof of macro, and don't distinguish between the two. By not distinguishing they can dupe the public into thinking these small changes prove the macro changes and the tree of life. A number of biologists do not agree that tree of life and macro changes are credible or factual. **Five reasons for this are cited**: **1**. Genetic limits and probabilities limit macro changes; the dog type always remains dogs. **2**. Genetic change is cyclical and not directionally upward as evolutionists assert; most mutations are harmful and not kept. **3**. Many structures and creatures are irreducibly complex: DNA, the cell, the eye, and the human brain. **4**. There are no viable transitional forms between major groups; the assertion that birds evolved from reptiles and scales turned into feathers, is false. **5**. Molecular and gene isolation is true; although about 90% of the DNA is similar between apes and man, this could be by divine design. It is also true that mice and men have a 90 % similarity. The DNA that is different is very important. Biologist Michal Denton states there is no evidence at the molecular level of the commonly stated evolutionary transitions from fish to amphibian to reptile to mammal(p.142-51). There are also huge gaps in the fossil record, with missing transitional forms. Darwin thought that fossil finds over time would prove the theory, but they have not. Evolutionary paleontologist S. Gould stated: "The history of most fossil species includes two features particularly inconsistent with gradualism:1. Stasis—species show no directional change, 2. Sudden appearance—species do not arise gradually—but fully formed" He then rejected gradualism and proposed punctuated equilibria, with fast changes over short periods of time(p.152). The missing links are still missing. Denton stated 99% of the biology of any organism resides in the soft anatomy which is not left in a fossil(p.153). With a few bones or even one tooth of a fossil, many assumptions are made often incorrectly. **That is why so many missing links have later been exposed as frauds.** Henry Gee, chief science writer for *Nature* also noted this(p.154). Atheists and Naturalists have a world view just as creationists do. The former can be more dogmatic and un-open to evidence than the later and propose theories based on little or assumed evidence(p.159). The **naturalists have much to lose in financial security, grants, prestige and even employment if they acknowledge design or a creator**(p.163). "In grammar school they taught me that a frog turning into a prince was a fairy tale while, in the university they taught me that it was a fact"(p.137).

"When we say moral law exists, we mean people are impressed with a fundamental sense of right and wrong. Everyone knows, for example that love is superior to hate and that and that courage is better than cowardice.

There is no land where murder is virtue and gratitude vice"(Geisler p.171). J. Budziszewski in his book *What We Can't Not Know* makes this point from research. We all know it is wrong to kill an innocent person for no reason. Seven points are made about moral law: **1. Moral law is undeniable**: Relativists are absolutely sure that there are no absolute moral values. However, they usually do not live or act that way and there is the inconsistency. If someone wants to kill or harm them they are sure it is wrong. Core moral values are true and transcend cultures and most believe it is wrong to torture babies. **2. Our reactions help us discover moral law**. When the Muslim terrorists flew planes into our buildings on 9/11 we all had a strong reaction of it being wrong. It may not always be the standard by which we treat others, but it is the standard by which we want to be treated. Bin Laden and his comrades may have thought it right; but not if the planes were flying into the houses of their own loved ones. Our consciences help us determine right and wrong as it is written on our hearts. **3. Without moral law there would be no human rights**: Thomas Jefferson wrote in the declaration of Independence: "We hold these truths to be self evident, that all men are created equal, that they are endowed by their Creator with certain unalienable rights, that among these are Life, Liberty and the pursuit of Happiness." The signers noted these as God given rights. Nazi war criminals were convicted of violating basic human rights. These rights are in international law but came from higher laws we all recognize. **4. Without moral law, there would be no good way to measure moral differences:** This is what we do when we compare the behavior of Mother Teresa and Hitler. When one says one set of moral ideas are better than another we rely on a higher moral standard. **5. Since we know what's absolutely wrong, their must be an absolute standard of rightness**. Relativists often claim there is no certain truth or right or wrong. However, they are inconsistent and make truth and right and wrong assertions all the time about their political causes, and about issues like sex and money. **6. Without the moral law, there are no moral grounds for political or social dissent**. Relativists are often liberal and oppose war, anti-abortion laws, anti-sodomy laws, and just about anything the religious right might support. Without moral law the basis for their position becomes largely opinion. **7. If there were no moral law, then we wouldn't make excuses for violating it:** Moral law calls us to go beyond tolerance to love. The plea to be tolerant is a tacit admission that the behavior to be tolerated might be wrong(Geisler p.172-92).

Some confusion about morals will be discussed. 1. **What people do and recent trends are different than what they ought to do**. A relativist might say relative to premarital sex or cohabitation: "Get with it, this is the 21st century." However there are also more murders now; should we get with that also because more are doing it.? This reasoning can also be applied to the pious killing witches in the 1700's. At that time some thought that their curses killed people (p.182). 2. **Absolute morals are true even if there are exceptions or dilemmas in particular situations**. Don't murder for no reason; don't rape; and don't torture babies are true morals. Even if only one absolute moral law is true, then the source for the law is true. Some situations may justify murder as exceptions. There are also some exceptions to natural laws. The basics are clear even if some difficult situations are not. Abortion is often cited as a source of moral disagreement. One view is that allowing liberty to a woman to control her own body is most important. The other view is that preserving the life of a baby is most important. The facts indicate that the unborn baby is a separate human being, not just part of a woman's body. Thus the right to life should supersede the right to liberty(p.184). 3. **Some evolutionist's arguments**: Morality evolved by natural selection and may be an instinct. If only materials exist, they do not have morality. An instinct may also be a gift from God and his programming. Instincts that pursue survival do not necessarily do good. Cooperative morals helped humans survive together. Why should the stronger cooperate with the weaker, when the powerful can survive longer by exploiting the weaker? Darwinism is by definition a non-intelligent process; it has no survival end purpose. Some human behavior is self destructive, like smoking, drinking and suicides. Some behaviors involve self sacrifice like a soldier dying for his country. These behaviors don't have direct survival benefit. Some will also say do what ever works or brings the greatest good to the most. We should ask by what definition of good—Hitler's or mother Teresa's? Also ask what ends should we work toward? They may say we gain morals by genetic and environmental factors like what our mother taught us. That shows morals are discovered not invented. The absolute moral principle is still true whether it came from our mother or not. Likewise we are taught the laws of mathematics by a teacher; but the laws are universally true. If there is no God and we evolved from slime, then we have no moral purpose higher than slime.(Geisler p.189).

Geisler notes some important points about the New Testament(NT) and other **documents about Jesus' history** in Chap. 9 of his book. He notes there are 43 ancient non-Christian authors that mention Jesus(p.222). There are 5700 hand written Greek manuscripts of the NT and 9000 manuscripts in other languages (p.225). Some authors critical of the NT state that it is unreliable, because most manuscripts are dated 200AD or older. Geisler refutes this. There are more early manuscripts of the New Testament or parts of it, than for any other ancient document. There is an undisputed fragment of John known as the John Ryland's fragment that is dated between 117-138 AD. There are 9 disputed fragments that date from 50-70 AD and were found with the Dead Sea Scrolls. These include parts of Mark, Acts, Romans, 1Timothy, 2 Peter and James. The fragments were found in a cave containing material from 50 BC to 50 AD(p.227, Web19). Some non controversial NT manuscripts are dated 100-150 AD. Geisler (p.235) asserts that all NT books were written before 100 AD. In letters written by early church fathers Clement, Ignatius and Polycarp, in 95-110 AD, they quoted passages out of 25 of the 27 books of the New Testament. Since Clement was in Rome and the others two hundreds of miles away in Symrna, this provides strong evidence of the **NT being written before 95-110 AD**. Geisler asserts that most NT books were written before **70 AD**, the date of the destruction of Jersulaem and the temple. It is hard to believe that the five historical narrative books of the gospels and Acts could leave out such an important fact, (destruction of Jerusalem) especially since Jesus prophesied in the gospels that the temple would be destroyed(Geisler p.237). Some dates of death are noted below(Web20):

o   Peter, crucified upside-down in Rome circa AD 64.
o   James, son of Zebedee was beheaded in AD 44,
o   Matthew killed by a halberd in AD 60.
o   **Saint James the Just**, (died AD 62), also known as *James the Righteous, James of Jerusalem, James Adelphotheos,* or *James, the Brother of the Lord*, was an important figure in Early Christianity. The *Catholic Encyclopedia* concludes that, based on Hegesippus's account, it is "probable" that James the Just is also James the Less, and in line with "most Catholic interpreters", that he is therefore James, son of Alphaeus as well as James the son of Mary.http://en.wikipedia.org/wiki/James_the_brother_of_Jesus

o   Paul was killed in about 65-67 AD

In addition the case is made that Luke records the death of Stephan, and James the son of Zebedee, so that would be after 44AD. The case is made that Acts was written before 62 AD or the death of James, the head of the church in Jersulaem, would have been recorded. Luke was written before Acts because in Acts 1, the writer Luke refers to his earlier gospel book. Luke 1:1-4 refers back to earlier sources which could also be the book of Mark. Paul writes his letter to the Corinthians in 55-66 AD. Many scholars note the 1 Corin. 15:3-8 refers to and early creed dating back to shortly after the resurrection. **These death dates argue that certain books would have to be before the death dates**(Geisler p.235-247). The recent Holman Bible asserts that Mark was written in 50-60 AD. In summary, the early eyewitness writings and the many copies of documents available argue for the validity of the documents.

The Apostles had little to gain from asserting their eye witness truths other than persecution (p.255). Luke's books were especially historical. In Luke's gospel he records 84 confirmed historical facts, in addition to 35 miracles(p.260). John provided 59 details that have been historically confirmed. Geisler gave **8 reasons the New Testament writers told the truth**: **1.** They told embarrassing details about themselves; **2.** They told embarrassing details and difficult sayings of and about Jesus; **3.** They distinguished Jesus' words from their own and did not brag about themselves. **4.** They included events about the resurrection that could have easily been checked. **5.** They included historical details and details about important people that could have been checked and refuted. **6.** They included slightly diverging details which argues against collusion. **7.** They challenge their readers to check out verifiable facts even about miracles. **8.** They abandoned their long held sacred beliefs and practices and adopted new ones, and would not deny their testimony even under threat of death.

The Absurdity of life without God

Craig discussed (p.51,65) the Absurdity of life without God. He shows the disastrous consequences of human existence, society, and culture if God is false. B **Pascal** stated this in his **Pensees** (Kreeft96)**.** Man is largely immoral and selfish. His knowledge is small in comparison to all knowledge of the universe. I am a mere speck in the universe and in time. I know that I soon must die, as all do. Man flounders un-tethered in uncertainty in his attempt at meaningful life. Many occupy their time with trivialities and distractions to keep their mind of this. Man's mind is his one asset that can lead him to a higher search. He is like a "thinking reed." He ends with his wager argument(p.54). Dostoyevsky and others have stated that if God is denied one is left with complete moral relativism; In some cultures then, almost any bad act goes and is difficult to condemn. He also discussed the problems of evil and suffering. Some suffering may perfect our character and some evil is the result of man's bad decisions.(Craig p.55).

S. Kierkegaard described that life can be lived on **3 different planes**: 1. The aesthetic plane which is the sensual level and pleasure centered—here one finds no ultimate meaning to life and no true satisfaction; 2. the ethical plane in which man lives by objective moral standards, may also lead to guilt and despair, as it is difficult to achieve; 3. The religious plane is one in which one finds forgiveness of sins and a personal relationship with God(Craig p. 56). Also see Sire97 p.94 for differing existential views. **F. Schaeffer** (1912-84) drafted the modern predicament and the western culture of despair. He believes the root of the problem is in the Hegelian philosophy and its denial of absolute truths. This extended to—once God is denied, human life become worthless and we see these fruits in relative morals, drugs and songs of despair as in Pink Floyd(Craig p.56). Schaeffer noted(1990 p.13-25) that Hegel began the dialectic thinking of seeking truth in synthesis, this led to Marxism. This was extended by Kierkegaard into existentialism. **With existentialism faith and significant personal experience are separated from reason** in which man is a machine and can't find a rational purpose. This lead to escape by jumping to experiences of non-reason and to drugs. Several statistical studies found a higher incidence of depression and suicide among those with no religion (web 90).

L. Eiseley described man as a cosmic orphan, since he is the only one who asks "Who am I? and Why?" However since enlightenment, when he threw off the shackles of religion, he tried to answer these questions without God. The answers are not exhilarating but dark and terrible; You are an accidental byproduct of nature, a result of matter, plus time, plus chance. There is no reason for your existence. All you face is death. Then man's life becomes absurd. Compared to the universe and time, we are but a speck(Craig p.57). JP Sartre said death is not threatening as long as it is of another remote 3rd person, but it becomes so when it is for us or close. Life without God and immortality is absurd. Life without ultimate significance, value or purpose: Scientists say the universe will end and also the human race. Then it makes no difference whether we exist or not. We are no more significant than a swarm of mosquitoes. Our lives are then ultimately meaningless. Absent God there are also no objective moral standards. Who is to judge that Hitler's standards were wrong for his culture? Morals then become relative to the maker's preference. My self interest and that of the herd do not always correspond. Freud says our actions are the result of repressed sexual tendencies. Feminists have raised a storm over his sexual psychology because it is chauvinistic and degrading to women. Some psychologists have modified their theory because of this. However, if naturalism is true this is inconsistent and nature should determine what sex is dominant (p.69). Skinner says our actions are all conditioned responses with no free will. Skinners behaviorism can lead to a society envisioned by G. Orwell in the *1984 movie*, where the government controls and programs the thoughts of everyone. Nietzsche said that atheism would usher in **Nihilism** and the destruction of all meaning and value in life(p.64). It is difficult for an Atheist to truly live by that philosophy. They tend to jump to some constructed upper standard for value and meaning(p.65). Just because I chose some meaning and you choose another, makes neither true. They are both pretend constructions. Humanists are inconsistent in affirming the values of love and brotherhood(p.66). Without God the problem occurs of there being no punishment for unproven evil acts and no reward for good deeds and life giving sacrifices. Torture of war prisoners becomes OK. Oppression of women in some cultures also becomes OK. The slaughter of innocent children in war becomes OK. Medical experimentation and torture that the Nazi Dr's did, becomes OK, as does elimination of the weak and sick. There is the present Indian Hindu practice of suttee—burning the widow at the funeral of her husband(p.73). The lack of objective morals is a good argument for college students. Help them to the logical conclusion of their morals, without criticizing their morals. They may assert that values are social conventions pragmatically adopted to ensure survival. Ethnic cleansings, apartheid, child abuse, and the Holocaust are good examples that then become OK.

A number of evolutionists describe their view without God(Ham, 2008 Chap.21 p. 210 "Evolution as a Religion or Philosophy" by Mitchell, T, and White, M). They quoted Ernst Mayr a noted evolutionist "Evolutionary biology, in contrast with physics and chemistry is an historical science—the evolutionist attempts to explain events and processes that have already taken place. Laws and experiments are inappropriate techniques for the explication of such events and processes. Instead one constructs a historical narrative, consisting of a tentative reconstruction of the particular scenario that led to the events one is trying to explain." Dr. Michael Ruse (p.213), a philosopher of science and evolutionist wrote "Evolution is promoted by its practitioners as more than mere science. Evolution is promulgated as an ideology, a secular religion—a full-fledged alternative to Christianity, with meaning and morality. This was true of evolution in the beginning and is true of evolution today." William Provine, a prominent Cornell Univ. biologist wrote "There are no Gods, no purposes, no goal-directed forces of any kind. There is not life after death. When I die, I am absolutely certain that I am going to be dead. That's the end for me. There is no ultimate foundation for ethics, no ultimate meaning to life, and no free will for humans, either."(p.213). The belief in molecules-to-man evolution can and does cause people to become atheists, stated Charles Dawkins, a leading author on evolution and atheism(p.214). Another atheist, Jeremy Rifkin stated "It is our creation now. We make the rules; we establish the parameters of reality. We create the world, and because we do, we no longer feel beholden to outside forces. We no longer have to justify our behavior, for we are now the architects of the universe. We are responsible to nothing outside ourselves, for we are the kingdom, the power, and the glory forever and ever."

The ICR web site gave these references(web 99): Weikart, R. *From Darwin to Hitler: Evolutionary Ethics, Eugenics, and Racism in Germany*, Palgrave Macmillan, NY, NY 2004. Dr. Weikart, head of the history Dept at California State Univ. He noted many quotes from German philosophers, on how Darwin's theories influenced Germany's amoral attitude to humanity in favor of racial hygiene, with infanticide, and racial cleansing. Evolutionary progress was rated as the highest good for society, and this established moral relativism. This included devaluing the disabled and killing the unfit. Darwinism provided a justification for the Holocaust. It later led to the lessoning of Judeo-Christian values and more moral relativism in the 20th century.

Evans, R.J., in his book *The Coming of the Third Reich,* The Penguin Press, NY, NY 2004 agrees with Weikart: "Huxley a well known evolutionist wrote in *Ends and Means* 1938, pp. 270-273 "Those who detect no meaning in the world generally do so because, for one reason or another, it suits their purpose that the world should be meaningless . . . For myself, as no doubt, for the most of my contemporaries, the philosophy of meaninglessness was essentially an instrument of liberation. The liberation was desired was . . . liberation from a certain system of morality. We objected to the morality because it interfered with our sexual freedom."(web 99). The AIG site also lists references on this topic(web 21).

Other Religious Views vs. Christian Definitions of God

Kreeft94(p.90-7) described the nature of the one God. God is partly a mystery, but is given some revelation in Bible. He has both existence and essence. He is **Infinite**—therefore one God. He is **Spiritual and immaterial**—not limited as matter is; He is **Eternal;** He is **Transcendent and Immanent**—Above all but in all, sustaining all, not Pantheistic; He is **Omniscient** all knowing and **Omnipotent,** all Powerful; He is **Good, Perfect, holy.** Some parts of these definitions come from philosophy and logic and thus rule out other types of Gods (Geisler p.197). The cosmological, teleological and moral arguments all aid the definition of God. Taliaferro(p.11) gave further description of the divine attributes of God, with scriptures.

Kreeft (p.342) cited **Smith**, Huston, *The World's Religions*: Other religions have some truth but not full truth. Here the law of non contradiction applies, as they can't all be true(p.344). The moral code in other religions is not as different as their theology.

Within Theism—mono theism vs. polytheism—Hinduism and Greek mythology. This has the weakness of the God's battling, dying and changing or holding different positions.
Within monotheism—pantheism (God=everything and is not transcendent.)
Within Theism—Deism; God is real but remote.
Within Theism—Unitarianism vs. trinitarianism (Father, Son and Holy Spirit).

Within Christianity—Cessationists vs. Continuationists (spiritual gifts continue) see S. Stroms article in the Journal of the Apologetics Resource Center, Mar.-April 2008

Pantheism: The belief is that all is God and there are no distinctions between God and non God. God is impersonal but human beings are also God. The apparent distinctions between things are an illusion, as all reality is spiritual. **Morality is an illusion. True knowledge is acquired through meditation.** Empirical knowledge is an illusion (Kreeft94, Meister p.48). Meister(p.48, Web22) stated that pantheism holds that God is not above all (transcendent) and not personal. Variations of Pantheism include Hinduism, Taoism and the new age movement (Web22, Geisler p.198). In addition, Animism and Buddhism have some similarities to Pantheism. A number of logical problems occur with Pantheism: The original creation, the existence of evil, the absence of clear morals, the absence of right and wrong, and the lack of God acting in history and doing any miracles. Is God evil since he is part of evil? A further logical inconsistency occurs with our transformation and becoming one with God by meditation as noted below: (Meister p.64). Also see Cornish, Part 9 for other religions.

A. We are one with God
B. God is the changeless **impersonal** all.
C. We (god) need to move beyond our ignorance and become enlightened by realizing our own divinity. (How can we be one with the impersonal-**Aren't we personal**?)

Polytheism: There are many Gods and Goddesses (Kreeft 352, Web22). Historically Hinduism has some elements in common with this as does Greek mythology, the Sumerian and Egyptian Gods and the Roman religion. Shinto and Mormonism have some traits of polytheism (Geisler p198). Some problems also occur with this belief: God cannot be infinite or omnipotent, as only one God can be this. Some polytheistic Gods are not perfect or eternal as they die and do bad things. Can this explain good and evil by good and bad Gods and who is in control? Can the creation and maintained order of the universe and all the physical and mathematical laws operating in harmony be explained by this? **Wouldn't different Gods have different goals**? Why would they be in harmony?

Deism: God is real but remote and not presently involved in the universe(Kreeft 352). He created the universe and set up all the natural laws and left it to operate on its own (Web22). He is not described in any book like the Bible and he did not act in history and there are no true prophesies or miracles He did. It is related to Unitarianism and Universalism. We can only know God by reason and nature. Some logical objections include the following: What is the basis of morality and right and wrong? How can we depend on the physical universe sustaining itself and the laws of nature and science being true tomorrow? Nature is constantly changing. It's unlikely that all the verified history in the Bible, and the prophesies and miracles are untrue.

Monotheism: Other non-Christian beliefs like Judaism and Islam have fewer, but some limitations. Neither of these has the abundance or miracles found true, that Christianity does. Neither offers clear salvation by a known person and savior who claims to be God(Kreeft p.347). Muslims: "there is no God but Allah and Mohammad is his prophet." Kreeft (p.151).

The belief in Jesus as God and as Being Historical, and Being Resurrected

This distinguishes Christianity, and if true, rules out other religions as not having full truth(Kreeft p.347). "The doctrine that Christ is the only savior, does necessarily entail the conclusion that consciously professing Christians are the only ones saved." What then happens to those dying before Christ was revealed on earth? Jn. 10:30 "I and the Father are one" Jn. 14:9 "Whoever has seen me has seen the Father." The Bible claims the divinity of Christ as the Son of God, sinless, able to forgive sin, able to rename people, able to save us and the enfleshing of God and incarnation (Kreeft p.150-1). If Christ is God then he is omnipotent and present right now and able to transform our lives. This can be shock for new believers. A person can have 2 natures: material and immaterial and spiritual; body and soul. C.S. Lewis said the incarnation myth became fact. For an omnipotent God anything is possible, so it is possible if Christ was a Son. It's not a contradiction. Some animals have metamorphosis and transformation. Geisler discusses Jesus as being God and historically true in chapters 9-14 of his book, *I Don't have enough Faith to be an Atheist.*

The many prophesies in the Old Testament relating to Christ became true and the miracles were witnessed, including the resurrection of Christ. Kennedy (p.152) stated that **there are 333 prophecies about Christ made 400 yrs or more before his birth that came true.** Examples include being sold by a friend for 30 pieces of silver, being pierced by a spear, but having no broken bones, having lots cast for his garments, being nailed to a cross, etc. The odds of this occurring by chance are extremely rare. It is recorded in historical books that a person named Jesus lived and was crucified and died. This argument is made clearly in Strobel's book, *A Case for Christ,* which interviews many experts on this topic(Web 38). In addition, he notes (Strobel98, p.90) G. Habermas' book *The Verdict of History* which cites 39 ancient sources documenting Jesus' existence in history—Josephus, Tacitus, Pliney, Thalllus, and others (Web23). Wikipedia (Web 39) cited Josephus and the Antiquities as being accurate in describing the death of James the brother of Jesus by stoning. He claimed to be the Son of God and existing from the beginning of the world and God in flesh (incarnated). Kreeft (p.173) listed scriptures: 1Cor 12:3;15:3-8; Phil 2:11; Jn. 14:9. Most agree Jesus existed and was good and wise teacher; but he claimed to be God before Abraham. **Here are the only alternates**: Jesus claimed divinity (Kreeft p.171).

A. He meant it literally
   1. It is true—**he is Lord**
   2. It is false
      a. He knew it was false—**a liar;** How could he have so many disciples and do miracles?
      b. He didn't know it was false—**a lunatic**, same as above and the resurrection proved this.

B. He meant it non-literally, mystically—he is a Guru, does not fit with being a Jew, a historical religion and miracles. His resurrection was witnessed by many persons and written in the Gospels. The stone was rolled away, there is no corpse, and the tomb was empty(Kreeft p.195). Kreeft (p.178-198) has many arguments refuting alternate theories to Jesus' resurrection and also confirming it. The swoon theory is well refuted as there is evidence that he did die and it would be impossible to rescue him and keep it quiet. A brief summary below outlines the reasoning: It is very unlikely all the disciples would die for a lie(Kreeft p.182).

Jesus Died:	He rose	**1. Christianity**
	He didn't rise—The apostles were deceived	2. Hallucinations
	The apostles were mythmakers	3. Myth
	The apostles were deceivers	4. Conspiracy

Habermas (p 248-250) also asserted the resurrection. He cited several nonchristian references noting Jesus crucifixion(p.187-228). Jesus is the man buried in the Shroud of Turin and there is additional evidence—the resurrection(p.249). The Pope recently endorsed the Shroud(Web24). A number of books on Jesus being historically true are on the Habermas site (Web36). According to **Josh McDowell**, he was as an agnostic at college when he decided to prepare a paper that would examine the historical evidence of the Christian faith in order to disprove it. However, he converted to Christianity, after, as he says, he found evidence for it, not against it.(Web37). Geisler (p.300) quotes Habermas who reviewed all the theories opposing the resurrection in *The Risen Jesus and Future Hope*. "Skeptics must provide more than alternative theories to the Resurrection; they must provide first century evidence for those theories." **The historical facts** from many early Christian and non-Christian references support the following:(Geisler p.300)

1. Jesus died by Roman Crucifixion; Non-Christian writers confirm this.
2. He was buried, in a private tomb of Joseph of Arimathea, of the Jewish Sanhedrin
3. Soon after the disciples were discouraged, bereaved and despondent
4. Jesus' tomb was found empty very soon after his internment.
5. The disciples and Paul believed they saw and heard the risen Jesus
6. Due to these experiences the disciples' lives were thoroughly transformed and they were willing to die for this belief

7. Their proclamations of the resurrection took place very early in Jersulaem, the city of his death. The gospel message centered on this.

8. Sunday, the day of the resurrection, was the primary day of their worship

9. James the brother of Jesus was a skeptic before the resurrection, but was converted by seeing him. The same is true of Paul. Paul agreed with the apostles about the resurrection and this is in early creeds.

Other current facts include the following:

1. Three MD's note in the Journal of the AMA 3/21/1986 that medical evidence affirms that Jesus would have died from the whipping and the difficulty of breathing on cross, before being speared. The spear likely perforated the lung, pericardium and the heart.(blood and water from the wound).Geisler (p.305)

2. Historical evidence from crucified skeletons, show major body-bone damage and the likelihood of surviving this Roman execution is very remote.

Some common alternate theories include the following: (Geisler p.304-312; Kreeft 181-196)

1. **The Hallucination theory**: The disciples saw visions or hallucinations. He appeared to many people at different times and settings. The risen Jesus walked, talked, ate and was touched. Hallucinations are not generally experienced by groups of people with the same observations. Also a group of people do not have back and forth conversation with a hallucination or watch him eat. The Jesus Seminar (web40) supported this theory. They also invalidated 82% of Jesus' sayings in the gospels and favor the Gnostic gospels instead. They also invalided all miracles as being unnatural. The empty tomb noted by the Jews, has to be explained. Would the disciples steal the body and then talk of a bodily hallucination when they knew where the dead body was?

2. **The Swoon or apparent death theory**: He didn't die and escaped from the guarded tomb with a big stone in front of it. The medical

opinions are that he would have died and had no strength to escape. How could the guards have been overcome? Why would the disciples be overjoyed and transformed to see bloody and weak Jesus? Why would they then lie about his resurrection including his brother James and Paul? Historical evidence from crucified skeletons, show major body damage and the likelihood of surviving a Roman execution is very remote. A variation of this is that the disciples stole the body while the guards were sleeping. This is the excuse the early Jews stated to explain the empty tomb. How could someone move a great stone without waking the guards? They thus admitted the tomb was empty. Matthew 28:11-15 records that the Jews had to pay off the guards and promise to keep them out of trouble so they could maintain the story. How could a live Jesus hide, lie and remain silent for a long time? The Jews would surely have found him.

3. **A substitute took Jesus' place on the cross**: This is the explanation some Muslims offer and it is in the Quran; also that Allah raised him up. The Quran was written 600 yrs. after the crucifixion. How could everyone be so deceived—the guards who whipped him and put on the crown of thorns, the Jews who captured him and wanted him executed, and the disciples? Why would Jesus then have remained silent while alive and lie about his prophesized death as being a sacrifice for man's sins? The empty tomb is also a problem and it would have to also be assumed the disciples stole the body of another man.

4. **The New Testament writers copied pagan myths**: The apostles and New Testament were not inclined to myths. The first apostles were simple sincere peasants not cunning liars or experienced mythologists. They preached a resurrected Christ and died for it (Kreeft94 p.185). The change in the disciples from fear to strong faith and from cowardice to steadfast boldness is not explained by myth or even by a vision. If the apostles stole the dead body, why would they be overjoyed and transformed? The myth does not explain the empty tomb which was a fact. C.S Lewis who was an expert writer of myths, stated that the New Testament does not resemble myth literature. Other students of myth literature agree. When non-Christian writers talked about Jesus and his followers they were not talking about myths they were talking about actual

events and history. No Greek or Roman myth spoke of the literal incarnation of the monotheistic God into a human form.(Geisler p. 312).

Miracles

The cosmological, teleological (design) and moral arguments provide strong arguments for God, but don't require religion or the Bible.(Geisler p 216). C.S. Lewis stated: If we admit God we must admit a miracle. The first miracle is the creation of the universe and of all life Geisler (p197). **The God who created it is by the cosmological argument timeless, non-spatial, immaterial, outside time and space, infinite, all powerful, and personal.** Because of these characteristics God can do miracles anytime He wants (Geisler p.200). However as S. Cowan pointed out in "Discerning the Voice of God; the Apologetic function of Miracles" If God does a miracle, he has a purpose or reason for doing so, often as a sign that people will take note of and attribute to Him and his believers. However as Geisler notes, He does make Himself so obvious or so intervening in nature to cancel out our free will. God leaves us free will so He can woo us rather than command us(p. 201). He does provide a written history of His miracles in the Bible. Natural laws are not immutable. If God made them, He can overrule them or provide an exception to them; just as we can override the natural law of momentum of a baseball by catching or batting it(p.204).

The many miracles such as the resurrection in the Bible are somewhat unique to Christianity and will be discussed further. The more common definition is a supernatural event or "a special act of God that interrupts the natural course of events. "Alternatively, an event need not run counter to the laws of nature in order to count as miraculous. It might be seen as a special act of God because of its context. Examples would be the sudden remission of cancer, with or without therapy or treatment, after a Christian or group prays for a healing. Lewis (p.90-94) also noted a miracle is not an event without cause or results. (Geisler p.210) gave a table classifying all types of unusual events. With providence God uses natural laws at special timing to aid the believer. The cause may be God and the results follow known laws. Christian philosopher and apologist Dr. Winfried Corduan(Branch) responds to other skeptical objections, including those of David Hume and Antony Flew, in "Miracles and Their

Omniscient Critics." As you will see, most arguments against miracles claim that we could not have enough evidence for them to override our confidence in the laws of nature, or that science somehow makes miracles unlikely or belief in them irrational. Hume also stated that a rare event should not be believed over the most normal event. However, that has an immediate exception when a golfer gets a hole in one. It is a rare event, yet it is believed if it is credibly witnessed and written down. Also some rare events like the creation of the universe and first life have best explanation by an outside creator(Geisler p.206). Corduan aptly shows that all such arguments require that the skeptic be omniscient—which, of course, is impossible. No one has enough knowledge to make universal judgments ruling out all possibilities. The "scientific" worldview, a mechanistic view that claims everything that occurs happens only according to rigid scientific laws which totally control everything. Perhaps we should, with tongue in cheek, reply that it is the scientific naturalists who demonstrate the most "faith" in order to believe the plausibility of macro-evolution(Branch, C). Corduan's summary of arguments follows:

1. **The Critic is Omniscient and He knows infallibly that Miracles Are Impossible.** In other words he has a fixed mind set and is not open minded.
2. **A Critic Knows From Science That Miracles Are Impossible.** Have there been decisive experiments to prove that miracles are impossible? There have not been any, nor is it conceivable that there could be any. This is a philosophical stance. Miracles are a free act of an all powerful God.
3. **The Critic Knows That One Cannot Know That a Miracle Has Occurred.** Thus he has to deny all observed evidence in favor of maintaining his position. He has to deny other's observations as being in error. This also is illogical, as it denies the observed evidence and is omniscient. Lewis (p.73-5.; 159-171) was quoted below:

"Miracles defy the laws of nature." Experiments tell us what regularly happens. Some laws of nature have exceptions. **Science does not say there can be no exceptions; that is a philosophical assumption.** No one knows all the laws, they are still being discovered. Many have observed apparent miracles. Most alleged miracles may be false, so we need a criterion to judge them. Historical evidence is one criteria, our intuitive sense of logical fitness is another. **The grand miracle—incarnation**: That God became man, can be argued on historical grounds. The analogy from a story or symphony can be made: a piece is inserted; if it improves the work it is accepted; it integrates the whole. God becoming man is a little like God's rationality and spirit being in man. Adam's fall caused a need for redemption of all. If God came down he should improve and redeem. God never undoes or redoes anything but evil and its effects(Lewis p.173-213). Divine miracles glorify God and truth, not the performer or error. Satan can do counterfeit miracles (Geisler p.214).

Geisler asks why a number of religious scholars (like the Jesus Seminar group) don't believe in the resurrection. If one has a strong belief in science and naturalistic philosophy, and rules out divine intervention, one then denies all miracles. Then the standard of evidence becomes extremely high, making it almost impossible to prove a miracle. D. Crossan, one of the leaders of the Jesus seminar group, had a debate with Wm. Craig. Crossan's strong bias against all miracles was noted in this debate(Geisler p.315). Relative to this position or philosophy, the arguments of Corduan above are instructive. Some laws of nature have exceptions. **Science does not say there can be no exceptions and no God; that is a philosophical assumption**.

An important question concerns **whether God still does miracles today**. The Bible is filled with miracles which are very unusual and help prove its validity. In theory God could do a miracle whenever He chooses and did many of them to confirm new truths (revelation) in the Bible(Geisler p.216). Several types of miracles appear to continue, including new believers receiving the transforming Holy Spirit and the future end times fulfillments. There are two views on this called Cessationists and Continuationists presented by Stroms (Branch) "Contrary to what many Cessationists have said, signs, wonders, and spiritual gifts don't authenticate the apostles, but rather Jesus and the apostolic message about him. Furthermore, nowhere does the NT say that authentication or attestation was the sole or exclusive purpose of such displays of divine power. These supernatural phenomena also serve to glorify God (John 2:11; 9:3; 11:4, 40; Mt. 15: 29-31) to evangelize the lost (Acts 9:32-43), to display love and compassion for the hurting (Mt. 14:14; Mk. 1:40-41), and to build up the body of Christ (1Cor. 12:7; 14:3-5,26). Even if the ministry of the miraculous gifts to attest and authenticate has ceased (a point I concede only for the sake of argument), such gifts would continue to function in the church for the other reasons cited. Some have pointed to 2 Corinthians 12:12, where Paul asserts that "the signs of a true apostle were performed among you with all perseverance, by signs and wonders and miracles" (NASB). He does not say the insignia or marks of an apostle are signs, wonders and miracles, but rather that miraculous phenomena accompanied his ministry in Corinth as attendant elements in his apostolic work." Stroms (Branch08) provided more details on this debate.

Bergman 2011 made some good points on miracles and creation. He noted the creation ex-nihilo(out of nothing) is a long standing Christian and Jewish doctrine. John 1:3 implies it was created by the word of God. He notes the example, that Adam and Eve were created fully formed somewhat instantaneously and had the appearance of age on the days they were created. If one did medical estimations of the rate of bone ossification backwards the day after they were created, this may indicate they were 20 or more yrs old. Other tests on the rate of DNA degradation may indicate a very young age. Is this deceptive by God? This can also answer the old question of the chicken or the egg being first. They could have been both created simultaneously as the chicken was fully functional. **Thus Bergman repeats the mature creation hypothesis, where things have the appearance of age**. This reasoning can be extended to all parts of creation as Col. 1:16-17 says everything was created by God. For the earth to have advanced life, he notes that the moon is necessary and so are many balanced eco-cycles:C, N, O, S. The bible states the trees were created with fruit and seeds. The fish were created swimming and birds flying. These are definitely miracles as is the resurrection of Lazarus and Jesus. So it is possible that this miraculous creation also applies to the stars and heavens. **The Apostles Creed states** the God created the heavens and earth. The more we apply naturalism to every step of the creation of the heavens over billions of yrs the more we deny miracles. It is not unreasonable to assume that God created the stars and their light in transit so that Adam and Eve could see them. Man would glorify God because he could see the glory of the heavens. Is this deception on God's part because it defies our recent back figuring of the stars separation due to the speed of light? God can do any miracle he wishes.

Dr. T. J. Tofflemire

The Truth of the Bible-Inerrancy

Theologians refer to inerrancy views rather than truth. Erickson (p.69) reviewed the three classical views of Bible inerrancy: **Absolute inerrancy, Full inerrancy and Limited inerrancy**. Absolute inerrancy holds that scientific and historical details are true in an exact manner. Full inerrancy holds that the scientific and historical details are true in an approximate phenomenological way. That is the writers made statements as to the way they appear to the human eye, using human language. For example, 2 Chron. 4:2 stated the diameter of the molten sea was 10 cubits and the circumference was 30 cubits. Using the πD formula, it would have circumference of 31.416 cubits. The verse is approximately correct and correct in the view of the writer. Thus this verse would fit into the full inerrancy view but is more difficult to fit into Absolute inerrancy. Limited inerrancy holds the Bible true in its salvation doctrines but may be in error in its historical and scientific statements. Erickson noted that there are some apparent or possible historic contradictions in scripture and also that numbers as used in the time of the writers were also more symbolic in meaning than they are to us now. Also later discoveries sometimes resolve the apparent differences in scripture (Erickson, p.69-71). He gave the **Full inerrancy definition** as follows: "The Bible, when correctly interpreted in the light of the level to which culture and the means of communication had developed at the time it was written and in view of the purposes for which it was given, is fully truthful in all that it affirms" (Erickson p.72). Most fundamental Protestants hold to full inerrancy not absolute inerrancy. The Bible was not intended to be a precise scientific handbook nor exhaustive in truth (Schaeffer 1976-p.76). Some items are not stated.

The International Council on Biblical Inerrancy(**ICBI**) of 1978-86 (Web25) gave a view that somewhat agrees with the absolute inerrancy view. Article 15 stated "We affirm the harmony of special with general revelation and therefore of biblical teaching with the facts of nature. We deny that any genuine scientific facts are inconsistent with the true meaning of any passage of Scripture." My view after reading all the articles: Art. 15 supports the idea that general revelation is an important area of knowledge that science, if correctly understood, would fit with special revelation in the Bible and not disagree with it. I don't agree that we should change what appears to be the straight forward reading of scripture to something very stretched, tenuous and different to make it fit with the latest vote of 80-90 % of scientists, when 10-20% of scientists offer a different view that fits with the Bible. It is sometimes difficult to determine which scientists are correct and what is the true general revelation. With more knowledge scientists sometimes change their majority view on an issue(web25).

One's view of scriptural interpretation and of creation can be affected by how one views the authority of the scriptures. The view of the Protestants is that scripture alone (Sola Scriptura) is sufficient to be the basis of Christian doctrine (web26). In addition, most protestant denominations also adopt many of the early creeds like the Apostle's creed. They may have slightly differing doctrinal positions, although sticking to a more strict interpretation of the scriptures. The Catholics, Anglican and orthodox churches, value the role of the church authorities to interpret scriptures and some have a more liberal interpretation of the scriptures (web26). Some common texts, reviewing and classifying scriptures, classify the book of Genesis as an historical book (Wilkinson, Hendricks). They classify **17 books in the Old Testament and 5 in the New Testaments as historical books**.

The Catholic view of creation is that Genesis should not be interpreted literally or as a historic book, but symbolically (Web 27). They also view scriptures to have limited inerrancy, which according to Erickson (p. 72) is a more liberal view of scriptural authority. In addition, Dr. Rowan Williams, the Archbishop of Canterbury, the *de facto* head of the Church of England (also known as the "Anglican" church),was featured in a wide-ranging interview with *The Guardian*—a left-leaning daily newspaper in the UK. His views were that we should not teach the creation views given in Genesis and it should not be treated as a historical book of the Bible (Web28).

A 709-page book by an Orthodox monk reviewed the history of Christian literature on Genesis and creation noted that the early Christian writings support a historical interpretation of Genesis. With many lengthy quotations from the 'Holy Fathers' of Eastern Orthodoxy from the fourth century to the present, the book reinforces the assertion that a Six-Day Creation about 6,000 years ago, followed by a global catastrophic Flood, was the historic teaching of the church until the 19th century (web29).

Ham2011(p.213-25) discussed the authorship of the Pentateuch-Moses or the Documentary Hypothesis(DH). The DH held that four different authors wrote the four differing sections J, E, D, and P reflecting the differing names for God and then it was complied and edited by a redactor. Ham noted that many of the authors for this view were Jewish, skeptics or liberal theologians. It was also noted that there were no complete documents for the J, E, D or P ever found. Ham then cites about 25 scriptures implying that Moses wrote or gave the law. Some will be cited: Ex. 17:14 "Write this for a memorial in the book and recount it"; Num.33:2 "Now Moses wrote down the starting points of their journeys at the command of the Lord"; Mal. 4:4 :Remember the Law of Moses, My servant, which I commanded him in Horeb for all Israel, with the statues and judgments"; John 5:46-47 Jesus said "Moses—because he wrote about me. But if you don't believe his writings,"—); John 7:19 "Didn't Moses give you the law?"; Rom. 10:5 "For Moses writes about the rightness which is of the law." If one holds to Full Inerrancy of the scriptures, it is logical that one would hold to Moses writing most of the Pentateuch. There are a few exceptions, as when he was dead, Joshua may have completed his document, Deut. 34:5-12. Using an uninspired redactor to edit the books degrades scripture. The PCA report supports Moses authorship as does the Holman Study Bible.

The Pentateuch was read by Solomon at the temple between 951-1016 BC(Web93). The text including Job had been written by Moses between 1491-1406 BC. After Moses, the tests were carefully recopied by scribes. The Greek language Old Testament (OT) was written after the conquest of Alexander the Great around 130 BC and is known as the Septuagint. Some existing manuscripts of parts of the Old Testament date from 200-150 BC from the Dead Sea Scrolls find. McDowell(p.70) documented the very accurate copying and checking of the OT.

"Belief in a historical Genesis is important because progressive creation and its belief in millions of years (1) contradicts the clear teaching of Scripture, (2) assaults the character of God, (3) severely damages and distorts the Bible's teaching on death, and (4) undermines the gospel by undermining the clear teaching of Genesis, which gives the whole basis for Christ's Atonement and our need for a Redeemer. **So ultimately, the issue of a literal Genesis is about the authority of the Word of God versus the authority of the words of sinful men"(web30).** The differing views of creation relate to how to view the scriptures and were also discussed in the prior section on World Views. The Full inerrancy view agrees with the ICBI, supports an historical Genesis and agrees with most of the authors cited in the following few paragraphs. It makes the arguments for lack of internal Bible contradictions stronger.

Kreeft94 stated there are some internal and very few external contradictions in the Bible. Internal ones are not substantive and show the different views and perspectives of the authors. Haley(p.x) in his classic book on Bible Discrepancies stated "I—avow, as the issue of my investigations, the profound conviction that every difficulty and discrepancy in the scriptures is, and will yet be seen to be, capable of a fair and reasonable solution." Archer also agreed. Remember the elephant viewing example with reporters giving different perspectives as different views. Taylor (Ham 2008, 2010) maintained the Bible is inerrant in the original scriptures. A quote on discrepancies follows:

Commentary on Haley's book Jan. 6, 2003 By **Edward J Vasicek**
This review is from: Alleged Discrepancies of the Bible (Paperback)
Although this work is old, it is, in many ways, still up to date. It brings together Scriptures that apparently contradict one another and shows how they can be reconciled. These discrepancies are resolved hermeneutically (interpretationally), not so much archaeologically. Therefore, most resolutions do not depend upon discoveries made in the 125 years since the book was originally authored. One could probably find similar reconciliations by digging through commentaries, but we often want a quick and ready answer, and Haley often comes through. His answers are brief and understandable—no fluff. Although not all of his reconciliations are satisfying, most are. This is a reference book, not a book for reading. But it sure comes in handy. Gleason **Archer's book**, "Encyclopedia of Bible Difficulties" is much more thorough about the subjects it covers (and I highly recommend it), but it only address a fraction of the passages addressed here by Haley. Along with Bullinger's "Figures of Speech Used in the Bible," both of these 19th century volumes have no worthy modern replacements.
Archer, Gleason L New International Encyclopedia of Bible Difficulties. Zondervan

Taylor wrote "Isn't the Bible Full of Contradictions" p.283-297 of Ham, AIG 2008. He stated (Taylor p.284) "If the Bible is truly from God,—if two parts seen to be in opposition or in contradiction to each other, then our interpretation of one or both parts must be in error." Ps. 119:160 "The sum of your word is truth" Titus, 1:2 "God who does not lie" However if a student is determined to find an error in the Bible he can as it can become a self fulfilling act(p. 285). **Only the original manuscripts are maintained to be inerrant**. Translation to other languages can introduce errors but they are usually minor. Presuppositional discrepancies can occur if one starts with naturalistic assumptions—like the world and man is very old. Reading a phrase out of context can also cause an apparent error, examples: Ps 14:1 "The fool has said in his heart there is no God;" here one could wrongly take out the four words "there is no God." Also note Ecc. 7:29 "God made man upright", and Ps. 51:5 "Behold, I was brought forth in iniquity" In context—Ecc. is referring to Adam and Eve, while, David in the Ps. is referring to his person. Thus there is no discrepancy between the two prior texts. Translational errors: Gen. 2:19 "formed or had formed" the 2nd is correct; note Lev. 11:13-20 vs. 19 bats are listed with birds or fouls. The Hebrew word owph means has a wing, which a bat and insects do. Language can also change over time as has occurred with the 1611 KJV vs. present English for the word replenish, which in 1611 meant to fill and now means to refill. Idioms or common usage: Lev.11:20-23 "Insects that creep on all fours." This is referring to the colloquial use of walking on all fours. Also locust and similar insects do walk on four legs and jump with the other 2(p.294). Jesus' resurrection after 3 days depends on how days are counted(p.295). The Cainan in Luke 3:36 genealogy is a copying error not present in the original manuscripts stated Dr. John Gill (Taylor, p.296, Ham p.113).

Sproul(p.138) made a case for the Bible being inerrant and inspired. Some say the Bible is the word of God, because it says this about 3000 times. However, the reasoning is still weak; just because a book, any book, says it is the word of God does not make it so. The case is supported by history, miracles, and prophecy being true. Even philosophers say it's a book of history, which makes it different than many other books of faith that are not history.

The following confirmation of the word logically is given by Sproul: p.141

1. The Bible contains reliable history
2. The Bible records miracles as part of the history (fulfilled prophecy is a miracle)
3. The miracles authenticate the Bible's messengers and their message
4. Therefore the Bible message ought to be received as divine.
5. The Bible message includes the doctrine of its own inspiration.

6. Therefore the Bible is more that a generally reliable record; It is a divinely inspired record.

Truth of the Bible in General

Arguments from Prophecy: Kennedy (p.152) stated that there 333 prophecies about Christ made 400 yrs or more before his birth that came true. Examples include being sold by a friend for 30 pieces of silver, being pierced by a spear, but having no broken bones, having lots cast for his garments, being nailed to a cross, etc. The odds of this occurring by chance are extremely rare. He also noted that there are 2000 other prophecies in the Bible that came true(p.155). There are many concerning the ancient city of Babylon. Records show it was a magnificent city surrounded by walls 200 ft high and 178 ft. thick at the base. Nevertheless it was prophesied that the walls would be completely destroyed and the city would never be rebuilt. It is also odd that the city was never rebuilt and is a desolate area in Iraq now (Kennedy p.157). Also no prophecy has been disproved; Up to 300 Prophecies are known true about Christ (Kreeft94 p.217).

Arguments from Archaeology: McDowell (Chap.3 and 13) noted that archaeology confirms the Bible. N. Glueck stated (p.89) "Scores of archaeological findings have been made which confirm in clear outline or exact detail historical statements in the Bible." For example the walls of Jericho have been found fallen outward, which is odd but true (McDowell p.95). They are dated 1500-1400 BC in agreement with Bible history (web70). Many biblical cities and characters have been verified in other documents. W. F. Albright, a noted archaeologist stated "There can be no doubt that archaeology has confirmed the substantial historicity of the Old Testament tradition."(McDowell p.372). An important discovery was of the ancient Elba clay tablets in Syria(Heeren p.84). These tablets confirm ancient writing, parts of the creation story in Genesis, and biblical character names and laws (McDowell 375,6). Clay tablets have also been found confirming the tower of Babel history (p.378). Some artifacts from Saul, David and Solomon also exist (McDowell p.380). H. Morris (98) stated that **two great non-Christian archaeologists, Nelson Glueck and William Albright stated that the Bible was the single most accurate source document from history.** Kreeft noted (p. 217) "Nothing in Archaeology has disproven scripture:" Source:B. G. Wood *Biblical Archeological Review,* Mr.-Ap. 1990. Beechick (p.92) outlines why Egyptian history and dates may be wrong and gives older dates than biblical history and genealogies. Heeren (p.18) noted that archaeologist Wm. Albright discovered some Bronze Age cities with mounds that had inscriptions of Arriyuk, Abraham, Eber, and Laban all biblical names from Genesis Chap.14 that dated about 2000BC. Albright said this confirms the history of the Old Testament(Heeren). Wilson's(web77) article also supports the history of the Bible. Abraham's city of Ur has been found and his negotiations with the Hittites. A good summary of archeological findings is also given by Branch in 2011.

Arguments from Historical Records: Habermas cites **17 nonchristian historical references to Jesus' existence**, 11 for his death on the cross. There are about 7 nonchristian references and 11 more nonbiblical ones referring to the resurrection. Historical data includes primary and secondary written sources and archaeology (Hab. p.219-25). It has sometimes been alleged that the Bible has been copied so many times that it cannot be reliable. "Yet historical research confirms the reliability of the Bible. The number of ancient manuscripts is large, and the time scale between when the originals were written and the oldest extant copies is small which minimizes the possibility of transmission errors. By these criteria, the Bible is one of the most reliable books relative to early manuscripts. Contrast this with the works of Plato. Ancient copies of Plato are far fewer in number and the time span of transmission is much greater than for the Bible. It would be inconsistent for someone to deny the historical reliability of the Bible, while embracing the historical reliability of any other ancient document" (Lisle p.100, Haley 41, Morris09, p.94). The Old Testament is also more accurate that any other ancient writing. The Samaritan Pentateuch is from 400 BC, the Septuagint Greek from 280 BC, the dead sea scrolls in 0 AD, and the Latin Vulgate in 400 AD (Morris09 p.94).

The New Testament(NT) has good manuscript evidence (Hab.p.276)**:** There are over 5000 copies of the early manuscripts, while many other classical works have only 20 or less copies. Out of Livy's 142 books of history there are only manuscripts for 107. None of the NT cannon documents are missing. The Gospels were written by eye witnesses or significantly influenced by first hand testimony. Early nonchristian reviews by historians and government officials confirm the main elements of NT history. Geisler(p.225-247) **confirms** in detail the **early writings of the NT** gospels, Acts and Paul's letters, and their reliability. Many of the books give many factual and historical details that could have been checked(Geisler p.252-273). Also see p.35 and the apostle's death dates.

Arguments from Numerics and Theomatics or from ELS Code: Sabiers' book (p.40-50) notes that most sentences, and many names in the Bible follow a numeric pattern that can't be explained by chance, when one uses the original Greek or Hebrew texts. In the Hebrew and Greek alphabets each letter stands for both a letter and a unique number. Thus each word, phrase, and sentence has a numerical value. The probabilities are very high of divine inspiration. Del Washburn (web 80) draws similar conclusions in his books *The Original Code in the Bible* and *Theomatics II*. Satinover (p.1) noted that there is an equidistant letter sequence (ELS) code in the Torah (1st 5 books of the Bible) and he asserts that God must have dictated the exact words and order to Moses to keep the order of letters. Rigorous statistics has shown that some code words appear with meaning defying probabilities of 1/million or more. For example when Leviticus 1:1-13 is written on a rectangular grid, the name Aaron appears 25 times in ELS code. The chances of this occurring are less than one in 4 million(p.35).

Summary: There are five points that show the Bible to be true history: Prophecies being fulfilled creating high probabilities of truth, archaeology verifying it, historical literature documenting it is true, numerics supporting it, and its lacking of substantial discrepancies. When looking at ancient historical documents the Bible is unique in its degree of truth. It also differs from books of other religions which don't have the details and reliability of history in the Bible. The philosopher Magee (p.57) pointed out that the **Christian religion is a history with assertions and beliefs, rather that a philosophy.**

Early History and Lineages

There are many evidences the Bible is true from arguments above. It is held to be divinely inspired by God and fits the Full inerrancy view. Let's assume the Bible history is true and try to see how to square that with other history accounts. One of the stronger arguments is the lineages in the Bible from Adam through Christ which are about 4000 yrs. according to Usher's chronology (Finegan Table 196, p.405). This has Adam's creation at 4004 BC, Christ's birth at bout 4 BC, and the flood at 2349 BC. This is one of the more cited chronologies, although some biblical scholars hold to other ones (Ham2008 p. 185). The Eusebius chronology dates Adam at 5200 BC(Finegan Table 97, p.190). Some authors, that are not well accepted, date Adam as early as 11,013 BC (Camping p.101). Some conventional historians and theologians date man's activities and artifices' back to this time (10,000 BC) (Pierce-Ham08 p.180). Ham disagrees with the Camping analysis. This topic of old dating and calendars is very complex.

Creation Wiki (web93) gave a concise analysis of the times from the death of Terah to the birth of Jesus. Here there is a dispute of about 215 yrs: "The genealogy is precise and detailed from the first day of creation to the death of Terah. Ages are given for the birth, next son in line, and death of all the patriarchs reported to have lived during that period. There is some dispute about Terah's age at the birth of Abraham, but the record from there is once again fairly clear until the death of Joseph. From then until the Exodus of Israel, however, the Bible text lends itself to two different interpretations that differ by 215 years. The chronology of the kings of Israel beginning with Solomon and continuing to Zedekiah is subject to multiple differing interpretations of concurrence of reigns, viceroyalties, and the like. The Bible also does not give a precise length for the period from the end of the kingdoms of Israel to the New Testament era, though most authorities, both biblical and secular, are in accord on the date of the ending of those kingdoms." Two main differing views are noted: Usher and Thiele. The Usher view is more biblical based and is used by AIG and ICR. The Thiele view reconciles the I &II Kings lists with Assyrian tablets. It is accepted by some seminaries and by Fulbright and McFall. The two views differ by about 45 yrs.(web93).

Freeman wrote in (Mortonson08 Chap.10) "**Do the Genesis** 5 & 11 **Genealogies Contain Gaps?**" The short answer is **no**. Freeman did extensive seminary studies and articles on the gaps question; his chapter of 30 pages summarizes much of the work. He reviews the literature and cites 100 references and many different viewpoints on the gaps, with pro and con being given. He (p.308) maintains that Gen. 5 and 11 are correct and unique in that they give years and numbers while many other genealogies no not. There are different genre(types) of genealogies. For example Ezra 7 aims mainly to establish ones right to a certain office, and thus does not include every generation. The Gen. 5 and 11 ones have ages and also the toledoth format(these are the family records or generation of). Some genealogies are more horizontal (Gen 10) with the purpose of showing the spread of humanity to the nations and locations(p.290). **Gen. 5, 11 also agree with the earliest versions of Luke 3 and the Samaritan Pentateuch and with 1Chron.1:18** all of which do not have a 2nd Cainan. He notes the oft repeated argument that "When X had lived Y yrs. and fathered Z, should be interpreted that X had lived Y yrs. and became the father of someone in the list of descent to Z" is false, based on clear hermeneutics(p.303). One of the common reasons for doing this is to stretch the ages of man to agree with the traditional scientific view of ages of man older than 6000 yrs.(p.305). The ancient Masoretic text of Gen.11 does not have a 2nd Cainan, but some of the Septuagint texts do. Niessen argues that the latter(Septuagint) is an inaccurate revision of the former (p.309-10) to agree with Manetho's inflated Egyptian king list. As a result the Septuagint adds 586 yrs to the genealogy and has different age numbers. The Samarian Pentateuch does not have a 2nd Cainan. Luke's genealogy text copies dating after the 4th century have the 2nd Cainan, but the texts prior to the 4th century including Josephus do not list a 2nd Cainan(p.313). Thus it was concluded that a 2nd Cainan did not exist. The Gen. 11 text is correct. Another discussion of the possible gaps and lineages is given by Pierce and Ham (Ham08,p172-182). They refute the argument of begat not meaning father/son relationship by many other usages. They argue that Mat.1:8 is not a complete chronology due to the wording; Mat. 1:8 is also from the viewpoint of Joseph's linage rather than Mary's. The topic again appears complex. Hodge (Ham08, p.185) gives a table of differing author's chronologies varying from 3836-5501 BC. The topic is of key importance and many scholars disagree on it, so **Freeman's summary is briefly noted**:(p.306-7) 1. **All biblical genealogies do not agree when all lumped together, but this ignores genre**; different ones have different purposes. A simplistic argument is then—since all genealogies do not agree; the Bible is inconsistent and cannot be relied upon. See the Bible inerrancy section. 2. Most genealogies do not fit a standard 10 item list, so this can be dismissed; 3. The overlapping life spans do not disprove anything, as it is possible. 4. The X fathered Z fits good Bible hermeneutics, while X fathered a line leading to Z does not.

If the biblical chronologies are correct, it means the time from Adam to Christ was probably no more than 5200 yrs. This implies a young human history and probably a young animal history when compared to what conventional scholars would say. Some bits and theories of history will be explored. Beechick04(p.50-52) in a book of a probable story format, claims that Adam and all the favored line Seth, Enoch, etc. were interested in astronomy and signs in the stars they were also preachers of righteousness. Cain's line was worldlier but pursued metallurgy, music and weaponry and built a small city separated from where the favored line lived. Noah and his favored line to Shem and to Abraham also had interest in the stars(p.48,66). The favored line kept written genealogical records that were passed down. Beechich04 (p.153) cited Morris *The Genesis Record* and claimed that Hebrew word "**toledoth**" translates into English as generations this used frequently in the Bible as a concluding phrase "these are the record of the generations of" or "the account of" See Gen. 5:1; 6:9; 10:1; 11:10; 11;27. The history preceding was written before the patriarch died. The evidence of star interest and astrology is noted by Allen (p.1). The earliest star notes are of the Zodiac from Sumerian, with six signs Taurus, Cancer, Virgo, Scorpio, Capricorn and Pisces. This progressed to 11 and then 12 signs. The names of the months seem to have some correlation with the 12 signs as early as 2000 BC (Allen p.2). Hebrew antiquities have long recognized Enoch as inventor of the Dodecatemory divisions (12 signs or houses of the zodiac); and both Berosus and Josephus declare that Abraham was famous for his celestial observations and taught the Egyptians astronomy. A search of Wikipedia/Zodiac (Web31) reveals shared common star descriptions among ancient civilizations as does Allen's book. This supports the contention that they could have been passed down from Adam's and Enoch's early interest. Morris1989 (p.266) agrees and cited E.W. Maunder in *Astronomy of the Bible* who noted that many star pictures reflect crushing of the serpents head and wounding of the redeemer's heel. He said 1/3 of the constellations show events of Genesis Chap. 1-10(Morris1989 p.267).

Beechick04 (p.108-112) claims that Cush and his son built the Nimrod the tower of Babel(Bel). Bel was the serpent himself. He(p.106) claimed very perverted worship and sacrifices and séances were conducted by the priests of Cush. They even killed some of the priests of the favored line of Noah. The early history of the true God became greatly perverted and only the somewhat distorted flood legends remained at Babel. Nimrod's wife Semiramis became a noted queen. The tower was also to honor the sky Gods and the stars and Nimrod and his queen. There may have then been earthquakes and storms and there was the confusion of the languages and the dispersion. There was probably fear of part of the tower falling and looting in the city, as order could not be maintained (p.115).

Hodge (Han08,p. 299-31) used J. Usher's chronology and noted Babel 106 yrs. after flood at birth of Peleg (p.300), the Creation at 4004 BC, the flood at 2348 BC and Babel 2242 BC. Josephus also cited Babel (the dispersion of the nations) at time of Peleg. R. Koldewey excavated a structure thought to be the foundation for the tower built by Hammurabi (Ref. Down, David, "Ziggurats in the News" *Archeological Diggings*, Mar-Apr 2007, p.3-7). A number of Ziggurats and early towers have built in many countries. The table of nations passage in Gen.10 gives an outline of family groups that left the tower. **Cooper, in the book** *After the Flood*, **documented genealogies from ancient historical records for the royalty of many nations:** Britons, Danes, Anglo-Saxons, Irish, Norwegians and Franks. Noah's son Japheth is documented to father the Gaul's, Goths, Bavarians, Saxons, Romans and others(Cooper p.306, Ham08,p304). He asserted that the **Genealogies in the table of nations in Gen. 10 were shown true** by many pre-Christian documents with 99% accuracy(Cooper p.12). The descendants of Noah can be traced to starting many nations (Ham 08 p.308). Ancient biblical names are repeated in languages, city and river names. There are over 6900 spoken languages in the world and these are attributed to about 100 language families(p.310). At least 78 languages are believed to have started from the dispersion at Babel. Modern Hebrew came from Eber and Noah's grandson Aram was the father of Aramaic which Jesus spoke. Languages do change with time into various dialects. It is known the English language has changed greatly over the last 1000 yrs.(p.311).

Beechick (H110-1) noted the general discrepancy of the Usher biblical chronology with conventional history with the latter going back to about 10,000BC. She noted that the Manetho king lists for Egypt may be inflated and are not based on the original documents. The BC Dark Age may also be inflated(p.113). James (1993) wrote a scholarly book on early history that also asserts the inflation of the Egyptian king lists and of the dark ages. Dendro-chronology(tree rings) also argues for a history back to 4000 BC(James Appendix 1). The following is quoted from the Creation Wiki article on Biblical Chronologies(web83):

"Skeptics often criticize the Bible because its chronology disagrees with the standard chronology of ancient Egypt. However, this argument assumes that the *Egyptian*, rather than *Hebrew* chronology, is correct. One might just as easily argue that the Egyptian chronology is wrong, because it disagrees with the Hebrew. In fact, there is no original "Egyptian chronology." Egyptian historical accounts record the lengths of the reigns of kings and dynasties, but do not tell when these kings and dynasties ruled in relation to each other. The Standard Egyptian Chronology was developed in the early 20th century, based on the assumption that no two Egyptian dynasties ruled simultaneously, (which is demonstrably false), and a series of inferences and calculations based on the so-called Sothic cycle, (an assumption without any substantive evidence to support it). In contrast to this questionable Egyptian chronology invented in the 20th century and based on false assumptions and hypothetical calendars, the Biblical chronology records not only the birth and death of many of the patriarchs, but also reports their lives in relation to each other, and, in some cases, gives the *month*, *day*, and *year* when important events occurred. As a result, some creationist archaeologists (and secular Middle Eastern historians like Velikovsky) argue that the standard Egyptian chronology is erroneous, and in need of revision. They reject the two assumptions above, and have proposed a revised Egyptian chronology, consistent with the Hebrew chronology and with the archaeological evidence."

Pierce, L. wrote in *Creation* **22**(1):46-49 (Web32) "The year was 331 BC. After Alexander the Great had defeated Darius at Gaugmela near Arbela, he journeyed to Babylon. Here he received 1903 years of astronomical observations from the Chaldeans, which they claimed dated back to the founding of Babylon. If this was so, then that would place the **founding of Babylon in 2234** BC, or about thirteen years after the birth of Peleg. This was recorded in the sixth book of *De Caelo* (About the heavens) by Simplicius, a Latin writer in the 6th century AD. Porphyry (an anti-Christian Greek philosopher, c. 234-305 AD) also deduced the same number."

"The Byzantine chronicler Constantinus Manasses (d. 1187) wrote that the Egyptian state lasted 1663 years. If correct, then counting backward from the time that Cambyses, king of Persia, conquered Egypt in 526 BC, gives us the year of 2188 BC for the founding of Egypt, about 60 years after the birth of Peleg. About this time Mizraim, the son of Ham, led his colony into Egypt. Hence the Hebrew word for Egypt is Mizraim (or sometimes 'the land of Ham' e.g. Psalm 105:23,27)."

"According to the 4th Century bishop and historian Eusebius of Caesarea, Egialeus, king of the Greek city of Sicyon, west of Corinth in Peloponnesus, began his reign in 2089 BC, 1313 years before the first Olympiad in 776 BC. If Eusebius is correct, then this king started to reign about 160 years after the birth of Peleg. Note that Babylon, Egypt, and Greece each spoke a different language. These ancient historians have unwittingly confirmed the extreme accuracy of the biblical genealogies as found in the Hebrew scriptures."

"An interesting piece of information comes from Manetho, who recorded the history of Egypt in the third century BC. He wrote that the Tower of Babel occurred five years after the birth of Peleg. Manetho, *The Book of Sothis*, Harvard Press, Cambridge, MA, p. 239 (Loeb Classical Library 350). Manetho was the victim of many Egyptian fairy tales in constructing his chronology of Egypt. The Egyptians would place the Flood and Peleg's birth much earlier than the Bible, but still they linked the Babel incident with Peleg's birth." Pierce's work above is not well accepted by conventional historians. The minority view may be correct, however.

Languages

According to Usher's chronology the creation of new languages and dispersion of peoples occurred from Babel in about 2242 BC. Some reference on the spread and development of languages will be discussed. The chapter on the origin of languages by Gitt (p.209-220) is important. Refer back to the paragraph on p.33 section on Information.

Morris (web39) noted that **man has a unique language section in his brain not found in animals** and quoted Dr. Chomsky, a linguistics expert: "Human language appears to be a unique phenomenon, without significant analogue in the animal world." Some linguists note that it is possible that there was once one language, but at a time in the past the people and races rapidly dispersed and their languages changed. Yet it is difficult to explain how the phonologic sound component" ever become so diverse. There is a **present trend of simplification and blending of languages**. "Not only so, but the history of any given language, rather than representing an increasingly complex structure as the structure of its users supposedly evolved into higher levels of complexity, seems instead to record an inevitable decline in complexity." "It is significant that Chomsky, though an agnostic, still regarded human language as "miraculous", distinguishing humans from animals."(web 87). Indeed, the use of language cannot begin to be understood until some connection is made between processes of thought and processes of speech. That's why language is so miraculous. "Most today would say that first language learning is a mixture of genetic maturation and social learning. What is remarkable (and miraculous) is that it begins spontaneously in the normal child, and that adults do not in any formal sense "teach" language. When they correct children it is usually on matters of truth or appropriateness. Only a minority with interest in language will bother to correct the language itself. Chomsky often uses the term "creative" when referring to the ability of the child to acquire a grammar. Menyuk concluded that the average child gets its grammar by age three, though Chomsky is more cautious and merely regards it as very early acquisition"(web 87,94). Chomsky also viewed much language ability as innate(web 94). Demme and Sack(web 91) noted music like language is complex and unique to man. Musical imagery requires exceedingly sensitive and refined systems for perceiving and remembering music, systems far beyond anything in any nonhuman primate.

The following was noted from Comrie, B. et al, *The Atlas of Languages:* **No languageless community has ever been found**(p.7). **There is a huge gulf between apes and man in languages and communication**. Apes have been taught some human sign language of a two yr. old or less. They cannot be taught our speech sounds and don't have the vocal ability of man; the shape of the mouth, pharynx and larynx is different. Hodges (AIG) also agrees. Grammar is beyond them. Most languages are equally complex and have grammar rules. Human language is very versatile and it can be transferred to writing or signs (p.7). It can produce an infinite # of sentences that have never been said before and still be understood. There may be a single origin of all languages. The 5000 plus known languages can be grouped into about a dozen clusters(p.7). The great known language families are Indo-European(I-E) and Sino-Tibetan. (p.16). The I-E finding started with Sir Wm. Jones noting similarities of written Sanskrit to Latin and Greek(p.40). Thieme (64-74) traces the I-E origins and spread. The I-E is centered in middle Europe and includes England, but did not originally extend south of the Baltic Sea. Certain words like beech (tree), turtle, wagon and salmon are common to it. It treats relatives in a patriarchal way. There is also evidence of an early common numbering by 10's. Languages do undergo consolidation and divergence and change all the time (Thieme p.68). Greenberg has proposed a vast Eurasiatic family before I-E (p.28,38 charts). Genetics and languages are related in a possible Nostratic super family(p.74). Hebrew is from the Semitic family which came from the Afro-Asiatic root, which came from the Nostratic super family. Over the past several 100 years languages are dying out and consolidating. Hodges (Ham08,p.299-311) noted "It must be pointed out, though, that we cannot go back too far in time. Core vocabulary is stable, but does change. In some languages this change has been measured for more than 2,000 years. The result shows that 19.5% of the core vocabulary changes every 1,000 years."

Comrie (p.164-5) noted the **earliest writing** is Sumerian writing from clay tablets found in the city of Uruk dated 3400 BC. This was non-phonetic and symbolic or logographic. Later the Sumerians added some phonetic characters. Their writing system was developed further by the Assyrians and Babylonians in Akkadian which has some limited phonetics (p.167-170). Egyptian writing was probably influenced by Sumerian. Earliest hieroglyphs in Egypt were noted in 3100 BC; symbols plus a little phonetics(p.170). The ancient Semitic language of south Arabia was written in a script which evolved from a proto-Canaanite system in 1300 BC. Phoneticians recorded their NW Semitic language with a consonant script in 11th century BC in Mediterranean. It had 22 characters and it may have influenced Hebrew. A Canaanite Semitic language, Moabite, is closely related to Hebrew(p.177) and is preserved today by the Samaritans. The Semitic language was assigned a date of 1500-1600 BC(p.174). By the 9th century BC Aramaic spelling(like the Phoenician with only consonants) had been adopted into Hebrew. The Minoans were on Crete and had a pictographic script in 1500-2000 BC. The Greek alphabet was developed in 8th century BC had some similarity to phoneticians. In the 7th century BC Etruscans in Italy modified Greek and formed Latin.(p.188). In **summary, the earliest known writings from this Atlas were 3400-3100 BC**. These dates may not be certain, but adding a 1000 or so yrs to the Usher chronology as in the Eusebius chronology by Finegan (p.190), possibly fits with Bible history.

However, an earlier written Semitic or Hebrew language is theoretically possible as noted by Bodie Hodge (Web33) but there is not much archeological evidence for it. Hodge also noted that the similarity of written Sanskrit to Greek implies an earlier root language. Wikipedia(Web34) noted "The pre-Classical form of Sanskrit is known as Vedic Sanskrit, with the language of the Rigveda being the oldest and most archaic stage preserved, its oldest core dating back to as early as 1500 BCE. This qualifies Rigvedic Sanskrit as one of the oldest attestations of any Indo-Iranian language, and one of the earliest attested members of the Indo-European language family, the family which includes English and most European languages." "**Classical Sanskrit** is the standard register as laid out in the grammar of Pāini, around the 4th century BCE. Its position in the cultures of Greater India is akin to that of Latin and Greek in Europe and it has significantly influenced most modern languages of the Indian subcontinent, particularly in India and Nepal." **In summary**, Sanskrit is a more phonetic language with letters rather than pictograms. The archeological evidence is that the earliest written languages were pictograms with a little phonetics added, but by 1500 BC there were written phonetic languages including a Semitic language. This appears to fit with Usher's date for Babel as 2242 BC. Some have stated that Noah had a written language and records. Perhaps they were more pictorial, but numbers and names would be needed as in the "**toledoth**".(See Early History section.)

B. Creation Science

Cosmology—the Big Bang Singularity to Billions of Stars and Galaxies vs. God's Design

This topic is fairly complex, so a summary of arguments and differing views will be offered initially from a few references (Williams2005, Moche and Web 41 wikipedia.org.). Then some view of experts will be noted. Williams is an excellent read and Riddle2004 a good DVD. Heeren and Ross (2003,web 42) both favor the big bang and subsequent inflation, but reason that God caused and guided the process. The inflation has to be a very precise and guided process for it to occur(Heeren). This is the most common view stated by astronomers and encyclopedias. The most common scientific theory is the big bang theory—that everything began from a singularity explosion 13.7 billion years ago. This was followed by immediate but precise inflation explosion(s). Then the hot gases of hydrogen and helium from the explosions collapsed under gravity to form the Milky Way galaxy and star called our sun. The cloud of gas is theorized to also contain dust and rocks created from supernova explosions of nearby stars. Later, the debris began the process of accretion by gravity to form the planets (web 42). Moche (p. 117) explained "A protostar is a star in its earliest phase of evolution. Protostars form **by chance at high density clumps**, inside huge turbulent gas (mostly hydrogen) and dust clouds that exit in space. **Perhaps** a shock wave from an exploding star (supernova) triggers the process. The use of the bolded weasel words appears common in many conventional astronomy texts as the details of how everything formed appears not well known. Just how did the galaxies, stars and orbiting planets form in some areas, but not in others and at regular distances? Gravitational contraction of the cloud and protostar causes the temperature and pressure inside to rise greatly. When the temperature in the protostar's center reaches 10 million K, nuclear fusion reactions start"(Moche).

Williams (2005 p.58, 95) questioned the assumptions of the previously stated process. Physicists assume that all the matter and energy of the universe was concentrated into a point called a singularity. The energy converted into matter and the matter re-condensed into organized stars and galaxies. This is metaphysics not physics, as the laws of physics break down in a singularity and are not well known. There is a theoretical logic problem here, in that, if there was a beginning in the singularity, what caused it? With the 50 exact cosmological constants being fine tuned afterward, doesn't this imply intelligent design by a creator? The laws of physics say that hot gas from an explosion would just keep on dispersing or it could re-collapse back into the singularity. A precisely mixed inflation is needed to greatly expand the gas cloud to the point where it was dispersed enough to form the many galaxies millions of light years apart. Then the re-clumping of gas into stars is assumed to occur. The inflation is theorized to have expanded the universe at much greater than the speed of light (2005 p.125). Once the gas cloud is inflated, the pressure within the gas cloud is too great and gravity too weak to allow condensation into stars to occur from conventional physics. Dramatic cooling and a shock wave from a nearby supernova are invoked to give some possible mechanism for a localized gas cloud to be forced to collapse, against its own pressure. Supernovas have been observed, but **no one has reported seeing a new star created near a supernova**, as is theorized. If the gas cloud is highly compressed and of the right mass it will form a star and the gravity of that mass will balance the outward pressure. If the mass were too small it would again disperse, and if the mass is too great, it could theoretically form a black hole. The last few sentences, both creation and naturalist scientists agree on, as we can see operating stars (2005 p.58, 95). One of the things physicists know is that conversion of energy to matter in the laboratory always creates exact matter and antimatter pairs. If those pairs come back together they will annihilate one another and revert back into energy. This matter and antimatter problem is not well accounted for in the big bang theory and often it is assumed that somehow the matter slightly exceeded the antimatter and this resulted in all the galaxies and matter we see(Wikipedia, Heeren p.221). Several other assumptions are made via density fluctuations or some other method to get the inflated gas cloud to form many different galaxies, which are large clumps, and stars which are smaller clumps, to be assembled and dispersed as they are (2005 p.132). **The patterns that the galaxies form with some being spirals,**

some beautiful clusters, and some irregular are not easily explained from one big uniform big bang explosion (2005 p.149). New galaxies, new stars are not observed. We have all see aerial fireworks displays. We know they are planned by intelligent design, not by a random chance action. If the raw materials for fireworks were mixed randomly with no planning, what do you think would be the likely result? You might see no beautiful pattern at all.

Another apparent fact has been found from current star and galaxy observations and maps. It is called the cosmological principle. This means that the universe looks the same from any and every position within it (2005 p.133). This raises another question of whether the universe is finite or infinite. Most scientists believe it is finite, because it has an assumed starting time and mass from the big bang. Some scientists think that some evidence shows that our Milky Way galaxy is at the center of the universe and there are concentric spherical shells of galaxies and stars that are more remote from us (2005 p.135-6). In order to balance the universe explosion into the known universe, dark matter also is assumed with a mass of many times the known or observed matter. The ratio of dark matter to observed matter varies with the galaxy observed. For the Milky Way galaxy the ratio is about 5/1, for elliptical galaxies it is about 8/1 (2005 p.139). The model of Hartnett(2007) explains this without using dark matter.

Planet formation is another difficult problem to explain by cold accretion from dust and small rocks, but this is the standard naturalist theory. Earth is theorized to have been formed about 4.6 billion years ago from a contracting cloud of gas and dust (Moche1996 p. 228). Scientists are not sure why the inner planets are rocky like Earth, Mars and Venus, while the outer planets like Jupiter and Saturn, are gassy. This is not typical around other stars (Lisle07 p.80). Small particles of rock and dust are not known to stick to one and another in space. There is a disc of dust and rocks circling Saturn, but the materials are not known to be accreting together. Van der Waals force or gravity is not great enough to make small rocks or particles stick together. Once a planet is large enough to have some gravity it will hold particles that hit it. Meteorites will stay with a planet they hit, if they are of the right size and not burned up by the atmosphere. Meteorites are generally already fused rock and are thought to have been previously fused by high temperature. If the whole earth was initially very high temperature and then, cooled, how would one explain the vast amounts of water remaining? **We again have some unexplained breaking**

of the known laws of physics to form the planets and galaxies by the naturalist's theories (2005 p.151-7). The numerous heavy elements on earth in the bottom of the periodic table are also difficult to explain by dust accretion, unless the dust of some very old stars and supernovas was involved. Most of the big bang emission was thought to be hydrogen and helium and a few lighter elements (2005 p. 322).

Ross(2003) offered the conventional theory of universe creation and gave 8 arguments for the existence of dark matter which includes ordinary dark matter and exotic matter (EM) (p.36-50). Both are invisible because they do not give off light: EM doesn't interact much with radiation. **Earth the right place for life**: Sagan and Shklovskii noted a just right star and planet is found in only .001% or less of stars. Only 5% of the galaxies are spirals. Other galaxies spew out harmful radiation or are unstable. There is one supernova every 50 yrs, but they make heavy elements. Fluorine is not from supernovas, but from white dwarf stars. The sun earth distance is just right; gravity of earth and atmospheres is just right to hold oxygen and water. Earth's rotation is just right, and its tilt and moon. Jupiter removes comets from hitting us. With the earth there are now about 40 fine tuned parameters for life(p.139). Planetary formation has not been observed, although there is a theory for it(one planet for every 1000 stars). Probability for all parameters of planets and stars for life was 10^{-53}(P142). A number of secular astronomers and physicists have come to faith by these findings which indicate very high probability of design. For life to form, 40 different elements must bond together in molecules. The electromagnetic force must be just right for this as must the size and orbits of the electron. The proton and neutron must also have just the right mass, and the strong and weak nuclear forces must be just right (p.114).

Riddle (2004) provided a good summary of arguments for Biblical creation of the stars and galaxies in a possible young universe. He noted that Gen. 1:17 states that "God made the two great lights— **as well as the stars**." This is in opposition to what secular astronomers say; that stars were formed by gas and dust collapse by the force of gravity(natural processes). He quotes four secular astronomers who say that no one has every observed a star forming. The processes itself goes against the known laws of physics, as heat would cause the gases to expand, not collapse. "The complete birth of a star has never been observed. The principles of physics demand some special conditions for star formation and also for a long time period. A cloud of hydrogen gas must be compressed to a sufficiently small size so that gravity dominates. In space, however, almost every gas cloud is light-years in size, hundreds of times greater than the critical size needed for a stable star. As a result, outward gas pressures cause these clouds to spread out farther, not contract." Don DeYoung (Ph.D. in Physics), Astronomy and the Bible, 2000, p. 84.

"Precisely how a section of an interstellar cloud collapses gravitationally into a star . . . is still a challenging theoretical problem . . . Astronomers have yet to find an interstellar cloud in the actual process of collapse." Fred Whipple, The Mystery of Comets, (Washington, D.C.: Smithsonian Institute Press, 1985), pp. 211, 213.

"Despite numerous efforts, we have yet to directly observe the process of stellar formation . . . The origin of stars represents one of the fundamental unsolved problems of contemporary astrophysics." Charles Lada and Frank Shu (both astronomers), "The Formation of Sunlike Stars," Science, 1990, p. 572.

"There is general belief that stars are forming by gravitational collapse; in spite of vigorous efforts no one has yet found any observational indication of conformation. Thus the 'generally accepted' theory of stellar formation may be one of a hundred unsupported dogmas which constitute a large part of present-day astrophysics." Hannes Alfven (Nobel prize winner), Gustaf Arrhenius, "Evolution of the Solar System", NASA, 1976, p. 480. (Riddle 2004)

In addition the star formation number calculations indicate a problem: Scientists estimate that there are 100 billion galaxies (10^{11}). Scientists estimate that there are 200 billion stars per galaxy. If we allow for the universe to be 20 billion years old, then we can perform the following calculations for how fast stars had to form:

o   100 billion x 200 billion / 20 billion years = 1 trillion stars per year forming.

o   This equates to 2.7 billion stars forming every day for 20 billion years.

Yet we don't see stars forming today. Astronomers have identified what they believe are star nurseries which are dense hot gas clouds like the Eagle and Horsehead Nebulas. The Horsehead Nebula has been observed to be expanding. It is uncertain if any stars have formed here. They could have been hidden behind the cloud, but observed after the cloud expanded and became more transparent (Riddle 2004).

Riddle also noted **five evidences for a young solar system: 1**. Recession of the moon from the earth is a problem as going back 4.5 billion years would put the moon contacting earth; **2.** There are two classes of comets, young and old, coming from the Kuiper belt and the Oort cloud. "The existence of the Kuiper belt and the Oort cloud of comets has not been verified. Perhaps there is an alternative: The presence of comets may be evidence that the solar system is not as old as is often assumed." Don DeYoung, Ph.D. Physics, Astronomy and the Bible, 2000, p. 49-50. Because the comets burn up in thousands of yrs. as they come close to the sun, this indicates a young solar system. **3.** The age of the Sun: The sun should grow brighter with age. If the sun is 4.6 billion years old, it should have brightened by about 40%. The average temperature of the earth has recently been 59 F. This change in brightness changes the average temperature of the earth by about 32 F, so that it would have been 27 F. **4.** Supernova remnants(SRNs) are not that numerous. They are the remains of star death explosions which have been observed. See a table of the predicted and observed SRNs below:

SRN Stage	Number of observable SNRs Predicted if our galaxy is:		Actual Number Observed is
	Billions of Yrs Old	7000 yrs old	
First	2	2	5
Second	2260	125	200
Third	5000	0	0

5. Spiral galaxies wind up too fast to be billions of years old.

Faulkner (p.50-53) noted that blue stars burn very intensely and should last no longer than a few million yrs. This poses a difficult problem for astronomers, because the blue stars appear evident throughout the history of the universe of an assumed age of about 14 billion yrs. No new blue stars, and no stars at all have been observed to form in recent history; Why would they exist today unless the universe is young? Present interstellar gas clouds are observed to be generally of low density and low temperature. There is no reasonable mechanism that has been proven to cause these gas clouds to contract to form new stars. The postulated mechanism is that shock waves from a nearby supernova explosion caused the gas clouds to compress and form a star. However in a beginning universe, according to the big bang model, there may have been very few supernova explosions to cause the shock waves. He also noted that the spiral galaxies argue for a young universe.

Hartnett (2007) offered a unique theory of universe formation incorporating time dilation. He builds on the Humphreys model, the Moshe Carmeli theories. A physicist, M. Carmeli extended his concepts to the cosmos and developed a cosmological special relativity (CSR) theory. His new theory predicted the universe must be expanding and developed a space-velocity and equations to explain the redshift without using dark matter or dark energy. Carmeli expanded on his theories in 2 books: *Cosmological Relativity* and *Cosmological Special Relativity* (Hartnett p.42-44). Hartnett extended this theory to explain the rotational speed of spiral galaxies without dark matter (p46-48). He also explained the space time and space velocity dimensions and the puzzle of starlight travel to the earth by time dilation. In his Appendix 6, he gives equations and graphs for time dilation where time was much faster in the universe relative to earth time(p.222-230). **This is a way to explain how billions of yrs. time could have passed in the universe expansion while only day's time appeared to pass on earth.** Time dilation due to velocity or gravity differences of observers is an accepted principle (web60). **Humphreys offers a second time-space model allowing a days time on earth with billions of yrs in the cosmos.** He and Williams(p.72,134) also noted that **traditional cosmologists assume a priori that the universe has no center** and looks homogeneous, the same in every direction. This is to maintain a naturalistic and anti-biblical view. **There are a number of evidences that we are near the center of the universe.** The red-shifts are clumped in regular patterns around preferred values. This suggests shells of galaxies proceeding outward from our center measuring point. If the measuring point is mathematically shifted a few light yrs. away from us, the red-shifts no longer clump. The angle of polarization of radio waves coming from distant galaxies suggests a cosmic N and S pole. A large scale map of the galaxies known as the Sloan Digital Sky Survey indicates the galaxies are distributed in concentric shells moving out from our galaxy(p.136). It makes a huge difference to mathematical models like big bang ones if the universe has a center. **Humphreys** has one the few models with our galaxy at the center. He noted that in the book *The Large Scale Structure of Space Time* by Hawking and Ellis, the book states that an assumption was made, that the universe has no center and no edge. Big bang models are then built off this naturalistic assumption. Humphreys also notes that this even applies when the universe was very young. **One would think the big bang model would have a center as it started from a singularity, but it**

does not! Gravitational fields would be different in a universe that had a center than in one that does not. Gravitational time dilation is an accepted fact as noted in Wikipedia. Humphreys also noted that Einstein stated that space is an **ether**, like a fabric to contain the galaxies. It is possible that the ether was stretched out and this would cause red shifting also. Humphreys(p.34) offers the theory that God stretched out the fabric of space with water and elementary particles on day two of earth time. Some big bang models including that of Alan Guth have the universe initially expanding at much greater than the speed of light (Humphreys p.98). The clumping of the redshifts at million light yr. distance intervals from us is a problem for the big bang theory. Ross (2004 &web69) has criticized Humphreys and Hartnett models as not being true.

Let's explore the **biblical view of creation**. Gen 1:1 says "God created the heavens and the earth." Williams said there are numerous references in the Bible to God having stretched out the heavens: Ps. 104:2; Isa. 42:5, 44:24, 45:12, 48:13, 51:16; Jer. 10:10, 51:15, Zech. (2005 p. 241). Ps. 19:1 says "The heavens declare the glory of God and the firmament showeth his handiwork." This gives evidence of design as does Proverbs 3:19: "The Lord by wisdom founded the earth; by understanding he established the heavens." Gen.15:5, 22:17 Jer. 33:22, says the stars are countless as the sand grains on the seashore. A reasonable estimate might be 10 million billion stars (2005 p. 247). This number of stars from a big bang is difficult to conceive of. However, Ps. 147:4 states He determines the **number** of the **stars** and calls them each by name. This implies that they are not infinite in number. The Milky Way Galaxy alone is reported to contain over 200 billion stars and the universe is believed to contain 100 billion galaxies (M1996 p.139). Williams (2005 p.313) gave a scorecard comparing the big bang to biblical creation and found the logic of the Bible more consistent by scores of 4 correct for the big bang to 20 correct for the creation (2005 p.321-5). Williams (2005 p.182) theorized that God could have created the galaxies and stars at different sizes and ages of development all at once. Then due to relativistic time dilation, the star light all arrived visible on earth during the time of man's life. Gen 1:14 says "Let there be lights in the firmament of heaven to divide the day from the night; **and let them be for signs, and for seasons, and for days and years**." Mat. 2:2, 9-10 tells of the star in the east as a sign to follow to Bethlehem to find the baby Jesus. Our calendars are built on the orbits and rotations of the earth and moon. Uniquely formed galaxies in spirals are difficult to explain by random density gradients. If they were billions of yrs. old they would be wound up and no longer appear like recent spiral formations (2005 p.323).

A few chapters of Ross2004 are summarized. **Chap. 13** The Big Bang p.139-148 The Bible supports the stretching out of the universe with many verses. There is considerable scientific support for the expansion of the universe from a point or singularity. The red shifts and cosmic background radiation support this along with Einstein's equations. Also distant galaxies appear closer together in direct proportion to their distance from us. Also the abundance of elements heaver than helium decreases indirect proportion to their distance from earth. The CBR increases in temperature with distance from the earth. There is also time dilation in gamma ray bursts (p.147). **Chap. 14** Signs of and Old Age (p.149-59). Four signs that all agree are the redshifts and expansion, the CBR, stellar burning and the abundance of radioactive elements. He (p.156) noted that the entire spectrum of new, to middle aged, to old stars are seen throughout the universe as noted in the Sloan digital sky survey(web 102). Also the universe appears flat(p.154). **My comments:** One can conceive of portions of the big bang model as described by Herron in **Show me God** and in Wikipedia. Here it was noted according to standard cosmology, the temperature in the early bang would be too high for atoms and not until after 380,000 yrs when it decreased to 3000^0K could atoms form. One has trouble visualizing any model to make physical sense of all the Chap. 13 & 14 notes. Simplistic common sense would say the universe has a center and an outer expanding periphery. Common internet figures of the big bang show it starting from a center(web 103). A flat universe is difficult of conceive of in a 3D world, although scientists hold to it. If there was a hypothetical oven the center, why would the temperatures be coldest there? It is also possible that God guided galaxies and formed stars throughout history rather than all star creation being naturalistic and random. However this would go against the idea that God finished his creative work on day 6. We know that God does miracles today and maintains the universe by these verses: **Col. 1:17** "He is before all things, and by Him all things hold together."; **Heb. 1:2-3** He has spoken to us by His Son, whom He has appointed heir of all things and through whom He made the universe. [3] He is the radiance of His glory, the exact expression of His nature, and He sustains all things by His powerful word. Job 34:13 Who gave Him authority over the earth? Who put Him in charge of the entire world? The Reasons to Believe web site talks of the moon being formed from a collision of another planet with earth; thus forming the earth and moon and cloud of debris that took many yrs to settle. An article by Faulkner (2012) disputed this. He noted that the Titanium and Oxygen isotope ratios are the same on the moon and earth but not in extraterrestrial bodies.

In **summary**, there is considerable evidence for God's work in the universe's creation by either traditional cosmology with the big bang, or without the bang. **God's fine tuned miraculous touch must have worked either way**. Heeren stated(p.199) "The more we discover about how the universe works, the more we understand that our universe's laws are set within very narrow, very critical parameters. Without a combination of the wildest possible coincidences, a universe capable of sustaining intelligent life would be impossible. Even unbelieving physicists have come to agree with the Bible's assertion that our universe has been very precisely prepared for us; they routinely tell us that the universe's conditions were very carefully chosen, adjusted or fine tuned." Einstein wrote "That the harmony of natural law reveals an intelligence of such superiority that, compared with it, all the systematic thinking and acting of human beings is an utterly insignificant reflection"(p.201). Three lines of evidence support creation: Thermodynamics, Einstein's general theory of relativity, and the observations of astronomy. The 1st law of thermodynamics is $E=MC^2$ the conservation of mass and energy. Gen. 2:1 "Thus the heavens and the earth were completed in all their vast array." The 2nd law says the contents of the universe are becoming less ordered and more random. The useful energy will be used up. The entropy (the amount of disorder) increases with time. The earth's magnetic field is decreasing and its rotation is slowing(web 57). Ps. 102:25-26 "In the beginning you laid the foundations of the earth, and the heavens are the work of your hands. They will perish, but you remain; they will all wear out like a garment. Like clothing you will change them and they will be discarded. "Isaiah 34:4 All the heavenly bodies will dissolve. The skies will roll up like a scroll, and their stars will all wither as leaves wither on the vine, and foliage on the fig tree." Note the gap theory would allow the big bang cosmology. However the big bang models are based on the naturalist atheistic assumption that the universe had no center and no edge. **Models using our universe as a center provide a mechanism for time dilation.** Time could have been very slow on earth and very fast in distant space as it was stretched. This could possibly fit with our present observations that some universes are now millions of light yrs. away. Humphreys' and Hartnett's models provide for the possibility of time dilation. A video providing evidence of the Wonders of God's Creation in a visual form is **God of Wonders** 2008.

A summary by Riddle 2004 follows concerning the big bang: Evidence appears to support the big bang only when contradictions are ignored (as in textbooks). The big bang model is constantly changing to match the data. The big bang model cannot explain much of the observed data. "In a nutshell, the Big Bang, or, as some cosmologists prefer to call it, 'the Standard Model of Cosmology,' goes something like this. About 15 billion years ago, the universe erupted from an enormous and still unexplained event—often referred to as a singularity'—from which all of space and matter were created. That's why you can't say it was an explosion. Nothing can't explode. And at the instant of the Big Bang, there was something. It also didn't happen anywhere—that is in a single location—but everywhere." Kenneth C. Davis, *Don't Know Much About The Universe*, 2001, p. 298.

Geology and the Flood

Snelling (2010) in the *Earth's Catastrophic Past* traces the history of the change in thought from biblical geology to uniform ages. His two volume work is very detailed. Before 1830, the main viewpoint of geology followed that of the creation account and of a world wide flood(p.85-6). After the influence of Darwin and of Lyell, the biblical view is completely ruled out and replaced with uniformitarianism and evolutionary naturalism. Only those geologists with a strong faith will question the conventional view. Recently catastrophes in geologic processes have been recognized as important but still within the long ages naturalistic framework. Some areas of geology don't require a lot of this framework, like mineralogy, petrology and exploration geophysics(p.189). Examples of the trend toward **uniformitarianism** include the J. Hutton book in 1785 *Theory of the Earth* that notes the present is the key to the past; then J. Playfair 1802, then C. Lyell, *Principles of Geology* 1833; (p.477); Snelling(2009 DVD) stated that Lyell had an agenda of freeing geology from the Bible and the flood as evidenced in his letters. His geological theory was completely uniformitarian, with no catastrophes. This theory won out, but has now been considerably modified to include some catastrophes(p.480). **Many**

conventional geologists (JH Shea, UB Marvin, RH Dott, ND Newell, JE Eaton, and DV Ager p. 482-3) **state that most of the sediments and fossil depositions are from catastrophic processes** and there is good evidence of some well documented catastrophic depositions (bolide and asteroid impacts, turbidity currents from deep underwater landslides as in 1929 Grand Banks off S. coast of Newfoundland, Ventura Basin of Calif., the Storegga of Norway, and other large floods like the Scablans of Wash.) Ager further states "It is obvious to me that the whole history of earth is one of short sudden happenings with nothing much in particular in between." Ref. D.V. Ager, 1993, *The New Catastrophisim*—Cambridge Univ. Press, Cambridge. To put is another way, **the big sedimentary layers we observe were deposited quickly**, and the ages of time come in as the gaps in the geological record. The gaps then become a circular rescuing argument that begs the question of the long ages(p.486). The ages are supported on other arguments not based on sedimentation rates. Ager holds to the traditional geological ages. Even though most geologists argue against a world wide flood and biblical based geology, Dr. Snelling and some other geologists argue for it. More recently non-biblical geologists use the term actualism (observed geological processes) to replace uniformitarian which is out of favor, as many catastrophic process have been noted(Reed p.7-8).

Many geologists now agree with neo-catastrophism, the idea that big floods caused rapid water deposition of certain layers (Morris07 p.97). They then believe that these layers are separated by millions of yrs. of time due to imposed fossil dates. However, the surface features like ripple marks, raindrop impressions and animal tracks provide evidence for rapid deposition features. Such features would have been eroded away or disturbed by bioturbation in long periods of time (98). Burred sediments show a marked lack of soil layers which should have occurred repeatedly over millions of years. Other evidence or recently buried sediments include undisturbed, unfractured bedding planes, polystrate fossils, soft sediment deformation like dikes, and the limited extent of nonconformities(108-115). Coal beds have many vertically buried trees which are difficult to imagine or explain with standard uniform assumptions. They are also bedded over clay which is not a good soil or typical soil for a marsh. Spirit Lake, formed after Mt. St. Helen's has many buried trees that with time, pressure and heat, could form coal (106,117). Morris noted the false report of the geologist Charles Lyell that the erosion rate of Niagara Falls was 1 ft/yr, when local residents stated it was 4-5 ft/yr(web 64,65,66). This was used to disprove James Usher's book on chronology and rate agreeing with scripture(Morris p.46). Since 1942 the erosion rate of the falls has been slower due to reduced flow.

The following **biblical arguments are given for the global flood**(Snelling p.73): These arguments are difficult to refute, unless one relegates Genesis to just being myths and fables. The sons of Noah and their genealogies seem historically verified. (See the history section)

1. The Bible states that the flood wastes rose and prevailed upon the earth, covering all the mountains, for a period of 5 months, and that an additional 7 months were then required for the water to recede so Noah and his family could go out.
2. The water of the flood covered the highest mountains to a depth sufficient for the ark to float over them (draft about 22 ft, p.35)
3. The expression "fountains of the great deep were broken up" is clearly indicative of vast geological disturbances during the flood, and incompatible with the concept of a local flood, especially when the disturbances continued for 5 months.
4. The construction of the Ark with a capacity of at least 41,000 cubic meters just for the purpose of carrying a few animals and 8 people through a local flood is utterly inconceivable(p.73).
5. If the flood was only over a limited area, then there would have been no need for the ark at all, for there would have been plenty of time for Noah's family and the wildlife to escape the danger area.
6. 2 Peter 3:3-7 notes the flood in the context of a major event like the end times fire, and stresses scoffers will not believe these events. If the flood were merely local, why would it be mentioned?
7. Jesus several times uses the flood and the days of Noah in reference to the end times and his 2nd coming. If the flood was not global why would he do this?
8. The human race was likely widely distributed before the time of the flood due to population growth estimated to be 1-3 billion people(p.74).
9. The stated purpose of the flood was the punishment of sinful mankind; such a purpose could not have been achieved by if only a small part of humanity had been judged. Genesis and 1 and 2nd Peter state that only Noah and his family survived.

10. God's covenant with Noah after the flood becomes meaningless if another major part of the population survived. The Genesis account talks of the earth being filled with violence and wickedness and needing judgment.

Snelling (p.83) also noted the many **flood legends** among various peoples. Some of the earliest flood stories are on clay tablets dated 1880-2100 BC. The Gilgamesh legend from the Babylonians has marked similarities to the Genesis account. When one reads some of these legends as in Tigay(p.4-5) it was noted that **a mythical legend** was notably different than the more **factual Bible version**. For example the Bible gives dimensions, number of days of waiting, sending out a bird to test for vegetation, and final docking and unloading. On the other hand, the Gilgamesh Epic is about a king who is 2/3 divine and survived the flood and seeks immortality by eating a plant on the bottom of the sea. However, the plant was snatched by the serpent. It is polytheistic with mention of other Gods, and an imaginative story. For example, he slays the Bull of heaven (a star formation). He also bemoans the fall of certain game implements into the neverworld. It is possible such legends were made to venerate the king and not to tell history (Snelling p.87). **He suggests that a there were written records on the ark of the genealogies that were passed down through Noah**. After the dispersion of the peoples at Babel, the following flood stories became distorted by the many groups who were pagan. **After the language confusion, it took many years for languages to develop again to the point of being written**, resulting in the so called Dark ages (Snelling p 289). Cooper noted (p.17) much of Egyptian history going back to 1000BC held as the view of God as the creator. The sons of Ham settled Egypt after the flood by several sons who were named Cush, Put and Egypt "Mizraim" (Holman Study Bible p.13). Mizraim was also known as Menes and formed the city of Memphis on the Nile.(Beechick p.138). Menes was the first king of Egypt (web 45). **Possible distortion and adding years to the Manetho king list in Egypt may** have occurred making history there appear longer than it was(James p.220). Relevant archeological evidence supports the biblical chronology from Abraham onwards (Snelling p.289). Beechick(p.146) also asserts that Shem finished the genealogical records after Noah's death. **Shem met Abraham in Ur and gave him the old genealogical records** in the language of Edenese and taught him some about astrology. Shem also knew of Job who lived in the land of Uz(Beechick p.143). Job lived in the post flood period and has some details on the ice age that followed the flood in his area (Job 37:9-10) (Snelling p 289). Also see the history section.

Questions that people ask about the feasibility of the ark are answered in the Woodmorappe book *Noah's Ark a Feasibility Study*, ICR, 1996. A DVD by Tim Lovett titled *Noah's Ark*, explains the seaworthiness and construction of the ark. Ham (2006 p.125) also gives general information on the flood and the ark. Snelling(p.125-181) also answers many questions about the ark, the care of the animals and the post flood distribution of the animals. In taking animals by their kinds, only 16,000 animals would be needed, although 43,000 could be carried(p.137). Snails and insects could have been carried on floating logs and vegetation mats as would plants and seeds. The Bering Strait is a land bridge where animals probably migrated (web 49).

Baumgardner gave and detailed a 3D **mathematical model that explained the massive global plate tectonic activity during the flood.** The massive volcanic activity and separation of the continents are also explained and modeled. This fits with the breaking of the fountains of the great deep in Genesis and the beginning of the following ice age. Snelling (p.365-415) gave details on plate tectonics supporting the spread of the original continent into separate continents. Many geologists have written on this plate separation in the past, noting evidences of very similar rocks and fauna where the continents separated(p.366-70). A brief summary of Snelling is given by Tofflemire (2010). Hess and Vine noted that there was an upwelling of magma previously at the mid Atlantic ridge and other ridges; this lead to separation of the continents which have lighter rock than the deep basaltic ridges(p.374-5). Volcanic activity occurs along the ridges which currently spread at 1-10 cm/yr(p.383). There are also areas of subduction where the basalt descends. Snelling also has a video *Geology* describing how the plates separated to form the continents. **A summary of some of the Snelling 2010 chapters follows:**

Chap. 87 Catastrophic Plate Tectonics—The Driving force of the Flood(p. 691): There is much evidence that the basaltic crust of today's ocean floor is younger that the Paleozoic (early) portion of the continental sedimentary rocks with fossils. Presently the basaltic sea floor is spreading at the ridges at about 1cm/yr and the ancient sea floor has been replaced(at present rates this would take 200 million yrs—Hess p.375). The pre-flood cold dense ocean lithosphere was heaver than the underlying hotter rock and was unstable(p.691 Austin). This represented a huge store of gravitational potential energy. Laboratory experiments by several scientists show that silicate rock can lessen its viscosity by orders of magnitudes with increased temperature and stress(p.692). Baumgardner also noted this in his research in 1987 and made a numerical model of the old sea floor runaway. Because all the current oceanic crust seems to date from the flood and post flood times, it is apparent that the pre-flood lithosphere was subducted during the flood. Subsequent collisions of continental fragments at subduction zones are the likely cause for the mountain folds and thrust belts(p.605). The model indicated that the old dense lithosphere subducted downward to a lower mantle level. Seismic topography has located this cold dense layer and validated the model(p.696). Vardiman below also noted the sea floor was newer than the Cretaceous period (p.1057).

The mantle circulation in the Baumgardner model could also have the disturbed the earth's magnetic field, causing it to rapidly reverse and a confirming record of these reversals is found in the present mantle floor(p.697). This was confirmed by the research of Coe and Prevot "Evidence suggesting extremely rapid field variation during a geomagnetic reversal" *Earth and Planetary Science Letters.*,92, 1989. Part of the mantle circulation during the flood was the hot rising magma, which caused steam jets entraining sea water and sending it into the atmosphere, causing intense rain. A major sediment type deposited during the flood was limestone. The carbonate for this could have come from several sources: Degassing of cooling magmas would have released CO^2 to the sea water which formed bicarbonates. The carbonates could have precipitated from heated sea water. Pre-flood deposits could have been eroded and re-deposited or uplifted. The conveyor belt action of the old subducting sea floor would have scraped off sediments and piled them up on the continents. This along with a global flood and tidal waves could have deposited a lot of sediments rapidly and this is what the Paleozoic and Mesozoic layers reflect(p.701). These sedimentary layers are not easily explained by slow and gradual processes that we see today. Today sedimentation occurs around continental shelves and river deltas and very few fossils are preserved there. The massive volcanism stated in the flood model would have produced vast amounts of flood basalts and explosive ash deposits over large areas and that is what we see a record of. Continental crust folding due to subducting slabs and uplift due to isostatic disequilibrium from varying densities, could explain some of the mountain building(web63).

Chap 96 Post Flood Ice Age: Conventional geology places the ice age in the recent Pleistocene spanning 1.8 million yrs. with 4 or more advances and retreats(p.770). There are many varying theories for this, all of which have serious difficulties. To produce an ice sheet, the winter snow must survive in the summer and continue to build in the winter; the cooler summers are difficult to explain. With cooler summers, absent volcanism heating the ocean, there is not much evaporation to yield precipitation. So how could the great snow and ice deposits form? Some theories (Milankovitch 100,000 yrs) state there were orbital or tilt changes with the earth. The flood volcanism warmed the oceans 20 C. The post flood time is at the Cretaceous/Tertiary boundary, related to Oxygen isotope changes(p.773). Volcanism decreased as evidenced by less ash in the Tertiary. Heavy rain occurred over the middle latitudes and snow storms over the poles. Clouds and ash blocked the sun. **The high ocean temperature drove the process**. This is all described in mathematical model by Vardiman(P.774). **Ice cores** in Greenland and Antarctica indicated many snow layers, **that could as well be explained by many storms per yr. as by one season /yr**(p.777). The glacial ice advances and retreats were frequent at the edges and slow in the thick central areas. The model indicated a 700M thick layer over the N. pole and 1200 M over the south(p.776)

Chap. 97 Ice Age Changes (p.779): In the mid latitudes there was heavy rain and cool weather, except near oceans; Ice building occurred on poles, as the skies were cloudy, with the sea level dropping (50-60M); land bridges were exposed at Bering Strait and English Channel. The ice age period was 500 yrs, with 200 yrs in the melting phase (Skies clearer, summers warmer, winters cold, edges of glaciers melt). Ice dams burst and caused erosion, Glaciers (Laurentide Ice Sheet) formed the great lakes and outflow was the Niagara gorge. Niagara Falls recession estimated at 4-5ft/yr would take 7000-9000 yrs. However early high flows cause faster erosion accounting for 4000 yrs. Winters got colder as did oceans near poles as more ice intruded the ocean. Permafrost soils formed. Sea levels rose. The present ocean floor has an average of 200 M of carbonate ooze and shells. At current rates of 1-3 cm/1000yr this would take millions or yrs. However the flood and ice age deglaciation could account for this in 1000-2000 yrs(p.786). There was also a sudden change from sand to silt deposition in the Mississippi delta as the rains slowed. Snelling also discussed the formation of the coal and oil deposits from the flood(p.959-976).

In Chap. 63 p.489 Snelling stated that the all **Paleozoic and Mesozoic(P&M) strata were deposited during the flood, while the Cenozoic strata were deposited Post-flood.** Modern geology allocates 480 million yrs to P&M strata. Calculations show that using no greater flood velocities than we observe today in a common flash flood, can deposit an average thickness of 700 M of sediment (the average thickness of the P&M) in 8.4 months. A global flood could have done much more. Some strata are of large horizontal extent including the Permian of western Canada that covers 470,000 sq. km. The Dakota sandstone formation of the US covers 815,000 sq. Km. The white chalk beds (upper Cretaceous) have black flint nodules that cover part of England, N. Ireland, N. Germany, Poland, Bulgaria, Egypt, Texas, Arkansas, Alabama, and W. Australia. The three fold Triassic has distinctive red and green marls and is found in Germany, Birmingham England, E. and W. US and in Spain(p.491). Chap. 65 p.509 notes the Coconino sandstone covers, Arizona, New Mexico, Colorado, Kansas, Okla., and Texas as noted in Fig 44, p.1082. The **Tapeats sandstone** (p.529) is part of the Sauk mega-sequence and **covers much of the American continent** as in Fig. 45 of Snelling below (It would take a big flood to do this).

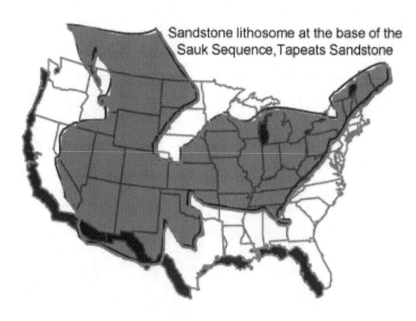

Sandstone lithosome at the base of the
Sauk Sequence, Tapeats Sandstone

Chap. 89 The Destructive power of Floods and Ocean waves: A hurricane, flood or Tsunami may do more in a day than ordinary process of nature do in 1000 yrs(p.713). A flood in India was noted to move blocks of granite of 350 tons. A flood in Utah in 1903 moved rock 20 tons in weight. They cut a canyon 70 ft. deep in rock. A very unusual flood erosion occurred in Wash. state called the Channeled Scabland. The water for the flood came from Lake Missoula in NW Montana formed from glaciers. Several geologists wrote of it including Chamberlain, and Betz. The lake may have covered 3000 sq. miles. Deep gorges or coulees were cut in solid basalt, including Grand Coulee which is 50 miles long and 2 miles wide, with walls 900 ft high. At flows of greater that 30 ft/sec cavitations occur and this is believed the case for this flood (p.715). The destruction of Mt. St. Helens was also noted (p.717). A canyon 700 ft deep and several miles long was formed. Tsunamis have also been known to cause much destruction. (p.720).

Chap. 70, 120 Coal Deposits: Coal is formed from accumulation and compaction of dead plant material(p.549). Often leaves, stems and tree trunks are found in coal beds. There are two theories of coal formation(p.550):**1.** The growth in place swamp theory, which is uniformitarian, and **2.** The plant transport and deposition theory, which is catastrophic. Although the 1st theory is widely held it makes little sense and has never been observed. How can swamps be hundreds of miles long and thick enough to yield a 100-300 ft thick coal layer? It would take 5-10 times the thickness of peat moss to form one unit of coal. Thus we are talking of moss beds up to 3000 ft. deep. A number of coal seams also have buried marine fossils, which argues against fresh water marshes, and boulders and tree stumps which argues for catastrophic deposition. How can the bottom of a buried tree in a layer be millions of yrs. older than the top?(p.555) Upright polystrate tree stumps often found in coal beds, argue for rapid catastrophic deposition as in the flood. Millions of yrs. of sedimentary history are also stated to have passed with the trees arguing against this. Similar trees are found in Spirit Lake from Mt. St. Helens, forming a decaying vegetation mat(Snelling p.959). The flood model also explains marine fossils found in the coal.

Chap. 76. Summary: p.607-10 There are **5 evidences of catastrophic deposition of the main fossil sedimentary record: 1.** The rate of sediment accumulation when observed in floods today is many orders of magnitude greater than that assumed in the large geologic record. Thick layers of sediment have been deposited in hours and days, that in the geologic record are very often assumed to have taken millions of yrs. Therefore realistic sedimentation rates during the flood could have produced the sedimentary geologic record. **2.** Widespread, rapid water-deposited sediments are very common in the geologic record. Many layers cover continents and display horizontal continuity. The nature of these sediments and the internal structures within them can only be explained by catastrophic deposition. There are many well preserved marine fossils in many of these deposits. Some of these deposits are now miles high and contain mainly marine fossils. The sediments deposited do not appear to have been eroded from nearby sediments but possibly from sediment transported great distances. This is logically explained by a world wide flood. The alternate explanation is that there were many continent-world wide floods and each of these was separate by millions of yrs of inactivity. **3.** The Fossil graveyards give good evidence of very rapid deposition and burial world wide to preserve the great detail without degradation. The coal beds on many continents also argue for rapid catastrophic deposition. **4.** Boundaries and time gaps: Many boundaries between layers show flat and knife edge cuts where a new sediment layer was deposited on top. If millions of yrs. occurred between the layers one would expect hills and valleys and many erosion features. For many of these layers, the erosion features are typical of a brief time, not millions of yrs. **5.** Soft sediment deformation: Following the deposition of many thick sedimentary layers, whole sequences were deformed by earth movements and uplifts to form mountains and plateaus. This often resulted in fracturing of the older Precambrian basement rocks but not in the flood deposits which were smoothly folded sometimes at large angles. If these flood deposits had sat there millions of yrs. one would expect hardening and fracturing. Snelling stated these 5 facts provide **strong evidence the sedimentary layers** with fossils **were deposited quickly** and not over hundreds of millions of yrs. Morris2007(p.96-119) agreed and provided a number of pictures of the folded sediments and layer interfaces.

Geology is a complex discipline and only a few of the points made by Snelling have been noted. Some **summary points from Snelling's DVD,** *The Flood* and a few other authors will be cited. This is an excellent summary video. He first raises the question of **how did the marine fossils get on the continents a mile high in the Grand Canyon and 5 miles high in the Himalayas?** 95% of all fossils are marine fossils and there are virtually no marine fossils found now in the ocean basins. Thus the slow and gradual present processes do not explain this past. In the Grand Canyon there are many layers of marine fossils, separated by millions yrs. of unknown history according to secular geologists. To get the marine fossils on the continents the ocean had to flood the continents and then the continents had to be uplifted. To account for the many fossil sedimentary layers in the Grand Canyon, the oceans had to flood very high on the continents many times and the continents had to rise and sink repeatedly like a bobbing cork. Snelling stated this is very difficult to explain by known geological processes. Here **Occam's razor** applies in that one simpler model explanation is usually better than a highly contrived and complex model explanation. It is a known fact that the present ocean floor of basalt is younger and denser than the continents. It is also known from the science of plate tectonics that the ocean floor is spreading at certain areas and ridges and subducting under the continents in other areas. These are the plate boundaries where there is considerable volcanic and earth quake activity. The present slow and gradual rate of plate movement is a few cm/yr. Snelling also asserts that the old ocean floor is not presently found on the current ocean floor location, but is deeply subducted and is believed to have been located by seismic studies. The model that best explains all of this is a catastrophic plate tectonics model by Baumgardner. It is further described by the Chap. 87 summary from Snelling above. During the flood a number of catastrophic processes occurred: **1.** There was a less dense warm mantle layer under the old ocean crust. **2.** As the fountains of the great deep were opened, the ocean floor split apart, the old dense ocean flood started subducting beneath the continents, the continents split apart, and the less dense hot mantle began upwelling and spreading at ridges forming the new less dense ocean floor. Because of the upwelling and lighter density it caused the ocean floor to rise flooding the continents. **3.** There were repeated Tsunamis that flooded the continents and deposited the marine sediments. There were also steam jets at the upwelling ridges from volcanoes that carried ocean water into the atmosphere that returned as intense rain. The plate movements were at meter/sec rates and this also caused crushing and uplifting of the lighter continents and the forming of the Himalayas. The warmer oceans and evaporation lead to more precipitation over the colder poles and formed the great ice deposits at the poles and the following ice age. The pattern of fossil deposition matches the land animals being catastrophically buried last along with marine animals. Some of the sedimentary deposits like the Tapeats sandstone are continent-wide arguing for a global and not local flood. **4.** After the old ocean floor was completely subducted the rapid plate movements greatly slowed, the lighter continents rose and the ocean floor sank leading to some runoff erosion on the continents and forming of some canyons. Also, Snelling 2012 noted that there may have been many meteor impacts during the flood as many were in the top layers of sediments.

A brief summary of Morris's book *The Young Earth 2007* will now be given. **The way sedimentary rock with fossils are dated is to look up the index fossil in an evolutionary book that dates fossils as millions of years old.** Radioisotope dating is not generally done in this case. **Thus the rocks are dated by the fossils and the fossils by the rock layers. This forms circular reasoning** (p.11-13). Morris noted the false report of the geologist Charles Lyell that the erosion rate of Niagara Falls was 1 ft/yr when local residents stated it was 4-5 ft/yr. This was used to disprove James Usher's book on chronology and rate agreeing with scripture (p.46). Only igneous and metamorphic rocks are dated by radioisotopes. Basalt from melted lava can also be dated. Advocates say the dating clock is reset to zero when the rock melts. Three or four assumptions are needed for the dating to be true:**1**. No gain or loss of parent or daughter materials (a closed system) **2**. Known amount of daughter material present at the start, **3.** Constant decay rate. **4.** An earth old enough to have produced the present state through the observed processes. Dr. Morris states there are difficulties with all these assumptions. Water can cause leaching making the system unclosed. The daughter material amount may be wrongly assumed or vary with catastrophic events. Three different types of experiments have indicated the decay rates may have varied greatly. **A**) Helium atoms trapped in zircon crystals in rocks dated 1.5 billion years old showed evidence of them being only 6000 years old by helium diffusion. **B**) Uranium and Polonium halos are found together in rock of all ages, including flood rocks. The Polonium indicated a young age. **C**) Ancient carbon—bearing rocks contain substantial C14 indicating a young age. The incorrectness and lack of consistency of radio dating was also demonstrated. Many recently observed lava flows have been sampled and radio dated at .1-10 million years (p.48-68). There is also one lava flow that is spilled over on top of the Grand Canyon sediments. However, it was dated by Rb-Sr-Pb isotopes to be older the Grand Canyon sediments themselves, which is impossible (p.58).

This shows the **inaccuracy of some of the isotope dating methods**. A group of creation scientists formed a team "RATE" to conduct experiments on radiometric dating and the age of the earth. **They found many inconsistencies in conventional radioisotope dating methods**(p.49-60). Riddle in *Dating Fossils and Rocks* also notes the errors in dating methods and a number of evidences for a young earth. Likewise Snelling 2010 noted in Chap.100 that there are errors in the K-Ar dating methods due to invalid assumptions of the initial Ar40. There are a number of excess Ar40 errors documented, that invalidate the initial low Ar40 assumption and the dates. Also the rubidium-strontium(Ru-Sr) dating has problems (noted in Chap.101) that can invalidate the isochrones due to mobility of Ru and Sr. The Uranium-Thorium-Lead dating problems are noted in Chap 103. These are some the main dating methods for old rocks.

Morris made additional **young earth arguments** as follows: **1.** C14 is building up and not at equilibrium in the atmosphere. Calculations indicated a maximum age of the earth of about 10,000-15000 yrs (Morris p.78). **2.** The earth's magnetic field has been measured for 170 yrs. and showed a uniform energy decay rate with a half life of about 700 yrs. Some models of this suggest a young earth of about 8,700 yrs. Dr. Morris states "Old earth advocates maintain hope that somehow the dynamo theory can still be salvaged. At present, it conflicts with observations of rapid reversals in modern lava flows, sunspot cycles, minor convection currents in the core, and it has no support in physical theory. The only existing model for the magnetic field that handles all the data specifies a young earth and a recent creation. It is based on sound physics and its predictions have been proven by observation"(87). **3.** Using uniformitarian calculations, based on measured Helium emission and loss rates, the earth cannot be older than 2 million yrs, not 4.6 billion that evolution claims. From the rate of salt build up in the oceans would give the present levels in 32 million yrs, when considering all inputs and outputs. At the present rate of erosion, the continents would be greatly eroded in 14 million yrs. They are no greatly eroded continents and the very old sediments remain. Also from the rate of sediment input to the oceans (27.5 billion tons/yr), the present ocean sediment would be accounted for in 15 million yrs. Assuming the world wide flood would greatly shorten these times. Thus there are many different estimates that do not agree with the 4.6 billion yr. old earth (90-94). **4.** Records show population growth at 2%/yr. This rate explains our current population of about 6 billion based on a recent history of

5000 yrs. However, if we existed for about one million yrs. as evolutionists teach, the population should be massive and also the human fossil bones (74). In summary, the **Morris book presents many scientific arguments for a young earth** of 12,000 yrs. or less age and many more that disagree with the 4.6 billion yr. age. Also CMI (web92) gave 101 evidences for a young earth.

Biology, Genetics, DNA, and Missing links

Dr. **Sanford is an expert geneticist** who noted the following in the book *Genetic Entropy*(p.25): The entropy is the degradation of genes and nucleotides through mutations which has a net downward effect for which there is no escape and no upward creation of more complex genes occurring. The primary axiom is that man is the product of mutations plus natural selection. **He shows that genetics refutes upward evolution**. The frequency distribution of mutations is described: It is dominated by nearly neutral **mutations**, followed by minor negative ones, followed by **beneficial ones which are extremely rare**. The neutral and negative ones overwhelm and make very unlikely the survival on any positive ones(p.27-32). Mathematical curves describe these distributions. In addition researchers are finding that much of what was thought Junk DNA (non functional) is actually functional(p.20-21). Muller's Ratchet is described (p.169) as genetic degradation heavily loaded with mutations. "Everything about the true distribution of mutations argues against their possible forward evolution: (p.25). He gives the analogy of an instruction manual where letters are changed randomly by a copying scribe. If one started with a manual for a red wagon, the manual would be a book; for a jet aircraft it would be library. DNA is a very detailed information code for which the letters A,C,T,G are used. If letters were changed by copying them incorrectly in the wagon manual, is impossible to the get the jet aircraft library of manuals. One would get a degraded incorrect wagon manual(p.5-13).

Sanford noted that Bergman reviewed the topic of beneficial mutations from the literature in 2004. He found 453,732 mutations hits, but only 186 of those were called beneficial. When the 186 were reviewed, they were beneficial in a limited sense, but all involved loss of information(p.26). This has also been shown true of bacterial antibiotic resistance(p.17). Dr. Sanford was involved, along with other researchers, in doing accelerated plant mutation experiments using radiation and chemicals. Millions of plants were mutagenized and screened for improvements over two decades. Huge numbers of deformed aberrant plants were produced with almost no meaningful improvements. This effort was a failure and has been mostly abandoned. There are a couple of exceptions. One example is low phytate corn. This is an example of a net loss of genetic information where plants producing phytic acid no longer produce much of it. Some ornamental plants were produced which were dwarfs, which were interesting to the eye(p.27). Selection involves death of the weaker and survival of the fittest. However due to the population distribution statistics, the power of selection is limited. The lethal mutations are easily selected out, but the vast majority of mutations are near neutral and very minor, and make it difficult for beneficial mutations to ever survive, and change the genome. Many animals die due to environmental factors unrelated to their genes.

He gave the **example of a biochemistry textbook** compared to a simple bacterial genome. If random letter errors (misspellings, duplications and deletions) are generated, say 100 new errors per text, then the textbooks are given to students and they are tested on their biochemistry scores. The students with the best test scores are selected and their textbooks kept and again subjected to the error-changing procedure. Would you expect any improvement in the textbooks or in the students' test scores over time? Why not? Many of the errors will be minor(p.50). A number of factors, other that the book errors, influence the students' success. The statistics for the changes vastly support the degradation of the quality of the textbook, not its improvement.

Sanford also made the point that gene duplication does not increase new information. When one chromosome is doubled it is called aneuploidy; when many are doubled it is called polyploidy. Theses extra copies are not generally beneficial; and extra copy of chromosome 21 causes Down Syndrome. In plants, polyploidy disrupts the cell shape and also results in stunted and deformed plants(p.194-5).

The human genome is degrading at 1-2 % per generation of about 20 yrs. **Mutation is clearly implicated in aging** (p.145-155). He accounts for the long lives the Adam and early figures and the shorter lives now by a curve based on genetic degradation. Our genes will continue to degrade. Mathematical modeling curves are given for this (p.155). Sanford's Appendix 1 has many quotes from notable geneticists supporting the genetic trends cited in the book (p.161-181). Haldane made a **case for human gene degradation** ruling out gene improvement statistically(p.163). Degeneration of genes is the precise antithesis of evolutionary theory(p.206). If humans lived for 1 million yrs, their genes would be badly degraded at the 1-2 % rate.

Parker's book *Creation Facts of Life* will be summarized next: He is a biologist and paleontologist ; his book had many good arguments refuting upward evolution. Two complex parts of every living system are DNA and proteins. DNA is a coiled string with special base units (A,G,C,T) that link. Proteins are also chains that have amino acids that have links(p.22). The organization and informational coding of these is very suggestive of creative design and not of randomness(p.28). All of our physical characteristics are spelled out in the DNA. Miller's experiments to make amino acids don't come close to the complex organization of DNA and proteins. These experiments are unrealistic in explaining creation, because oxygen is excluded but it is present in almost everything including ancient rocks. Ammonia, if present would have dissolved in the oceans. The electric sparks that put amino acids together also tears them apart much faster. So Miller added a trap to quickly remove the amino acids. The trap involves creative design and is not common to nature. The amino acids created were a mixture including ones that are poisonous to life(p.26).

Similarly a **cell is a complex machine** with DNA, proteins, over 75 helper molecules (including RNA and special enzymes) all working together in harmony (p.29-32). "It takes a living cell about 4 min. to crank out an average protein (500 amino acids) according to DNA specifications"(p.34). This resembles creative design not randomness. "Life is a property of organization, not of substance"(p. 34). He gave the example of a book being written by an unknown method or author, with the materials being ink and paper. To get another better book one wouldn't expect the ink and paper to do the work by randomness, one would expect an author. "**The DNA codes** contain **more information** than a thousand volumes of literary works"(p.36). Evolutionists may argue that crystal formation demonstrates that order can appear spontaneously. "Crystal order, yes, specified complexity, no. The specified complexity in a DNA sequence is nothing like the ordered simplicity or repeat pattern on the ice crystal"(p.35-7). A crystal is a simple repeating pattern produced by the shape and charge of its constituents). **Francis Crick**, who shared a Noble Prize for the discovery of DNA's structure, **stated that life could not and did not evolve on earth** (p.39). Sir Fred Hoyle, a famed astronomer and mathematician, reached the conclusion after mathematical analyses, that believing life could result from time, chance and the properties of matter was like believing that a tornado sweeping through a junkyard might assemble a Boeing 747 from the materials therein(p.40). Dr. Michael Denton, a prominent molecular biologist wrote a book "Evolution: A Theory in Crisis" and stated the **chemical evolution scenario as an affront to reason**. Dr. Denton does not acknowledge being a Christian, but states that creation may have religious implications but so does evolution. Parker stated that belief in evolution means that there is no God and no creator who sets the rules. Human beings are free to be their own boss and set their own rules(p.11).

For comparative **similarities in structure** biologists use the term **Homology**. Why should a person's arm have the same kind of bone pattern as the leg of a dog or the wing of a bat? There are two basic ideas: The evolutionary idea is descent from a common ancestor. The creation idea is creation according to common design plans (43-45). Dr. Denton and Dr. Parker noted many inconsistencies in the evolutionary idea of descent from one simple ancestor (p.45-50) including the following: **1.** Most evolutionists do not claim that hind limbs evolved from forelimbs or vice versa or from a common limb. **2.** Sexual organs are difficult to explain as males and females are different. **3.** In frogs, 5 digits on limbs grow out from buds on a paddle, while in human embryos, the 5 digits form as the tissue between them is reabsorbed. "Here quite different gene-enzyme mechanisms produce similar patterns"(p.46). **4.** Structures in adult crayfish and lobsters are very similar. However the crayfish egg develops directly into the adult form, while the lobster egg reaches the same pattern by going through a free swimming larval stage. **5.** Convergent evolution pertains to organisms not closely related that independently acquire similar characteristics while evolving in separate and sometimes varying ecosystems. For example, the complex eye of humans is similar to that of squids, but they have very different ancestors. The creation explanation of using common design features varied for differing environments again makes sense. Some deep sea creatures have very unique lens systems to gather and focus light including lens cylinders, lens mirrors. They make ingenious use of physics and refractions that implies creative design, but have no intermediate evolutionary forms. **6.** Hemoglobin is a protein that carries oxygen in red blood cells. It occurs sporadically among invertebrate phyla in no obvious pattern and also in nearly all invertebrates and is even found in some bacteria. In all cases we find a similar molecule. This is difficult for an evolutionist to explain but easy for a creationist to explain by use of a common design feature. 7. Algae are usually classified into groups on the basis of their pigment (reds, greens, browns, and goldens). They can also be grouped on their structural complexity (unicellular, colonial, and multi-cellular) and grouped by their type of sexuality (iso, hetero, and oo-gamy). This causes problems for tracing their evolution, but no problems for using certain chosen design features in various combinations. **8**. Molecular biology and homology has been used with DNA to create evolutionary trees. However, this has many disagreements with the trees based on fossils or on comparative anatomy of larger structures and has created large controversies in the evolutionary camp. This paradigm is solved if one uses a mosaic of different created kinds that then can have genetic variation in kinds and undergo microevolution (p.52-3).

Human embryos appear to show gill slits, a yolk sac and a tail on first glance. The evolutionist believes these apparent structures are useless leftovers or vestigial organs of our ancestry. The gill slits are pharyngeal (throat) pouches that house some glands. The yolk sac is a temporary pouch for forming the first blood cells. The tail forms the coccyx or tail bone which is an essential bone structure to support muscles. A related **diagram comparing embryos** of other species with the human one was authored **by Ernst Haeckel** in the 1860. This diagram **was shown to be an exaggerated fake**. The diagrams, although fake, have been used for many years in biology textbooks as recent as 2005. This was used to support the now out of vogue throwback theory that the embryo is supposed to retrace the evolution of its group (p.54-61).

The **woodpecker** is an **example** of specially designed creature with many parts working together. If all parts didn't work the bird would probably not survive. The parts include the following: A very strong pointed beak, a heavy duty skull with shock absorbing tissue between the two eyelids that snap shut upon the strike, a long tongue with sheath that inserts into the nostril. A Platypus is also unique in combining parts that occur in widely varying species. The parts include the following: milk glands, a leathery egg, and electric signal sensitivity, a wide flat bill, and webbed feet. A **woodpecker and a basic cell have irreducible complexity** and are compared to a mouse trap. That is to say all parts must be present at once for them to function (p.63-67). Another example of a creature with this unusual complexity is the bombardier beetle. It creates a hot noxious gas by combining hydrogen peroxide and hydroquinones. It has special enzymes, pressure tanks, and special nerves and muscles to control its operation (p.100-1). Cleaning symbiosis is also difficult to support based on evolution of the fittest. The small cleaning bird or fish could be eaten by the larger predator.

Parker used the term **Microevolution** as something both creationists and evolutionists believe in. The loose definition of evolution being change through time is not very useful and misleading. Macroevolution is the term used for evolution from a few simple species to man. The classic **peppered moths** example widely used in textbooks as an example of evolution is somewhat contrived and not a good example of evolution. The light and dark moths were still present before and after the smoke pollution so only the dominance of the population changed not the genes. The moths used for the book pictures were dead ones that were glued to the tree and photographed (p.76-82). There are logical limits to variations or change in a species that have been observed as stated by a number of evolutionary authors like Denton and Lewontin. Another widely used **example of microevolution is Darwin's Finches** that developed different beaks. It is also likely that the originally created finches (as do all species) had genes that allow some variation and adaptation within kind (p.101-2). Parker stated that a giraffe's neck that stretched by evolution is unlikely. It also has auxiliary pumps to get the blood to its head when held high, and pressure reducers to lower the pressure when it drinks (p.105).

Mutations are mainly **responsible for diseases and degradation**. Parker gave **six reasons** why mutations do not explain evolution across kinds: **Reason 1**. Progressive mutations building on one another are mathematically improbable. They occur in one in every ten million duplications ($1/10^7$) of a DNA molecule. Two successive ones have a probability of $1/10^{14}$; three successive, $1/10^{21}$ and four—$1/10^{28}$. At the 3rd and 4th successions the ocean and the earth aren't big enough to hold all the organisms. Bacteria can be made antibiotic resistant by mutation, but such forms are cripples and do not survive well. "The antibiotic resistance carried by plasmids results from enzymes produced to break down the antibiotic. Their resistance is by design. It's possible God designed antibiotic resistance in bacteria and antibiotic production by fungi, to balance the growth of these prolific organisms in the soil."(p.109). "Contrary to popular opinion, drug resistance in bacteria does not demonstrate evolution. It does demonstrate natural selection, but only selection among already existing variations within a kind."(p.110). Denton, a molecular biologist, stated that the mathematical improbabilities of random mechanisms explaining all of evolution comes very close to a disproof of evolution (p.110). **Reason 2.** The chance of upward useful mutations is also low, in that at least 1000 harmful mutations occur for every helpful one. Perhaps a helpful change might occur, but it would be drowned in the sea of harmful changes before the new surviving population could take hold. Geneticists refer to this problem as genetic load or burden which weights down a species and lowers its quality. Experiments in inbreeding of fruit flies demonstrated mutations which were so bad as to almost destroy this select group. Because harmful mutations so outnumber good ones, it's considered illegal in many states to marry someone too closely related to you (p.114-5). Parker claims that the Florida panther became endangered by too many bad mutations in a limited group in Florida. Only after importing panthers from the western USA, to lower the genetic burden, did the populations do better(p.119). **Reason 3**. Mutations point back to creation in kinds with some variation in genes as being more likely (the biblical view). This is because of the huge genetic load and improbability of mutations from a single cell to everything. "Mutations are not genetic script writers; they are merely typographical errors. Typically, a mutation changes only one letter in a genetic sentence averaging 1,500 letters(DNA bases) long"(p.120) The information in a technical book, for example, cannot be reduced to or derived from the properties of the ink and paper used to write it. Similarly, the information in the genetic code cannot be reduced to, nor derived from the properties of the matter, nor from the mistakes of mutations: its message and meaning originated instead in the mind of the maker (p.122). **Genes of the same kind**, like those for straight or curly hair or those for yellow or green seeds, are **called alleles**. There are over 300 alleles of the hemoglobin gene. By definition, alleles are just variants of a given gene causing variation in a given trait. Mutations produce only alleles. For example one allele of the hemoglobin gene caused by a mutation is the sickle cell gene which occurs when only one DNA base is changed out for several hundred. Genes of the same creation kind can be objectively defined as segments on DNA that occupy corresponding positions (loci) on homologous chromosomes. Homologous chromosomes are pairs that look alike, but come from two different parents, so their genetic content is similar but not identical. These genes pair up and separate in meiotic cell division. They are also turned on and off by the same gene regulations. The word genon is used for genes that affect a different category of trait. These differing genons do not occupy corresponding loci on homologs and do not pair in meiosis. A complete set of DNA specifying a kind is called its genome. **The human genome includes at least 30,000 different genons** or traits and this is the called the depth of the human gene pool. The E. coli **bacteria pool is about 5000 genons** deep, while a virus pool may only be a dozen genons deep. The width of the gene pool refers the amount of allelic variation within kind. Among dogs the width of allelic variation is narrow for greyhounds, but wide for mongrels. However the depth of the gene pool is about the same for both dogs (p.123-5). Evolutionists assume that all life started from one or a few chemically evolved life forms with a very small gene pool. They also assume mutations and selections by struggle and death, enlarged the gene pool and overcame the genetic load of harmful mutations. Creationists assume each created kind began with a large gene pool, designed to multiply and fill the earth with great variety. "The evolutionary assumption doesn't work and it's not consistent with what we presently know of genetics"(p.130). Occasionally members of one kind may also lose the ability to interbreed with others in the kind as occurred for fruit flies. These subgroups can then be called a different species but they could also be called alleles (p.131-3).

A **1980 conference** of leading evolutionary scientists was held in Chicago to consider the question of whether **the mechanisms of macroevolution** could be extrapolated to explain macroevolution. The answer that they gave **was a clear no**, as summarized by Lewin in Science(Parker p.150). Parker stated the old evolutionary view is similar to assuming you could ride a bicycle from earth to the moon if you just pedaled long enough. "There are just too many logical and scientific limits to such an extrapolation"(p.151). Although many scientists recognize that molecules to man evolution is very improbable, some cite fossils as evidence of the long periods of evolution. **Fossils** help us with **2 types of questions**: First, what kinds of plants and animals once populated the earth? Second, how fast were fossils and the rock layers that contain them formed? The oldest period of history where there are fossils is the Cambrian period. This period show sea life including complex trilobites, and nautiloids and no earlier intermediate or simple like forms. This is a blow to evolutionists because the early simple forms are missing (p154-8). Darwin also noticed this and stated that the fossil evidence was "perhaps

the most obvious and serious objection to the theory"(p.159). David
Rump, a modern noted expert on fossils, stated the same thing (p.160-2).
Fossilized plants are similar to what we find today. This includes complex
algae that do photosynthesis. Fossilized plants can be classified by the same
criteria we use today; they argue for a special creation(p.163-5)

Among vertebrate animals the Archaeopteryx has been cited as a
missing link between reptiles and birds. Although it has some features
in common with a reptile it is still a bird and not an ideal example of
a missing link. It was long used as a publicized missing link but is now
mostly discredited. National Geographic did an article and display on a
dinosaur with feathers, which was a complete fake. Fossils of bird parts
were cemented together with fossils of dinosaur parts. The **Piltdown Man**
was also shown a hoax with an ape jaw attached to man's skull In fact there
have been so many publicized missing links that have later disproven,
that books have been written on them by various authors(p.171). Many
of these have been hoaxes and falsifications. The widely publicized
Nebraska man was later shown to have been wrongly based on the tooth
of a pig. The Neanderthals turned out to be people who suffered from
bone diseases. A recent candidate, the Australopithecus, is now considered
grossly apelike and not really related to man at all. A 1926 paper by H.
Osborn claimed that Negroes would be classified as a separate species
and not fully human(p.177). He was a leading evolutionist of the time;
this promoted Hitler's racism and the false claims of eugenics and the
super-Arian race. Australian aborigines were also one treated as subhuman
evolutionary links. Parker noted the evolution goes far beyond the limits
of science, and is more easily influenced by human bias (p.178).

Referring again to the 1980 conference of leading evolutionists, Adler
and Carey stated "Evidence from fossils now points overwhelmingly away
from the classical Darwinism which most Americans learned in high
School"(p.186). "**In the fossil record the missing links are the rule**. The
more scientists have searched for the transitional forms between the species,
the more they have been frustrated." "Gould and Eldridge are simply
saying that most kinds of fossilized life forms appear in the fossil sequence
abruptly and distinctly as discrete kinds, show relatively minor variation
within kind, then often abruptly disappear"(p 187). Denton states that
although the transitional forms are missing, evolutionary thought today
provides the priority of the paradigm (i.e., the assumption that evolution is
a fact) takes precedence over common sense and the facts (p.190).

The 2nd question was **how fast** were the **fossils formed**? Most scientists agree the past fossils were formed rapidly under flood conditions. The old belief that the fossil deposition occurred very slowly has been cast aside, because organisms would decay by bacteria and rot to dust in long periods of time. The debate then is over whether there were many little floods or one big flood forming most of the fossils (p.192). The two interpretations of a common sedimentary fossil column are shown in Parker's fig. 32(p.197). The common evolutionary belief is that the ages of fossil depositions were eons apart and caused by many different floods. **The creationist belief is that the depositions occurred in about one yr. during the great flood** of Noah, **with the lowest elevation organisms (sea life) being buried first and the highest elevation life being buried last.** There is now a growing school of evolutionary geology with many members called neo-catastrophists who believe a massive flood or floods did occur (p.195-7). Parker further compares the two views in the *Fossil Book* and provides considerable documentation for the creationist *view*. The older uniformitarian school grew out of the theories of geologist Charles Lyell at about the time of Darwin. This slow and uniform theory can explain some erosion and deposition we see, but so can rapid erosion and deposition explain some events. More scientists are recognizing that very slow deposition does not create many fossils, as they decay away first. Some depositions with fossils are in fact spread out over vast areas, even continents. The Morrison Formation with its dinosaur remains covers much of the mountainous west, while the St. Peters Sandstone goes from Canada to Texas. Most scientists agree that there must have been massive floods of a type not seen in the better recorded history of the last 4000 yrs. "**Evolutionists believe that the land plants did not appear until 100 million years after the Cambrian trilobites died out. Yet over 60 genera of woody plants spores, pollen and wood itself have been recovered from the lowest trilobite rock (Cambrian)** throughout the world. This evidence is so well known that it's even in standard college biology textbooks." Some evolutionists say that despite the contrary evidence they still believe that plants evolved much later. The creationist does not argue despite the contrary evidence; he argues because of the evidence that was present near the same time(p.199). **Misplaced fossils are very common** so evolutionists have developed **terms for them like a stratigraphic leak** (it was deposited too low in the column), **reworked specimen** (it was deposited too high in the column), and **paraconformity** (a smooth continuous deposition into another misplaced geologic age), a disconformity (where a layer—age is missing). **"In fact the only way to recognize a paraconformity is by a prior commitment to evolutionary theory.** There is no physical evidence"(p. 201). Parker states further, "perhaps the actual physical evidence is correct and it's the evolutionary time scale-based on faith in evolution—that's wrong"(p.201). There are **many polystratic fossils.** As the name implies they **may extend through many rock layers** or strata. For example, fossilized trees have been buried vertically through many ages of sediments. **Evolutionists have no explanation for this, but creationists do.** There were not many ages, only a year (p. 202). "Polystrates are especially common in coal deposits." Many scientists are considering the rapid flood deposition theory as opposed to the old slow swamp plant deposition theory for coal. Dr. Steve Austin did his doctoral dissertation on coal geology. In this he states that coal was formed from plant debris deposited under mats of vegetation floating in sea water. His model explained many features of coal that the swamp model could not explain. Even more important, his theory is the first ever to predict the location and quality of the coal"(p.203). A dramatic confirmation of the processes theorized by Dr. Austin was confirmed in small scale by the 1980 eruption of Mt. St. Helens. The volcano sent mud and debris in a wave that sheered off millions of trees. The trees floated out on a large lake, became water logged and sunk down into the recent mud deposits. The whole mass is now reminiscent of early coal deposits and has polystrates(vertical trees in it). Creationists believe that many volcanoes went off during the great flood and sheered off trees and vegetation which floated and were deposited in sediment in a few years, not millions of years.

Other facts and theories that support rapid deposition and climate change causing rapid large animal death include the following: Many volcanoes going off during the Noah's flood would explain the warming of the oceans, the cooling of the high land areas, the deposition of massive ice fields, and the rapid killing of animals. Ice during the peak of the ice age covered about 30% of the earth surface(p.207-9). More details on the Ice Age after the volcanoes and great flood are given in paper and books by Michael Oard(p. 208). **There are many living fossils (very old organisms living today)** some of which are a problem for evolutionists. Some of these included lampshells, nautilus, certain fish and many plants. Some species do not seem to have evolved much from their fossils dated millions of yrs ago.

Dinosaur bones have been found repeatedly with soft fleshy looking tissue with supple bone cells and translucent blood vessels and blood cells, in fossils presumed to be 80 million yrs. old. How could fresh tissue and dinosaur DNA last this long without degrading?(p.210-12). Creation scientists have formed a RATE team investigating radioisotopes and the age of the earth. They have evidence that the earth is thousands of years old and not billions of years (p.212-3). There is evidence the Grand Canyon with its fossil record could have been formed recently by catastrophic flood and uplift processes. There is an approved USGS paper Lake Missoula by Harlan Bretz and a paper and video by Steve Austin on the Grand Canyon. Austin has also done papers on the rapid effects of Mt. St. Helen's valley formation and deposition (p.216-230). Patterson (2007) and Sarfati (2003) also discuss the improbability of evolution. Purdom (2009) is an expert molecular geneticist who has some good DVD's. Some excellent (web 53-56) articles are also available from AIG. **In summary, the weight of these arguments against upward macroevolution is very strong. Thus microevolution within the biblical kinds is very likely.** Riddle in *The Fossil Record* also concurred and noted the many missing links that have been disproven.

Both Riddle in ***The Origin of Humans***, and Patterson in *Evolution Exposed* discuss the origin of humans(web 84), as does **Rana in *Who was Adam***. Rana noted (p.59) that molecular clocks can be set on DNA changes. Humans display much less genetic diversity than any other species, which implies that they are young and from a single location near Africa(p.60). MtDNA research on mothers' genes indicated the following: Wilson's 1991 study indicated a beginning of woman's genes about **200,000 yrs ago** in Africa. A recent Swiss study in 2000 indicated a start 171,500 +-50,000 yrs. ago from Africa(Rana p.63). Correction for heteroplasmy in addition to homoplasmy to could shorten these ages to 50,000 yrs(p.64). The rate of mutations is assumed constant in history, but it is known that changes in the level of radioactivity can change the rate. The father's Y chromosome's mutations have also been backdated. One study indicated male origins about 40,000-60,000 yrs. ago and another 35,000-47,000 yrs. ago. Out of Africa was also indicated(p.66). Rana also noted (p 71) that various disease organisms associated with humans hand been backdated: Malaria parasite 50,000 to100,000 yrs, and Lice-72,000 yrs. Patterson (p.48) and Harrub(web 88) indicated that **several assumptions went into setting the mtDNA clocks: First**, they compared mtDNA from humans with that from chimpanzees, and then used paleontology and additional molecular data to determine the age of the supposed common ancestor. This (and similar calculations on other species) revealed a mutation rate in the range of 2% to 4% per million years. **Second**, they compared the groups in their study that were close geographically, and took the age of the common ancestor from estimated times of settlement as indicated by anthropology and archaeology. Again, 2% to 4% every million years seemed reasonable to them so a rounded mid average of these two estimates was 200,000 yrs. They also assumed a constant mutation rate back in time. Harrub (web 88) noted that some studies have challenged these assumptions and mutation rates. The Parsons study found that mutation rates in mitochondrial DNA were **eighteen times higher than previous estimates** (see Parsons, Thomas J., et al. (1997), "A High Observed Substitution Rate in the Human Mitochondrial DNA Control Region," *Nature Genetics,* 15:363.") Gibbons noted **using the new clock, she would be a mere 6,000 years old**. Gibbons, Ann (1998), "Calibrating the Mitochondrial Clock," *Science,* 279:28-29, January 2." These challenges are not well accepted, because of the attempt to fit to the older dates, which are closer to fossil finds for Homo Neanderthals that are dated up to 130,000 yrs ago(Rana p.36). The many fossils for Hominids (bipedal apes) in Africa are dated much earlier—several million yrs. ago(Rana p.31). Snelling and Morris indicated in the prior section these dates and the dating system are based on index fossils and radio-dating which he indicated may both be in error.

   Rana in *Who was Adam* will be summarized further: Conventional biologists say man evolved from chimps, and Neanderthals were a side path. Many hominid fossils have been found: The Piltdown man found in 1912 was proved a fake in 1953; orangutan and human parts were mixed and teeth were filed. A few scientists did fraud to gain recognition. Most are honest(p.28). Some creationists capitalize on this fraud, but it does not convince scientists unless an alternate theory is proposed to explain the other known **hominids** of which there are many fossils. Ross uses this term hominids for **bipedal primates**, while biologists let it include humans also. Ross maintains the **modern humans**, Homo sapiens sapiens, have always been different. Some biologists use **archaic Homo sapiens** for Homo erectus and Homo Neanderthals that are supposed to live 500,000 and 130,000 yrs. ago(p.31). "However, nearly all paleoanthropologists agree that modern humans appear in the fossil record not much earlier than 100,000 yrs. ago"(p.30). The bulk of the record, with many hominid fossils, occurred in Africa and is dated several million yrs. ago(p.31). Some of these used very simple stone pieces. These hominids appear distinct from chimpanzees and Rana terms them novel bipedal apes(p.33). These hominids had a larger brain than chimps but still had the longer arms, shorter legs for climbing and may have knuckle walked like apes. It is claimed that about 2 million yrs. ago that some hominids of the Homo genus appeared—Homo habilis, H. rudolfensis, homo ergaseter; then came homo erectus about 900,000 yrs ago with a brain size of 1200 cc. This was still different than modern humans(p.35). Homo Neanderthals appeared in Germany about 130,000 yrs. ago and had a brain size similar to humans. Edward Rubin of the Lawrence Berkeley National Laboratory in Berkeley, California, states recent genome testing of Neanderthals suggests human and Neanderthal DNA are some 99.5% to nearly 99.9% identical(Wikipedia web 89). This is a much closer DNA match than is true for humans and chimps. However Rana noted(p.184) studies from the Max Planck Institute that indicated the mtDNA fragments from Neanderthals and humans were very different. Also Neanderthal's tool making was very simple like in the late Stone Age. Riddle held that Neanderthals were humans, while Rana did not, and cited some differences. This poses some questions: There appears to be a progression of hominid creatures between chimps and man. If they were all created on day 6, how would early man react to them and why were they created? Is it possible that Adam's line mated with them as in Gen. 6:2? What would happen then, giants? If they coexisted, it is logical that the smarter humans would dominate, and the hominids would persist more in areas where humans were absent. It is also possible the God wanted to view the different behaviors of man and hominids and not make their differences too obvious.

Noel (web 106)offered an interesting assertion that the Neanderthals became the Basques. The Basque people have a high percentage of Neanderthal genetics, and thus a higher than usual percentage of Rh negative blood. It has been identified in recent DNA analysis of Neanderthal bone marrow that Neanderthal had no blood components for A, B, or Rh, which came during later genetics. "Some 55% of Basques have Group O blood, one of the highest percentages in the world. Even stronger evidence comes from the Rhesus factor, discovered only in 1940. The blood of most humans (and, apparently, all other primates) contains this factor, and is called Rhesus-positive or Rh+ blood. Blood lacking this factor is called Rhesus-negative." The Basques are well-known to have the highest percentage (around 33%) of Rhesus-negative blood of any human population, and so are regarded as the original source of this factor. In the United States, some

15% of the 'European' population is Rh-negative, while the percentage in the 'Asian' and 'Black' population is much less than this."

Several articles in Answers 2012 (Menton), address early cavemen. The authors claimed the many early bipedal beings, including homo erectus, were actually humans descended from Noah. They cite that these beings had tools, buried their dead and must have been able to make boats to cross seas, as evidenced by their migrations. The articles don't discuss whether there were earlier bipedal primates that had fossils, assuming none were younger than Adam. It was noted that all these fossils are in the Pleistocene layers, with only homo erectus going back into the lower Pleistocene. The Pleistocene is also the post flood ice age, dated at the Babel dispersion of 2250 BC. It was also held that the Neanderthals and the Denisovans had DNA similar to humans; genetic diversity and drift account for their physical differences.

Rana in *Origins of Life* Chapters **5, 6, 10, 12 will be summarized** briefly and discussed. **Chap. 5** An early or late appearance:p.63-79 The abbreviation **Gya** will be used for billion yrs. The earth's oldest rocks are found in Greenland-3.8 Gya, 3.3 Gya in NW Australia and SE Africa. Stromatolites(layers of several bacteria) in Australia were built by cyanobacteria in Shark bay, a hypersaline area-dated as 3.3-3.5 Gya(p.65-7). This implied shallow ocean environment. Threadlike microfossils were also found in cherts (3.3Gya) associated with kerogen tars in Australia(p.68). M. Braiser thinks they were deposited by chemical process under hydrothermal conditions; some others think that microbes operated in these hydrothermal vents. Carbon 12-14 ratios and Raman signatures support 3.3 Gya (p.69). Nitrogen 14-15 also supports this as may S-32 enriched sulfide deposits(p.70). There are kerogen and graphite deposits that are also dated by C12-14; also apaties although this has been challenged. Some are troubled by any dates before 3.8 Gya as this was the time of heavy asteroid bombardment(p.72). Banded iron formations may have formed in ocean with nutrient up swelling of iron and silica acted on by and affected by cyanobacteria and oxygen.1.8-3.5 Gya(p.75-6). The **Weight of evidence is that cyanobacteria existed early**. These were complex bacteria like today's and show that many complex bacteria existed then both aerobic and anaerobic(p.76-7). Some think the anoxygenic bacteria were first. There was a complex ensemble of biochemical processes and organisms(p.78).

Chap. 6 Slow or Sudden Arrival: p.81-92 Earth's origin 4.57 Gya, Moon 4.47 Gya; Fossils of bacteria back to 3.5 Gya; There is evidence of the sun's variability in luminosity and of ionizing radiation events in early history of solar system before 3.9 Gya. **There was heavy bombardment of asteroids and comets** that tapered down 4.4-3.5Gya; with a temporary **peak at 3.8-9Gya**; this is called **the Hadean era**. This would have exterminated any life, melted the earth's crust and evaporated the oceans. Low tungsten 182 rocks in Greenland dating 3.7-8 Gya give evidence of the meteorites. Also moon rocks and the moon's regression rate give evidence of it being formed by a collision of a medium sized planet with earth 4.47 Gya. This also caused a new earth atmosphere to form. Some of the first earth rocks are dated 3.85 Gya; before that time most rocks melted; Zircon crystals(which have high melting points and resistance) give evidence that the earth's crust melted and re-solidified 3.9-4.4Gya. It is known the RNA breaks down at high temperatures and could not have survived this period. It was noted that life must have appeared in a time window of less than 50 million yrs. and. perhaps 10 million or less(p.85). This would have included many complex bacteria and cyanobacteria including RNA and DNA. This invalidates some naturalistic models that say life evolved over longer times, which is very improbable. Fossils appear closely dated to the first rocks and show complex bacteria.

    Chap. 10 Codes of Life:p.135-41 **The cell uses 20 different codes of amino acids to make proteins**. The amino acids have a range of different physical and chemical properties. They form polypeptide chains and arrange themselves in 3 dimensional space. **The probability of one, 100 amino acid long chain assembling correctly is one in 10^{191}**(p138). Physicists say any probability greater than one in 10^{50} is considered impossible. **Making 20 proteins by chance is more impossible.** DNA and RNA are ever more complex.

    Chap. 12 Life's Minimum Complexity p.160-8 Recently molecular biologists have used a top down approach to track life forms. They are discovering new genomes and tracking them back to the most similar prior ones called the **LUCA** (last universal common ancestor). This has proceeded to identify the near beginning, the simplest functional bacteria. **For a bacteria to survive independently, it requires about 1500 gene products**(p.161). Parasites live off of other organisms and need at least 500 genes; but they can't perform certain life functions and are thus not independent. The cyanobacteria found in early fossils, have about 1700 genes. As noted previously, even one protein with its 20 amino acids is considered impossible to form correctly by chance, let alone 1500 genes.

The probability of 1500 genes forming correctly by chance is one in 10^{112500}. Not only must the genes form, but also the DNA, RNA and cell walls are needed. Prior to the 1990's the bacteria was thought simpler, but it is now known to be complex and impossible to form by chance.

Chap.14,16 shows that panspermia is very unlikely as is original life on Mars. Any old life on Mars most likely came from a collision with earth that sent life forms into space.

Snelling (2010 Chap. 52)noted similar findings to Rana about the early rocks, Stromatolites, and microfossils. He gave some nice charts showing the progression of these early fossil finds in the Precambrian. The Cambrian portion of the Paleozoic period is dated about .5 Gya. This is where the Cambrian explosion begins with Trilobites, vertebrates, and land plants. However, Snelling states the Paleozoic and Mesozoic strata were deposited during the flood, while the Cenozoic strata were deposited Post-flood, and the Precambrian pre-flood. Snelling admits that this tends to support the progression of life forms argument, that simple bacteria and algae were first(p.353). My brief thoughts follow: It appears then that the Precambrian with its algae is considerably older that the Cambrian. This poses a problem for the literal days and all vegetation being created in one day. One could possibly assume the radiodating is wrong and these vast time frames could be compressed, or even that there was a change in radioactive decay rates at the time of the flood. Still the progression of fossils would remain, showing that the algae considerably preceded the land plants. Gen. 1:9-11 talks of the land and water being separated before plants on day 3. Perhaps days 1,2,3 were longer than 24 hrs as this constitutes a trinity and a mystery miracle.

Thomas 2012 gave an interesting write up on the origin of Dogs. It indicated they developed from wolves rather quickly. Experiments have demonstrated that foxes have been bred quickly into a domesticated variety. About 200 breeds of dogs were produced in 300 yrs. Tompkins 2012 studied human and chimp gene similarity and found only about 86-89% similarity.

C. Theology, Problems, Values and Uses

Theology: There have been a number of challenges to apologetics by theologians. The differing creation views were discussed under the sections on world views. The truth of the Bible section also touches on this topic. Those believing in Full Inerrancy tend to also believe the Bible is historically true. **Craig**(p.12), a seminary professor, noted that a number of seminaries don't teach apologetics and are fideistic, separating faith from reason. He said the **primary way we know Christianity is true, is by the self-authenticating witness of God's Holy Spirit** (HS). The experience of the HS is veridical (truthful) though not necessarily irresistible for him who has it. As in Gal. 3:26 God has sent the Spirit of his Son into our hearts, crying Abba Father; Rom. 8:15-16 The Spirit bears witness to our spirit that we are children of God; Thus evidence and arguments may support the believer's faith they are not the primary basis of it(p.46). Thus we must distinguish between knowing and showing Christianity is true(p.43). The knowing is by the HS. John: 6:44 No one comes to God unless the father draws him. What is the role of arguments and evidence then? Martin Luther termed two kinds of reason: Magisterial (where it trumps the gospel) and Ministerial (it cooperates and servers the gospel). As Anselm put it, **reason helps us understand and defend our faith**. Thus we have a dual warrant to believe, the HS and reason. This can strengthen our faith and help us share more boldly. There are limits to arguments of man. If our arguments are wrong or not convincing enough, it is still the believer's responsibility for his belief. If one believes the magisterial role is primary, then his belief is dependent on our arguments being true(p.50). Nevertheless, Craig states he has met many non-Christians who came from a conservative Christian background, but were turned off to the gospel, by being told just to believe and not ask rational questions. By giving some rational arguments and answering their troubling questions, they made a decision for Christ. In summary, success in evangelism is simply communicating about Christ, with arguments if needed, in the power of the HS and leaving the results to God. Effectiveness in using apologetics requires study and practice. One must determine if the non-believer is throwing up an intellectual smoke screen or has true questions. The arguments given need to be tailored to their true questions(p.60). Now some more general challenges to apologetics will be given.

Sproul's book *Classical Apologetics* will be briefly reviewed. Some theologians subscribe to presuppositional apologetics, PA. Van Til says(p.186) says that without knowing every thing about God, we can't argue for anything about Him. The thesis of agnosticism is that it impossible for finite beings to know anything about the infinite. Henrich Heppe summarizes the **Reformed doctrine of the incomprehensibility of** God(p.94). **The finite cannot perfectly grasp the infinite**. Van Til says we must start with God. He also says it is a sin to start with our autonomy; we should start submitted to God. **PA has become ultimate Fideism riding under the banner of super rationality.** Sproul(p.212) said we must start with our minds in thinking; there is no other place to start. The counter argument to PA is that it abandons apologetics in the process, and loses all arguments of reason; for reason first decides who or what we will believe (p.188). Sproul states we can and do know something of God. We start with our rational minds. We can conceive of finite and infinite as they are the basic terms of mathematics. **General revelation logically and historically precedes special revelation** (the Bible). The ontological, teleological and cosmological arguments for God are sound. **Natural theology shows there is a God and if there is a God, miracles are possible.** With no God, miracles could be attributed to random chance (p.146). With no miracles, there would be no resurrection, as some very liberal theologians say. If there is a God, it is also logical that he would reveal His plan for us to us in writings, like the Bible (special revelation). The Bible confirms general revelation: **Ps.19** "The heavens declare the glory of God, and the sky proclaims the work of His hands. Day after day they pour out speech; night after night they communicate knowledge." **Rom. 1: 18-20** "For God's wrath is revealed from heaven against all godlessness and unrighteousness of people who by their unrighteousness suppress the truth, [19] since what can be known about God is evident among them, because God has shown it to them. [20] **From the creation of the world His invisible attributes, that is, His eternal power and divine nature, have been clearly seen**, being understood through what He has made. The Roman Catholic council stated: 1 "Reason and Faith do not contradict one another" There must be no reduction of faith to reason and no reduction of reason to faith. Natural revelation or general revelation is given by God. Natural theology is reasoned about God by man. Natural Theology(Aquinas promoted) stands as an opposite to Fideism (p.27). Sproul (p.141) gave **the following confirmation of the word (Bible):**

1. The Bible contains reliable history
2. The Bible records miracles as part of the history with witnesses
3. The miracles authenticate the Bible's messengers and their message
4. Therefore the Bible message ought to be received as divine.
5. The Bible message includes the doctrine of its own inspiration.
6. Therefore the Bible is more that a generally reliable record; It is a divinely inspired record. Tofflemire 2010 offers a more detailed summary of Sproul.

Tillich used a method of correlation to support an apologetic argument for God. He develops the Ontological argument of our being and God's necessary being. According to the classical philosophical concept, **reason is the structure of the mind which enables the mind to grasp and to transform reality.** The denial of reason in this sense is anti-human and anti-divine. Man is finite but can ask about the infinite which indicates he is separated from it. He becomes united again through Jesus Christ (p.62-73).

Schaeffer is quoted from(web79) "Schaeffer's *A Christian Manifesto* was published in 1981. The name of the book is intended to position its thesis as a Christian answer to *The Communist Manifesto* of 1848 and the *Humanist Manifesto* documents of 1933 and 1973. Schaeffer's diagnosis is that the decline of Western Civilization is due to society having become increasingly pluralistic, resulting in a shift "away from a world view that was at least vaguely Christian in people's memory . . . toward something completely different". Schaeffer argues that there is a philosophical struggle between the people of God and the secular humanists. In a sermon also titled "A Christian Manifesto", Schaeffer defines secular humanism as the worldview where "man is the measure of all things," and in the book he claims that critics of the Christian Right miss the mark by confusing the "humanist religion" with humanitarianism, the humanities, or love of humans. He describes the conflict with secular humanism as a battle in which "these two religions, Christianity and humanism, stand over against each other as totalities." He wrote that the decline of commitment to objective truth that he perceives in the various institutions of society is "not because of a conspiracy, but because the church has forsaken its duty to be the salt of the culture."

Follis summarized Schaeffer's life in his book *Truth in Love*. He noted some have criticized Schaeffer based on his apologetic books as being too intellectual and focused on rational arguments. He said this was not true; he was mainly an evangelist who reached out to others in love by the L'Abri center which was a work of love guided by God's spirit. The Schaeffers opened their home to visitors, cooked them meals and spent time with their needs. Many that came there were also discipled and became group and table leaders themselves. At times there were 140 people for dinner. Some stayed there for months; those who came included students, people in trouble and in confusion. Love and compassion were shown to all. Schaeffer's books grew out of discussions he had with visitors there. Schaeffer said there is no one apologetic, but conversations should be tailored to the individual and his needs. He taught and recognized love, prayer and the Holy Spirit were needed, along with pre-evangelism. Follis published in 2006 and offers some recent trends of interest(p.48-58).

Follis noted that in N. Ireland which is known as a Bible belt, many doubt the history and truth of the Bible, the resurrection of Jesus, and believe in synthesis rather that absolute truth, and many ways to heaven(p.140). He meets with students of a nearby university in a café, and notes they are open to discussion of religious issues as long as you are show concern and are open to free exchange of ideas. He also noted that Veritas Forums and debates are often successful in sharing truth. Although the demand for L'Abri centers, Forums and youth discussion has decreased from what it was in the 1960-70's there is still some demand, and people with questions. The rise of pluralism and of tolerance of all views has caused a decrease in the respect of clear truth and increase in the belief in moral relativism. Thus truth to fit personal taste is popular. If you try to support an inner spiritual Christian experience as your source of truth with a Muslim or a Mormon, you will not get far, as they will do the same. Discussions can be effective, but we need to listen to their views, before we speak. Recently, there is a greater emphasis of feelings and emotions being true or valued. Thus hedonism or being happy and seeking pleasure is prominent. Individualism and seeking self fulfillment, self satisfaction, and self aggrandizement are valued. The twin values of seeking personal peace and affluence are still important. Some affluence is needed to practice one's own seeking pleasure and satisfaction, and tolerance of all lifestyles is also promoted. Because of this, Dick Keyes of the Massachusetts L'Abri uses the term personal honesty rather than internal consistency of a world view. If you tell a student his view is not fully consistent and logical he may say "So what?" If you tell him he is not being true to himself or reaching his best potential, it sinks in as a concern. Widespread apathy and moral relativism prevails today. Sometimes they recognize that personal pleasure extended, is not all that fulfilling as in Ecclesiastes 1:17 and vanity. Most people accept the correspondence theory of truth even if they have not heard of the term. They value reality. As we push them off balance they must also feel our concern, or the effort will not be successful. It is good to build some relationship first. Some other evangelism books noted are—Barrs *The Heart of Evangelism*, Rietkerk *If only I could Believe*, and Keyes, *Beyond Identity*. These books note the importance of forming relationships. International students may accept the truth reasoning for Christianity, but hold back due to family or emotional factors. Today new believers desire personal experience more that truth and logic; so the churches often attract them by welcoming communities and fellowship, but spend little time on the details of the gospel. Follis cautions that faith is not primarily an emotional experience, but also rests on truth(p.156). Love is the final apologetic. For a summary of Follis see Tofflemire2011.

Schaeffer traced the history of religion, philosophy, law and society in his book *How Then Shall We Live*. He noted the renaissance brought humanism and secularism to the Catholic Church. In the north was the reformation which focused on man's importance as being made in God's image, but a sinner(p.80). The reformation and the **Bible answered the questions of the nature and dignity of man, the purpose for living and the source of true morals**(P.86). Humanism, although having man central, gives no real meaning for his existence. Biblical values gave people freedom without chaos because there, order and morals are given. Paul set an example of non violence here. **This was illustrated** in P. Roberts famous mural entitled "**Justice Lifts the Nations** (1905). Here a lady is holding scales in one hand and the other is pointing toward the Bible. On the Bible picture is written "The Law of God"(p 106). S. Rutherford wrote the book Lex Rex: Law is the King in 1644. "The book defends the rule of law and the lawfulness of defensive wars (including pre-emptive wars) (Web 101). The industrial revolution and philosophy of utilitarianism contributed to slavery which was a non Christian practice(p.116). This provides one example of abuse of the greatest good to the greatest number which was misused to justify it.

Logic flows naturally from a biblical worldview. Alfred Whitehead and Robert Oppenheimer, both non-Christians, stated that modern science was born out of a Christian world view (Schaeffer p.132). Many early universities were founded by the church. Schaeffer noted(p.138) that the universe is orderly with laws coming out of it. Einstein stated "I cannot believe that God plays dice with the universe." Science springs from looking for underlying causes and laws. It is logical that **laws come from a law giver,** rather than springing out of randomness. What changed then? Now the view is that everything is one big cosmic machine including man(p.142). This was influenced by Darwinism which progressed to social Darwinism and naturalism or humanism(p.150). Plato noticed something crucial in practical living: If there are no absolutes, then the individual things (the details) have no meaning. This is especially true in the area of morals. If there are no absolutes in morals or values beyond man's ideas, there is not a final standard; we are left with conflicting opinions and no meaning to life(p.145).

Man also disappears and is viewed as a form of determined or behavioristic machine in psychology and sociology. The Humanist thinkers either conclude there are no values and meaning or suddenly try to produce values and meaning out of rhetoric. The concept of an unbroken line from molecules to man, based on time and chance, leaves out the critical questions of how and why. Hitler and Himmler stated that the law of nature must take its course in the survival of the fittest and that Christianity and its notion of charity should be replaced by the ethic of strength over weakness. **The humanistic ideals did not work out in practice**(p.151). The early humanists were optimistic that man could find unified true knowledge based on reason alone; this failed and changed to pessimism. Four philosophers were influential in the change to pessimism and the first was J. Rousseau (1712-1778). He favored man's freedom from restraint to escape man as a machine. This view contributed to the French revolution and the yr. reign of terror in which 40,000 were beheaded. The new governments had a democratic goal, but had great violence between political and power fractions(p.155). Napoleon finally took somewhat dictatorial power. Rousseau's ideal was that the autonomous man fights all of society's standards, values, and restraints.

The 4th philosopher noted was S. Kierkegaard (1813-1855). He held that one can find optimistic answers in the upper level of faith outside of reason by **existentialism**. This is because reason leads to pessimism. **One must leap to faith outside of reason.** This is again a dichotomy. In our day the main view is again that man is a machine, as proposed by determinism and behaviorism. Without God it is still difficult to account for love, freedom, meaning and purpose. Although man is viewed as a machine, one cannot live as a machine, they must leap upstairs as Keirkegaard suggests to find any meaning(p.166). Modern people have put things "upstairs" in the area of non-reason in an attempt to find some optimism about meaning and values. A. Huxley(1894-1963) furthered existentialism and proposed drugs to give the high experience and wrote several books about it. He also used LSD. The **emphasis on hallucinogenic drugs** brought with it many rock groups(p.170) including Cream, Jefferson Airplane, Grateful Dead, Incredible String Band, Pink Floyd, and Jimi Hendrix. Some of the Beatles work also fit here. As a whole, the music was a vehicle to carry the drug culture and the mentality which went with it across frontiers which were impassible by other means. There is the culture of psychedelic rock fostered by the Beatles and Bob Dylan. The next area of religious experience was **Hinduism and Buddhism** where there is **a grasping of non-rational meaning to life. These seek truth inside one's own head by meditation, but negate reason and contradictions**(p.170). The occult religions and practices like white witchcraft, and Harry Potter have added to this. Healthy religious beliefs promote coping and avoid isolation(web90).

In recent times the **German theologians brought** in the **idea of biblical criticism** and relied on man's thought and **starting from man as the source of** reason and **wisdom** rather from God and thus using the presuppositions of rationalism(p.175). **This later converted to religious liberalism with the synthesis of rationalism** and Christianity. A. Schweitzer wrote a book *The Quest for a Historical Jesus* and noted that **if one did not keep miracles and the supernatural (the resurrection), not much was left of the historical Jesus.** K. Barth accepted the existential methodology and dichotomy and brought in the higher critical views. **This held that the Bible had many mistakes** but was nevertheless good in the areas of faith and experience. **They did not see the Bible as true relating to the cosmos and history.** Some held it is not true in giving moral absolutes either(p.176). Schaeffer noted as do liberal theologians, that **when the Bible history is considered unreliable, then there is no way to explain why evil or sin exists in all people**. This is close to the Hindu position that everything is equally in God, including good and evil. P. Tillich continued the rationalist tradition. In simple way it is theological word games. When he was asked if he prayed, he said, no he meditated(p.178). Some theologians think God is dead, relative to doing any miracles today. Nietzsche was a champion of the God is dead philosophy. **Without an infinite personal God all one can do is make game plans. Humanists may make this sound high and noble by saying doing the greatest good for the greatest number of people**(p.181). **Marxism-Leninism is also uses humanist ideas.** Materialism is its base philosophy, but the talk is of dignity and rights for the masses. In practice it is followed by a loss of human rights and free speech leading to dictatorship. A. Solzhenitsyn wrote of this in The Gulag Archipelago. About 15 million were killed in this revolution in Russia. A. Malraux stated that communism does not have human values in practice. It is only in talk. **In materialism there is no base for the dignity and value of the individual, only value for society and the masses**(p.215). **Law decisions are now governed by the majority view of society or by humanist legal challenges (sociologically acceptable). Abortion and same sex marriage are cases in point. Law and morals become a matter of averages. The Kinsey studies on sex are an example. Here statistics make behavior OK**(p.224).

Most recently people had two important values: personal peace and affluence. (p.205). Personal peace means to be left alone and not be troubled by other's problems. Because meaning had been placed in the area of non-reason, people turned to drugs more, as at Berkeley. **Many cities have degenerated with crime and drugs**(p.226). **When personal peace and affluence are top values how will we fare? If liberties are only taken away at small steps, will anyone object, as long as affluence is OK? Will the church be involved here or go with the majority flow?** Rome's decline was marked by the following:1. Love of affluence, 2. Widening gap between the rich and the poor, 3. An obsession with sex, 4. Freakishness in the arts, 5. An increased desire to live off the state(p.227). There are also lessons to learn for Hitler's ascent to power. Germany had economic problems and high unemployment. It also appears that he staged a terrorist type attack on the royal palace. Because of the fear of terrorism, this gave him the dictatorial power, and suspension of civil parliament rights, to declare a state of emergency—martial law, and take control. Modern governments have available to them forms of manipulation not available before: mass media, TV, internet, movies, and schools. Political ads are very media image savvy and often negative. Thus there is considerable sociological conditioning and convincing occurring already by the media(p.243). Subliminal adds on TV have proven successful but are now banned in the US, but strong appeals to emotion rather than reason are allowed(p.240). There are pressures in Government to control the people. People will accept some loss of freedoms to insure affluence (met needs) and personal peace. Threats to promote this include: **1.** Economic Breakdown, **2.** War and the threat of war, **3.** Terrorism and violence, **4** The redistribution of wealth, **5.** The growing shortage of food and resources, **6.** Control of Disease, and crime(p.246-54). My comments: This appears some what prophetic for a book written in 1976, as we see some of this today.

Schaeffer continued to track the battle between humanism and Christian values in his book, *A Christian Manifesto*, which will now be summarized: **Chap.1 p.17-30 The Abolition of Truth and Morality**: Permissiveness, pornography, humanism in public schools, breakdown of family and abortion are only **symptoms of a larger problem: a world view shift to naturalism.** Pietism contributed by making a sharp division between the spiritual and material world. True spirituality covers all of reality, and the Lordship of Christ all areas of life. The concept of materialism was promoted by G.B. Shaw, A. Huxley and by the *Humanist Manifesto*. Liberal theology was an attempt to merge the 2 views, where humanism is expressed in theological terms. Many denominations have adopted this view and come out in favor of abortion. Humanities are the study of literature, art and music. Humanitarianism—being kind to humans should not be confused with humanism which places man at the center and measure of all things. Some supporting Humanism include—J. Huxley, B.F. Skinner, J. Monad, and John Dewey. This philosophy of matter, energy and chance is also the base of Marxism. J. Bentham favored Utilitarianism in the law as did Oliver W. Holmes who said "The life of the law has been experience, not logic." British law was influenced by the Judeo-Christian view. Here law triumphed over kingly power. The king must be just, and not use excessive force on his subjects. This is the basis of English Common law and the Magna Carta. The protestant reformation contributed to this; where the written word was supreme over the church and the state. The **Humanists** push for freedom, but their freedom **can lead to chaos and slavery to the state**, as it has no intrinsic reason to be interested in the individual, but only in the masses.

Chap. 2 p.31-39 **Foundations for Faith and Freedom**: John Witherspoon was a Presbyterian minister and the president of Princeton and signer of the Declaration of Independence. He stood in the stream of S. **Rutherford who wrote the Lex Rex (law is King)**. Thus the heads of government are under the law. In the phrase "**certain inalienable rights,**" who gives these rights? They had the concept that God did. If governments did, then they can take them away. Also the **phrase In God we trust** is on our money. William Penn stated "If we are not ruled by God, then we will be ruled by tyrants." Originally the 1st amendment had two purposes: **1.**To prevent there being an official church of the USA **2.** To keep the government from interfering or impeding the free practice of religion. Justice Douglas wrote the majority decision in 1944 for the Ballard case: "**The 1st amendment** has a dual aspect. It not only forestalls compulsion by law the acceptance of any creed or the practice of any form of worship but it also safeguards the free exercise of the chosen form of religion." **Today it's used to silence the church**. Originally the founding fathers established a Chaplain for the congress. Also, the NW ordinance of 1787 set aside property for schools fostering religion and morality. Several state courts had indictments for blasphemy in 1811. In 1760 William Blackstone wrote Commentaries on the Law of England which was widely used. This noted two foundations for law, nature and revelation (the scriptures). In 1829, a professor of law at Harvard, J. Story said "There has never been a period in which **the Common Law** did not recognize **Christianity as laying its foundation.**"

Chap. 3 p.41-51 **Destruction of Faith and Freedom: Today law is secularized and sociological**: That means it favors what is good for society at the given moment, without having a fixed base. Chief Justice F. M. Vinson stated in 1950 "Nothing is more certain in modern society than the principle that there are no absolutes." W. B. Bell wrote that law has drifted away for the Constitution also in an effort to for pragmatic public policy(p.42). Thus **the meaning** of the interpretation **of the 1st amendment has shifted** from that of the original authors. Modern science was first produced on a Christian base. Now Carl Sagan is allowed to say on public television: "The cosmos is all that is or ever was or every will be." This is a creedal and not a scientific statement. Will Durant a humanist stated: "There is no significant example in history, before our time, of a society successfully maintaining moral life without the aid of religion." **The French revolution proceeded from a humanistic viewpoint into chaos and then a dictatorship by Napoleon.** Pluralism has evolved in the US to the idea that almost everything is acceptable. On public TV, euthanasia of the elderly and use of marijuana are presented as a personal choice, not as a matter of right and wrong. The Supreme Court ruling on abortion is an example of situational ethics and current opinion as opposed to firm source based law. This decision overthrew state laws prohibiting it. More theologians have also taken the side of the humanists in matters of life style and sociological law(p.50). Another example is a single federal judge with homosexual leanings overturning a California constitutional amendment approved by the voters(see proposition 8-Wikipedia).

    Chap. 4 p.53-62 **The Humanist Religion:** Both Humanist Manifestos I, II state that **humanism is a religion or faith.** A 1961 Supreme Court decision on the case of Torcaso V. Watkins defines humanism as a religion equivalent to other theistic religions or non theistic religions. **By 1961 the court had swung to favoring humanist views.** In a 1933 decision of the US vs. MacIntoch conscientious objection was considered, and religious belief was tied to a belief in God. In a 1965 case of the US vs. Seeger this shifted to a much broader view of religion than was stated as in the 1961 case(p.55). Public TV often shows humanistic views solely. When approached to show a view against abortion with medical data, in "Whatever happened to the Human Race" with Dr. Everett Koop, Surgeon General, they refused on the basis that they cannot show only one view. In the humanistic and materialistic view, God has no role, and there is no organizing principle in the world and no guiding true moral and ethical laws. On TV now, views are presented that may be quite different from the true facts of a case. This can sway public opinion to false views, even with respect to facts, when key facts are omitted.

    Chap. 5 p.63-71 Revival, Revolution and Reform: **The Lordship of Christ is over the whole spectrum of life. Revivals have been important.** J. Wesley is an example in England. He ministered to the coal miners and iron smelters. He formed them into groups where they could develop their own leaders. He helped them with social issues and working conditions. Some say he saved England from the French revolution. Lord Shaftesbury in England championed justice for the poor in the Industrial revolution. W. Wilberforce fought against slavery in England

and succeeded. These old revivals resulted in social action. Jeremy Rifkin wrote Entropy and the Christian view of Ecology in 1980. He noted there is a Christian view of ecology that has had an effect. The president of Wheaton College, J. Blanchard and of Oberlin College, C. Finney both were involved in Christian social action. They had the view that "if the law is wrong, you must disobey it". **They suggested civil disobedience, if necessary. The seeds of the Amer. Revolution were sown in the earlier religious revivals**. This was our heritage. The dignity of human life is not something peripheral to Christianity. Many issues spring from this, including abortion. Our freedoms without chaos or totalitarianism have been somewhat maintained. People have lived in the US for so long that **they take the Judeo-Christian heritage base for granted. It is eroding and being replaced with humanism and materialism.**

Chap. 6 p.73 **An Open Window**: Conservative political victories provide an avenue for growth of Christian values. The threats of drug culture continue as an escape. In Europe the idea of anarchy is growing. Nixon talked of the silent majority: It had **two values that persist: Personal peace and Affluence**. Personal peace means to be left alone and not troubled by other's problems. The desire for affluence makes a good economy an important value. The question is raised, are Americans still capable of informed self government? Politicians and the media can so easily mislead. The courts seem more inclined to making new sociological laws and the frequency of their overturns of congressional laws is increasing. The government constantly increases the country's debt and passes it on to the next generation. Will Christians ever stand up for biblical values and the Godly world view? Many court cases and challenges to Christian values have occurred and are listed(p.83-5). For Example, can a pastor counsel a parishioner without being sued? What if the patient-parishioner later commits suicide and wasn't seen by traditional psychologist-psychiatrists?

Chap. 7 p.89-102 The Limits of **Civil Disobedience**: Are we to obey the State no matter what? Some scriptures: Mat. 22:21 "Give unto Caesar what is Caesar's and to God what is God's" Rom. 13:1-4 This talks of submitting to the government and also doing what is right; 1 Pet.2:13-17 Fear God, honor the King and do good. Schaeffer stated that government, as all life, stands under the law of God. He suggests that when the government requires things that go against the word of God we should object and not obey. In the time of Rome Christians were thrown to the lions because they would not worship the Roman emperor. Wm.Tyndale translated the Bible into English and advocated the authority of the scriptures. He was condemned as a heretic for it and finally executed. **In almost every place where the Reformation had success there was some form of civil disobedience**(p.92). In Europe the Catholics persecuted the Protestants. Luther barely escaped death when he held to the truth of the Bible against the Catholics. He was protected by the Duke of Saxony using force for defense. Likewise John Knox of Scotland advocated the reformation and escaped to Switzerland, as did Calvin. At this time Mary Tudor of England imprisoned many Protestants. **Knox** wrote an *Admonition to England* against this and had it smuggled into England. **He developed the idea that the Christian can disobey the government and even rebel when faced with this tyranny**(p.97). The reformers were not against the government per se, just against ungodly laws not following the word of God. S. **Rutherford** followed Knox and **wrote** the **Lex Rex** in 1644. Wikipedia noted Rutherford was a Scottish Presbyterian theologian and author and one of the Scottish Commissioners to the Westminster Assembly and university professor. The Lex Rex was immediately outlawed in Scotland and England. Scotland condemned him to death for his views. They viewed it as going against the Divine right of Kings which held that the King ruled as God's agent and thus the King was the law. Rutherford argued that all men and the King are under the law of God. He also argued that the acts of state that contradicted God's law were illegitimate and were acts of tyranny. He said that the tyrannical power to oppress the people is not from God but a licentious deviation of sinful man. Since tyranny is satanic, not to resist is to resist God. The power to rule is given conditionally by God (or by the people-my note). Although the office of magistrate is to be respected, tyrannical and unjust and ungodly rule can be opposed. He also said that a single breach of conduct is not justification for opposition, only when the governing structure of the country is threatened and the welfare of the people in danger is rebellion justified. The Declaration of Independence is quoted; "That to secure these rights, Governments are instituted among Men, deriving their just powers from the consent of the governed,—That whenever any Form of Government becomes destructive of these ends, it is the Right of the People to alter or to abolish it, and to institute new Government."

Chap. 8 p.103-116 The use of Civil Disobedience: **The Lex Rex suggested several avenues** of resistance: 1. First protest by legal or written means, 2. Flee the area, 3. Use of force to defend one's self. One should not use force if one can flee. One should not flee if he can peacefully protest. When a higher state body commits unjust acts against a lesser body like a local government, the lower body may also object. Rutherford reasons that the lesser body is just as much chosen by God as the higher body. John Locke extended the Lex Rex rights to the following: 1. inalienable rights, 2. governments by consent, 3. separation of powers, 4. the right of revolution to unlawful authority(p.105). **These writings influenced the American Revolution and constitution.** In a fallen world, government often must use force to maintain law and order. There are **two guides** to the use of force: **1.** There must be a legitimate reason for it, **2.** The force must not be excessive and cross the line into unnecessary violence. James Madison wrote in the Federalist #145 "The powers delegated by the proposed Constitution to the federal government are few and defined. Those which remain in the state government are numerous and indefinite." Schaeffer notes that since then the federal powers have been greatly expanded. The original interpretation of the first amendment has shifted. Many ACLU court cases have removed any Christian religion from the schools and replaced it with humanism. Here state laws were overruled by federal court rulings, also going against the majority public opinion. Russian schools are geared to teach the materialistic humanistic view and the American schools are not much different. Some countries like Switzerland have much stronger local laws that are not overridden by the federal government.

Chap. 9 p.117-130 **The use of Force**: Occasionally the use of force or acts of rebellion against government policies does become necessary. One good example is the American Revolution. Without that there would be no America as we know it today. Other examples are those Christians who disobeyed Hitler to hide the Jews, and eventually fled the country. Another example is America fighting Germany in WW2. What would the world look like today, if everyone gave in and let Hitler take over the world? Schaeffer uses abortion as an example of a policy that justifies a demonstration before an abortion clinic, and other legal oppositions. In Russia, it was at one time illegal to teach any Christian religion to one's children at home, just as it was illegal for the early Christians to worship God in their homes. The right thing to do was to disobey the government. Much of liberation theology is built on the concept of man being basically good, and comes close to merging Marxist thinking with Christianity. The concept of the goodness of the common man was the basis of the French and Marxist revolutions. Both ended in totalitarianism and political chains. The kingdom of God should not be confused with a state social program. Our Declaration of Independence contains many elements of the reformation thinking of Knox and Rutherford. It speaks directly of citizens offering resistance to and abolishing an oppressive government and forming a new government. Schaeffer states "If there is no final place for civil disobedience, then the government has been made autonomous, and as such, it has been put in the place of the Living God."

Chap. 10 p.131-8 By Teaching, by Life and by Action: We need to return to the world view of our founding fathers. Rather than taking issues piecemeal, address the whole view. Isa. 59:12-16: "[12] For our offenses are many in your sight, and our sins testify against us. Our offenses are ever with us, and we acknowledge our iniquities: [13] rebellion and treachery against the LORD, turning our backs on our God, inciting revolt and oppression, uttering lies our hearts have conceived. [14] So justice is driven back, and righteousness stands at a distance; truth has stumbled in the streets, honesty cannot enter. [15] Truth is nowhere to be found, and whoever shuns evil becomes a prey. The Lord looked and was displeased that there was no justice.

He saw that there was no one, he was appalled that there was no one to intervene; so his own arm achieved salvation for him, and his own righteousness sustained him."

D. J. **Kennedy** has continued in the tradition of Schaeffer and has DVD *Citizens' Arrest*. There it is noted that the separation of powers by our USA founding fathers, used in our Constitution, were based on the idea that power corrupts and man is sinner, needing some restraint when in power. **Some quotes follow**: George Washington: "**Government is a dangerous servant and a fearful master**." James Madison:"If man were an angel, Government would not be needed." John Adams: "Because power corrupts, society's demands for moral authority and character increase as the importance of the position increases." "There is danger from all men. The only maxim of a free government ought to be to trust no man living with power to endanger the public liberty." The separation of powers into executive, legislative and judicial branches was based on this, as was the idea of bicameral legislatures, so no legislation could be quickly passed in the heat of the moment. Kennedy stated Government has changed from a mad dog to be fed for protection, to a fat cow to be milked for a handout. The concept of our founding fathers, of the Bible and of the Lex Rex was that Government was under God as our divine leader. **God is sovereign**. The power ultimately came from God. The problem is that man is sinful and selfish and power corrupts. **Now the concept is that government is sovereign** and supreme: Now the church is under the government and limited by it, and God is under the church. Socialism is legalized plunder. Forced taking from the rich and giving to the poor sets up injustices, with cycles of welfare with absent fathers. Benevolence in the Bible is supposed to be voluntary. When mandatory, it is not benevolence. Socialism is basically atheistic, holding that man is good, and that the present life is all there is. Therefore we should get out of it what we can. If man fails, he must be propped up(*Citizens' Arrest*). My comments follow: These authors have a conservative right-wing view. It is not said that all government social programs are wrong; some serve good purposes. Balance and measures of effectiveness are needed with the programs. Ham gave an update on the state of our nation in the DVD *Erosion of Christian America.* In he noted that our country was founded on principles and values from the Bible. If the Bible and God are removed the values become relative and changeable. Our society is removing God and the Bible. He quotes Ps. 33:12 "Blessed is the nation whose God is Jehovah" and Deut. 28:15 "But it shall come to pass, that if thou will not hearken to the voice of Jehovah thy God,—that all these curses shall come upon thee and overtake thee."

Schaeffer in his book *The God Who is There* lists a **few areas of theology** that have been pushed **in a negative direction** by philosophies of rationalism, dialecticism, and existentialism(p.51-65): 1. Nihilism or God is dead, 2. Acceptance of an absolute dichotomy between faith and reason, 3. Denial of miracles, 4 Denial of the divine inspiration of the scriptures, and 5. Denial of any useful science or history in the Bible. 6. Use of semantic mysticism or word symbols. **"The western mind is adrift on the sea of relativism and irrationalism and synthesis."** Synthesis says there is no difference between right and wrong, truth and untruth. The line of despair began in Germany spread to Europe and then to America. It started in philosophy and spread to art, music, general culture and theology. It was first called **rationalism and like humanism began with man** to find all knowledge, meaning and value, **without God**. Philosophy began with drawing circles or systems to encompass thoughts and reality. The next philosopher would cross out that circle and draw a new one. Eventually they came to the place where no circle was adequate, so despair set in, as there were no good systems, absent God, to give meaning and purpose to life(p.5-12). Hegel began the dialectic thinking of seeking truth in synthesis and this led to Marxism. With existentialism, faith and significant personal experience are separated from reason, in which man is a machine and can't find a rational purpose. A. Huxley and T. Leary favored drugs to achieve a first order experience and escape from the rational which has no purpose for man. These indescribable or drug experiences provide no true answers. Neo-orthodoxy and new liberalism followed from Heidegger who was an existentialist and atheist favoring Nietzsche and National Socialism. It is useful to look up Neo-orthodoxy and Liberal Christianity in Wikipedia. See p. 15. Schaeffer noted that these are characterized by a view of the scriptures as being full of mistakes and not divinely inspired. It also denies most miracles in favor of a naturalistic view. Once one removes all of the miracles of Jesus, there is not much Jesus left. Then belief in God and Jesus then becomes a complete leap in faith, with no reason or logic being part of it(p.83-90).

Bias and Deception in Evolutionary Arguments.

Tofflemire (2007) offered some additional summary arguments against evolution. A section on bias was included because it can be pervasive. Evolutionists portray the debate as scientific truth seekers versus biased religious believers. Another way of portraying this is a debate of **biased atheists** versus truth seekers who believe it is a sin to lie. Sarfati (2003 p.20-28) points out there have been many very misleading presentations by evolutionists that present distorted views, leaving out facts and sometimes even presenting falsified accounts(2003 p.28) to bolster their arguments. **A prime example of this is the Haeckel falsification** (Sarfati p.200) (Patterson p.96). Here, a known falsified diagram was published for about 50 years in school biology textbooks as an argument for evolution (web 61). Also in an effort to show land animals evolved into whales evolutionists have published fish-like transitional diagrams of the Pakicetus. However, this is now known to be a land animal that had four legs and walked. This misleading technique has often been used by evolutionists to fill missing links that are not proven and are often falsifications in details (Sarfati p.136-146). The **Piltdown man and Nebraska man** were both shown to be **frauds**(web 67). For a larger discussion of fraud and deception in the ape to human links see Riddle (2004 Origins). The evidence for strong bias in a scientific journal is found in the following information and quote from *Scientific American(SA):* "Thus, science welcomes the possibility of evolution resulting from forces beyond natural selection. Yet those forces must be natural: they cannot be attributed to the actions of mysterious creative intelligences whose existence, in scientific terms is unproved"(Sarfati p.83). If one automatically rules out any intelligent design argument, even if very compelling and logical, one has an atheistic-naturalistic bias and may not be open minded to all facts and arguments. However, they appear to accept all naturalistic assumptions, even if even far fetched and improbable. Sarfati (2003 p. 10) pointed out that SA also has an agenda of pushing abortion, human cloning and population control and was biased in staff hiring. They ruled out hiring a highly qualified staff writer after finding out he believed in God and was against abortion. The editor of SA was quite political on the controversy in a Kansas creation education court case, even implying that Kansas schools and colleges should screen out all applicants who believe in creation by God(Sarfati p.10-11). Thus, SA appears one sided and biased and open to consider only one set of views: the atheist-materialistic ones. Another example of deception is an important **false fact** published in an influential book *"Principles of Geology"* **by C. Lyell**. To support his assumption of gradualism in geology, he stated the **erosion rate of Niagara Falls** was 1 ft/yr when the observed rate at the time was 4-5 ft/yr. His estimated 35,000 yrs. of erosion of the falls has been proved wrong by history and recent geological reports (web58, 66). His work is thought to have strongly influenced Darwin and later theories of geology (Sarfati p. 28). More examples of evolutionary fraud in textbooks are in Tofflemire 2007 Appendix 3 and are also noted by searching by the word "fraud" in the AIG web site. McGrath (2007) in discussing Darwin's book *The God Delusion* notes considerable bias. In the classic pepper moths story in textbooks, dead moths were glued to the tree and photographed. This was claimed as poof of evolution but this is variation in kind. With Archaeraptor it was claimed dinosaurs turned into birds—a dinosaur tail attached to a bird and the fossils were cemented together(Parker 2008, p.165).

In most public schools it is difficult to teach the creation view. Some states have made it illegal to teach the intelligent design or creation view. A teacher can risk a lawsuit if creation were taught in an unbalanced fashion or in deviation from the school textbook. This may be due to the requirement to keep any religion out of the schools, to maintain the separation of church and state and the establishment of religion clause(web 59). This does present a naturalist theory teaching bias, which tends to reinforce itself. The bias continues in college, because most funding for research grants is only available in the naturalist theory areas not in creation view areas. The new movie ***Expelled-No Intelligence Allowed*** provides a documentary of bias in colleges. College professors are fired for just once mentioning intelligent design as a theory. There is no real academic freedom on this issue. The movie noted that Hitler and his medical staff believed strongly in Darwinism and Eugenics. Crippled people were gathered up and executed to improve genetics. It was also noted that strong Darwinism leads to atheism and world view strongly against belief in God. This results in militaristic oppression of anyone suggesting intelligent design.

My opinion as a scientist who has written 50 scientific papers and pursued and secured research grants, is that grants are commonly offered for research within the current paradigm and very few are available outside of the paradigm. It is also very difficult to publish any article in a peer reviewed journal that goes outside the current paradigm and questions its assumptions. There is considerable inertia in the system to change beliefs. Inertia can occur also among Christian scientists who may have entrenched positions, such as young earth vs. old earth. With evolution scientists greatly out numbering creation scientists, who have little funding, it will be difficult to convince the scientific community of research findings supporting a biblical creation view even if the findings have good evidence.

Quotable quote:

> "Science . . . is not so much concerned with truth as it is with consensus. What counts as "truth" is what scientists can agree to count as truth at any particular moment in time . . . [Scientists] are not really receptive or not really open-minded to any sorts of criticisms or any sorts of claims that actually are attacking some of the established parts of the research (traditional) paradigm—in this case neo-Darwinism—so it is very difficult for people who are pushing claims that contradict the paradigm to get a hearing. They'll find it difficult to [get] research grants; they'll find it

hard to get their research published; they'll, in fact, find it very hard."-Professor Evelleen Richards (science historian, University of NSW, Australia), "Lateline," Australian Broadcasting Corporation, October 9, 1998. (web 62)

History is full of scientists who believed in God and made great discoveries for science. Many of them did their work in a time when the church promoted learning and biblical creation of the world was an acceptable world view. Many biblical creationists love science. Most fields in science were developed by men who believed in the Bible.-Examples: Isaac Newton, Michael Faraday, Robert Boyle, Johannes Kepler, Louis Pasteur, and Francis Bacon(who developed the scientific method). Logic flows naturally from a biblical worldview. We were created by a very intelligent and logical God, and thus could be expected to also have logic and intelligence (Ham2006 p.206). During the Renaissance the many scientists supported a biblical creation view and some early universities were founded by the church (Williams 2005 p.34). Just because a view is widely held (the evolutionary view) does not guarantee that it is correct. One has the example of most believing the earth was flat at one period in history.

Some Possible Uses of the Material.

The statistics cry out that we are loosing 70% of our youth; they stop attending church and are influenced by Naturalism, with no God and no miracles. How sad it is for a parent to send a Christian child to school and have him/her return an atheist. Many Christian schools teach little in apologetics or world views. Ham and Hall (p.97) cite **a needed call to action**: Christian **schools** and the **church** need to **teach some apologetics** and worldviews to prepare the students. **Parents** need to choose schools and instruct their children wisely, as a Christian school name does not guarantee anything. Prov. 22:6 "Teach a youth about the way he should go; even when he is old he will not depart from it." Also in Luke 6:39-40-A pupil will be like his teacher. In public high schools, 52% loose their faith as Christians(p.40). God wants both our minds and hearts. Churches and schools that teach apologetics are **able to reduce this loss of youth from 70% down to about 26%** (web2a). Still most churches favor entertainment, devotions, and activities for youth, with no apologetics.

It is somewhat true that Christian apologists are missionaries to a select group of intellectuals; but, every soul won is precious to the Lord. Some great minds have been won by apologetics. C.S. Lewis was won; he was formerly an atheist. Engineers, people in medicine, and lawyers are good candidates for these apologetic arguments. When won, they can and have become very powerful assets for the Lord(Craig p.22). Bill Bright, the founder of Campus Crusade for Christ, was won in a college age church group(Bright p.22). As Schaefer, C.S. Lewis, and Lisle noted, everyone has a set of presuppositions that make up their world view. When we ask them questions we can expose these views, some of which have logical holes. Schaeffer called this taking the old protective roof off and did it successfully for 30 yrs in the L'Abri centers, which also showed love and concern for the visitors. Some have really not thought through their view and are still forming it. **Appendix 7** gives some questions to ask to explore their world view. The Answers in Genesis and Institute for Creation Research web sites are powerful tools; one can refer questioners to the sites to get answers to many questions they might ask. *The New Answers* book series is also useful to loan to a questioning friend. I have loaned such books to three friends and each has come to at least the following conclusion: **There is a plausible, and even scientifically supported, creation explanation to counter evolution, for most questions.** It then becomes more of a question of which view does one believe and what assumptions does one make? Even evolutionists have to make some initial assumptions, some of which are very weak. I noted that each who read the *New Answers* book had their faith strengthened. Many people are curious about answers to such creation questions; discussions on science and creation are more easily started in an office setting, than would a discussion of a question like "are you saved?" One can refer a person to a scientific book or web site, and this is generally considered acceptable. A seminar, debate or table at a college on the topic or creation vs. evolution would usually draw large interest. The **moral argument is very good** for use with students and adults. Some useful high school and college materials include—*Demolishing Strongholds* by AIG and *Case for Christ/ Faith* student editions by Strobel. A good adult small group lesson book is *Answers for Life* by AIG. The *Answers* magazine by AIG has sections for adults and youth. Sire2006 told how to apply apologetics in different settings and groups. Cornish also has an excellent book, *5 minute Apologist* that gave good brief arguments.

Beliefs are very common, even **among Christians**, in many misleading books, publications and TV broadcasts stating **that macroevolution is proven, animal fossils are millions of years old and man evolved from ape**. I was in a church of 400 members, which had a very successful Old Testament Bible class that used the AIG materials and shot many holes in these evolution assumptions. About 20-30 members attended the class. At the end of the class, a sermon was given before the whole congregation, in a question and answer interview format. This caused some stir in the church and considerable after discussion, as many people's beliefs were challenged. I was at several weekend seminars put on by AIG but held at local churches in Jacksonville, Fl. These seminars were very successful with both programs for the children and for the adults being held simultaneously. AIG has small pamphlets for handout that can be given out on various proofs of creation topics. There are times where discussion on creation facts can be brought into conversations. This can be done with dinosaur toys or movies and with programs or discussions of geology, astronomy, biology or nature. Ham points out that our culture has been indoctrinated in the secular evolutionary philosophy and considerable reeducation is needed (Ham2006 p.345). Questioning the proofs of the philosophy and pointing out obvious inconsistencies can be helpful. It is logical to proceed from natural revelation to special revelation. The first prepares for the 2nd and the 2nd confirms the 1st. Other creation teaching organizations like CMI, ICR, Apologetics Research Center, and RTB also have useful literature countering evolution and promoting a Christian world view.

Summary

Let's return to the analogy of putting parts of a puzzle of a world view together in a brief summary. **Truth** was defined as a **justified true belief.** In our reasoning we must start with the laws of noncontradiction and of the excluded middle and with basic logic. Either God exists or He doesn't and either Christianity is true or it isn't. Also if we don't start with the belief of our senses, mind and memory being mostly reliable, we can get nowhere, and are left with complete skepticism and knowing nothing. We note that reason supports faith. It is very difficult to rule out the possibility of God or to fully disprove God. The old arguments from ontology, cosmology and teleology support the existence of God and theism. Kreeft (see p.42) gave 20 arguments for God that, in total, make a very strong case for God. This is the heart of general revelation and natural theology. The nature of God can be described from this revelation to be infinite, all powerful, all knowing, personal, present, spiritual and immaterial, eternal and of the highest moral standards(see p.55). This rules out pantheistic and polytheistic Gods. Within theism this leaves Judaism, Islam and Christianity. The case was made for Jesus being divine and human as he said he was, and being resurrected (see p.57). Both He and the Bible are historically true. See p.65 about the truth of the Bible. Verified history, miracles and prophecy support this. In this respect the Bible is unique in that it has a long record of true history, miracles and prophecy. The genealogies in the Bible appear accurate as does the table of nations. There is no other book of faith that can compare to it. Liberal theologians question the miracles, the history and the divine inspiration of the Bible. In doing so, they weaken the whole message of the Bible, in favor of majority scientific view, denying most miracles. A straight forward reading of the scriptures supports a six 24 hr. creation and a world wide flood. Other creation views compromise scriptures to various degrees in favor of what the majority of scientists think. Ross stated that creation scientists should offer a testable model; his alternate views are given in Appendix 5 and 6. A minority of well qualified scientists and theologians have presented some evidence for the possibility of a young creation. A larger number of scientists support old earth creation or complete naturalism. There is strong evidence for an old universe and earth. In the final analysis it boils down to the question of whether one believes God's word or man's (scientist's) current word. One's view of inerrancy of the scriptures and how to correctly interpret them incorporating the findings of science is involved. Many of the scientists making up the majority view don't believe in the Bible. Some rule out even considering the Bible, a priori, because their naturalist evolutionary world view rules God out. Nevertheless our logical understanding is challenged on the issue of young earth and universe vs. an old one. General revelation and current science do contribute to our understanding of how God created, which on some questions is not well known or understood. The age of the universe and days of creation could be viewed as a topic open for discussion and more understanding. Many apologetic arguments can be made on the basis of God creating everything without specifying all the how's. I pray that Christian scientists and theologians can remain open to new understandings and revelations, rather than being entrenched in their stated positions. It is also my hope that some of this material in this book and on the web site will be useful in sowing seeds and in witnessing. For a few of my speculations see Appendix 6.

References Cited

Books, Journals and DVD's

Archer Gleason L *New International Encyclopedia of Bible Difficulties.* Zondervan

Allen, R.H. *Star Names: Their Lore and History,* Dover Public., Mineola .NY.1963-1899

Baumgardner, *John Global Tectonics and the Flood* DVD from Answers in Genesis 2006

Beechick, Ruth, *World History Made Simple,* Mott Media, Fenton, MI 2006

Beechick, Ruth, *Adam and His Kin: The Lost History of Their Lives and Times* Mott Media, Fenton, MI 2004

Bergman, Jerry "The Case for a Mature Creation Hypothesis" *Creation Res. Soc. Quarterly,* Vol. 48, #2, 2011, p.168-177

Boa, Ken and Moody, Larry "I'm Glad You Asked" Victor Communications, 1995

Branch, Craig Miracles ARC.apolgetics, Veritas: Miracles, *Journal of the Apologetics Recourse Center,* Mar.-April 2008

Branch, Craig "Amusing Ourselves to Death" *Areopagus Journal,* Spring 2010, Vol. 10 #2 and "Biblical Archaeology" Vol. 11 #3, 2011

Bright, Bill *Witnessing Without Fear,* Here's Life Publishers, 1993.

Burch, R. W. A *Concise Introduction to Logic,* Wadsworth Pub. Co. Belmont, Ca. 1994

Camping, H. *Time Has and End,* Vantage Press, Inc. NY, NY 2005

Comrie, B. et al, *The Atlas of Languages,* Facts on File, Inc. N.Y.1996

Cooper, Bill *After the Flood,* New Wine Press, Chichester England, 1995

Cornish, R. *5 Minute Apologist,* Navpress, Colorado Springs, Co. 2005

Craig, W. L. "The Existence of God" Chap.3 *Reasonable Faith* Crossway Books, Wheaton , Il. 2008 http://www.reasonablefaith.org/site/PageServer

Downs, T. *Finding Common Ground*. Chicago, Moody Press, (1999)

Erickson, M. J. *Introducing Christian Doctrine,* Grand Rapids, MI., Baker Book House Co. (2001)

Faulkner, D. "Unexpected Brilliance" *Answers* Vol. 6, #1, Jan. 2011

Faulkner, D. "Latest Lunar Hypothesis on the Rocks" *Answers* Vol 7, #3, p.38, 2012.

Finegan, J. *Handbook of Biblical Chronology* Hendrickson Pub., Peabody, Mass. 1998

Follis, B. A. *Truth with Love*, Crossway Books, Wheaton, Ill. 2006

Geisler, N.L. and Turek, F. *I Don't Have Enough Faith to be and Atheist* Crossway Books, Wheaton, Ill. 2004

Gitt, Werner. *In the Beginning Was Information*, Master Books, Green Forest, AK 2005

God of Wonders, Eternal Productions, www.eternal-productions.org 2008.

Green, Marjorie. *The Anatomy of Knowledge—Papers Presented to the Study Group*, Amherst, MA, Univ. of Mass. (1969)

Habermas, Gary *Historical Jesus*: College Press Publishing Co. Joplin, Mo. 1996

Hartnett, John. *Starlight, Time and the New Physics*, Creation Book Publishers (2007)

Haley, J. W. *Alleged Discrepancies of the Bible*, Whitaker House, Springdale, Pa. 1992

Ham, K and Beemer, B. *Already Gone*, Master Books, Green Forest, AK 2009

Ham, K. Editor *The New Answers Book 2*. www.masterbooks.net, Answers in Genesis (p.197 by Riddle) 2008. Taylor, Paul "Isn't the Bible Full of Contradictions" p 283-297

Ham, K. Editor *The New Answers Book 1*. www.masterbooks.net, Answers in Genesis 2006

Ham, K. *The New Answers Book 3* "Was there death before sin" p 109-17, Master Books Green Forest, Ak. 2010

Ham, K. *Demolishing Contradictions*, Master Books, Green Forest, Ak. 2010

Ham, K *Erosion of Christian America*, AIG DVD 2010

Ham, K. and Hall G. *Already Compromised*, Master Books Green Forest Ak. 2011

Hendricks, H.G. & Hendricks,W.D. (1991) *Living by the Book*, Moody Press, Chicago

Heeren, Fred *Show Me God*, Vol 1. Day star Pub. Olanthe, Ka. 2004

Holman Illustrated Study Bible, Holman Bible Publishers, Nashville, TN 2006

Humphreys, R. D. 'New time dilation helps creation cosmology' *Jour. of Creation* 22(3) 2008 http://creation.com/images/pdfs/tj/j22_3/j22_3_84-92.pdf *Starlight and Time* 1994

Humphreys, R. D. *Starlight and Time*, DVD Creation Ministries International. 2007

James, Peter *Centuries of Darkness*, Rutgers Univ. Press 1993.

Kennedy, D.J. *Evangelism Explosion.* Evangelism Explosion International, Tyndale House Publishers. Wheaton, IL (1996)

Kreeft, Peter *Christianity for Modern Pagans-Pascal's Pensees*, Ignatius Press, 1996

Kreeft, Peter & Tacelli, R. K *Handbook of Christian Apologetics*, IVP Academic, Ill. 1994

Lewis, C.S. *Miracles, Mere Christianity*, Harper Press, San Francisco 1952, Macmillan 1943

Lisle, Jason. *The Ultimate Proof of Creation*, Green Forest, AK, Master Books (2009)

Lisle, Jason *Taking Back Astronomy*, Master Books, Green Forest, AR. (2007)

Lisle, Jason "Faith and Reason" *Answers* Vol. 5, #4, 2010.

Lovett, Tim *Noah's Ark, Thinking Beyond the Box*, Answers in Genesis DVD 2007

Lumpkin, J. *The Lost Book of Enoch*, Fifth Estate Pub. Blountsville, Al. 2004

Magee, Bryan. *The Story of Philosophy*, NY, NY. DK Publishing (1998)

McDowell, J. *The New Evidence That Demands a Verdict.* Thomas Nelson Pub., Nashville (1999)

McGrath, A and J. C. *The Dawkins Delusion* Intervarsity Press Downers Grove, Il (2007)

Meister, C. *Building Belief.* Grand Rapids, MI. Baker Books, (2006)

Moche, D. *Astronomy, A Self Teaching Guide.* John Wiley and Sons, N.Y. (1996)

Morris, Henry M. *The Long War Against God*, Baker Book House, Grand Rapids, MI 1989

Morris, John. *The Young Earth*, Green Forest AK. Master Books (2007)

Morris, H. M. *Exploring the Evidence for Creation*, ICR, Dallas, Tx. 2009

Mortenson, T., Ury, T. *Coming to Grips With Genesis*, Master Books, Green Forest, Ak. 2008

Parker, Gary. *Creation Facts of Life How Real Science Reveals the Hand of God*, Green Forest, AK., Master Books, (2008)

Patterson, R. *Evolution Exposed* Answers in Genesis, Hebron, Kentucky(2007)

Popkin, H and Stroll, A. *Philosophy Made Simple* Broadway Books, NY, NY 1993

Purdom, G. The *Code of Life DNA, Information, and Mutation* and *Genetics, Evolution and Creation* Answers in Genesis DVD's, answersingenesis. org (2007, 2009)

Rana, F and Ross, H. *Who Was Adam*, NavPress, Colorado Springs, (2005)

Rana, F. and Ross, H. *Origins of Life*, Navpress, Colorado Springs, 2004

Reed, J. K. "Understanding Uniformitarianism" *Creation Matters* July 2011, Vol. 16 #4.

Riddle, M. *Astronomy and the Bible*, DVD from AIG 2004; and written study guide

http://www.answersingenesis.org/cec/study_guides/ AstronomyAndBible_MR.pdf

Riddle, M. *The Origin of Humans* DVD, from AIG 2004 and written study guide http://www.answersingenesis.org/cec/study_guides/ originOfHumans_MR.pdf

http://www.answersingenesis.org/cec/study_guides/fossilRecord_MR.pdf

http://www.answersingenesis.org/cec/study_guides/ DatingFossilsRocks_MR.pdf

Ross, H. *Creation and Time* Navpress, Colorado Springs, Co.1994

Ross, H. *The Creator and the Cosmos* Navpress, Colorado Springs, Co.1993

Ross, H. *The Genesis Question*, Navpress, Colorado Springs, Co. 2001

Ross, H. *A Matter of Days* Navpress, Colorado Springs, 2004

Ross, H. *More Than a Theory*, Baker Books, Grand Rapids, MI. 2009

Sabiers, Karl *Mathematics Prove Holy Scriptures—Russian Scientist proves Divine Inspiration of the Bible*, Bible Numeric's, Niagara Falls, Canada (1969)

Sanford, J.C. *Genetic Entropy*, FMS Publications, Waterloo, NY 2008

Sarfati, J. *Refuting Evolution*. Master Books, Inc, Green Forest, AR. (2003)

Satinover, J. *Cracking the Bible Code*, Harper Collins Pub. NY, NY 1998

Schaeffer, Francis *How Then Should We Live?* Crossway Books, Wheaton, Ill. 1979

Schaeffer, Francis, *Christian Manifesto*, Crossway Books, Wheaton, Ill. 1981

Schaeffer, F. A. *Genesis in Space and Time*, Intervarsity Press, Downers Grove, Ill. 1976

Schaeffer, F. A. The *God Who is There*—Trilogy, Crossway Books, Wheaton, Ill. 1990.

Scholes, A. and Clinton, S. "Levels of Belief in the Pauline Epistles" The Orlando Institute, 1991 http://www.toi.edu/Training%20Materials/ Biblical%20Syllabi/index.htm

Scott, Eugenie C. *Evolution Vs. Creationism, An Introduction*, Berkeley, Ca. Univ. of California Press, (2009)

Shodde, G. *The Book of Jubilees*, reprint from version by Goodrich, E. Artisan Pub. Muskogee, Ok 2005

Sire, James *A Little Primer on Humble Apologetics*, IVP Books, Downers Grove, Ill 2006

Sire, J. *The Universe Next Door*, IV Press, Downers Grove, Ill 2004

Snelling, A. *Earth's Catastrophic Past*, Geology, Creation & the Flood, Vol 1-2 ICR 2010

Snelling, A. *The Flood; Noah's Flood and the Earth's Age* DVDs from AIG, 2009

Snelling, A. "Order in the Fossil Record" *Answers* Vol. 5, 3 1, p.66-68, 2009.

Snelling, A. "Did Meteors Trigger Noah's Flood" *Answers* Vol. 7 #1, Jan 1012 p.69-71149

Sproul, R.C. et al *Classical Apologetics* Academie Books, Zondervan Corp. Grand Rapids, MI 1984

Strobel, Lee. *The Case for a Creator*, Grand Rapids, MI. Zondervan (2004)

Strobel, Lee. *The Case for Christ*, Grand Rapids, MI. Zondervan (1998)

Taliaferro, Charles "Divine Attributes" *Areopagus Journal*, Vol. 11, Num. 1, 2011.p.11

Thieme, Paul "The Indo-European Language" Scientific American, Vol. 199, 1958

Thomas, Brian. "On the Origin of Dogs" *ICR Acts and Facts*, vol. 41 #1, 2012

Tigay, J.H. *The Evolution of the Gilgamesh Epic*, Univ. of Penn. Press, Philadelphia 1982

Tillich, Paul, *Systematic Theology*, Vol 1.Reason and Revelation, Being and God, Univ. of Chicago Press 1951

Tofflemire, T.J. *A Creation versus Evolution Discussion Using Answers in Genesis (AIG) and Other References.* paper available from engtuffy@yahoo.com 2007

Tofflemire, T.J. *Defending Biblical Creation by Logic*, paper available from engtuffy@yahoo.com 2009a and on (web 85)

Tofflemire, T.J. *An Introduction to Philosophy with notes on Mathematics, Logic and God*, Paper available from engtuffy@yahoo.com 2009b

Tofflemire, T.J. *Some Alternate Views of Creation and Should Christians Believe the Six Day Creation View?* DT100 paper for the Orlando Institute, Sept. 2008c;

Tofflemire, T.J. summary of 2010 Popkin, H and Stroll, A. *Philosophy Made Simple*, Broadway Books, NY, NY 1993 available from engtuffy@yahoo.com

Tofflemire T.J. summary in 2010 of Kreeft, Peter & Tacelli, R. K *Handbook of Christian Apologetics*, IVP Academic, Ill. 1994 available from engtuffy@yahoo.com

Tofflemire, T.J. *Summary of Snelling's book Earth's Catastrophic Past* Sept.2010; available from engtuffy@yahoo.com, see web 85.

Tofflemire, T.J. summary in 2010 of Sproul, R.C. et al *Classical Apologetics.*

Tofflemire, T.J. summary in 2011 of Schaeffer, Francis *How Then Should We Live?*

Tofflemire, T.J. summary in 2011 of Follis, *Truth with Love, The Apologetics of F. Schaeffer.*

Tofflemire, T.J. *Time use in the Scriptures and a Summary article on Time*, see web site 2011

Ward, Peter & Brownlee, Donald **Rare Earth** www.copernicus-ny.com 2000. Summary by Tofflemire on the web site http://creationapolotetics.net 2011

Tofflemire, T.J. *Can Numerology aid in Interpretation of the Days and Aspects of Creation?* 2012

Tompkins, J."Human-Chimp DNA Similarity Research", *ICR Acts and Facts*, Vol. 41,#1, 2012

Wheaton, David, *University of Destruction*, Bethany House, Minneapolis, MN. 2005

Williams, A. & Hartnett, J. (2005) *Dismantling the Big Bang*. Master Books, Green Forest, A

Wilkinson, B.H. and Boa, K.(2002) *The Wilkinson and Boa Bible Handbook*. Thomas Nelson Publishers., Nashville, TN

Wise, K. "Lucy Was First", p 94-7, *Answers* July-Aug. 2011

Woodmorappe, John, *Noah's Ark a Feasibility Study*, ICR, 1996

Web

1. http://www.cultureandmediainstitute.org/specialreports/pdf/NationalCulturalValues.pdf

2. http://www.barna.org/barna-update/article/21-transformation/252-barna-survey-examines-changes-in-worldview-among christians-over-the-past-13-years

2a. http://www.nehemiahinstitute.com/

3. http://www.thenewamerican.com/index.php/usnews/politics/2978-obamas-;http://www.answersingenesis.org/articles/2010/03/08/state-of-the-nation

4. http://www.answersingenesis.org/

5. http://plato.stanford.edu/entries/truth/ Knowledge

6. http://en.wikipedia.org/wiki/Knowledge, Epistemology, Truth

7. (PCA) Report of the Creation Study Committee 1990 http://www.pcahistory.org/creation/report.html

8. http://en.wikipedia.org/wiki/Jesus_Seminar

9. http://www.alliancenet.org/CC_Content_Page/0,,PTID307086_CHID750054_CIID,00.html http://library.dts.edu/Pages/TL/Special/ICBI.shtml,

10. http://en.wikipedia.org/wiki/Galileo_Galilei

11. http://en.wikipedia.org/wiki/Apostles'_Creed

12. http://plato.stanford.edu/entries/frege/

13. http://www.sciforums.com/Newton-vs-Einstein-t-6684.html

14. http://en.wikipedia.org/wiki/Nazi_Party

15. http://en.wikipedia.org/wiki/Meta-ethics

16. http://www.answersingenesis.org/articles/am/v3/n2/marvels-of-monarch

17. www.ARCapologetics.org

18. http://en.wikipedia.org/wiki/List_of_religious_populations
19. http://en.wikipedia.org/wiki/Jos%C3%A9_O%27Callaghan_
    Mart%C3%ADnez http://en.wikipedia.org/wiki/7Q5
20. http://en.wikipedia.org/wiki/Apostle_(Christian)
21. http://www.answersingenesis.org/get-answers/topic/religion
22. http://en.wikipedia.org/wiki/Theism,   http://en.wikipedia.org/
    wiki/Knowledge
23. http://books.google.com/books?id=9nnTNwAACAAJ&dq=the+
    verdict+of+History&cd=1
24. http://www.washingtontimes.com/news/2010/may/02/pope-all-
    endorses-shrouds-authenticity/
25. http://www.Bible-researcher.com/chicago1.html.   http://library.
    dts.edu/Pages/TL/Special/ICBI.shtml
26. http://en.wikipedia.org/wiki/Sola_scriptura
27. http://www.answersingenesis.org/docs2005/1007authority.asp
28. http://www.answersingenesis.org/docs2006/0322anglican.asp
29. Orthodoxy and Genesis: What the fathers *really* taught A review of
    Genesis, Creation and Early Man, Fr Seraphim Rose, Saint Herman
    of Alaska Brotherhood, Platina, CA, 2000 TJ Archive > Volume
    16 Issue 3 > Orthodoxy and Genesis: What the fathers *really*
    taught http://www.answersingenesis.org/tj/v16/i3/orthodoxy.asp
30. http://www.answersingenesis.org/articles/wow/whats-wrong-
    with-progressive-creation
31. http://en.wikipedia.org/wiki/Zodiac
32. http://www.answersingenesis.org/creation/v22/i1/peleg.asp
33. http://www.answersingenesis.org/home/area/
    feedback/2006/1027.asp,
34. http://en.wikipedia.org/wiki/Sanskrit,   http://en.wikipedia.org/
    wiki/Vedic_Sanskrit
35. http://www.impactapologetics.com/default.
    asp?cookiecheck=yes&
36. http://www.garyhabermas.com/
37. http://www.josh.org/site/c.ddKDIMNtEqG/b.4023555/k.
    BE5B/Home.htm
38. http://www.leestrobel.com/
39. http://en.wikipedia.org/wiki/Josephus_on_Jesus#Reference_to_
    Jesus_as_brother_of_James_.28xx_9.1.29
40. http://en.wikipedia.org/wiki/Jesus_Seminar

41. H. Ross; A Beginner's-and Expert's-guide to the Big Bang: Sifting Facts From Fictions http://www.reasons.org/astronomy/astronomy-and-Bible

42. http://en.wikipedia.org/wiki/Origin of_the_Earth#Origin, http://en.wikipedia.org/wiki/Big_bang_theory, http://en.wikipedia.org/wiki/Time_dilation

43. http://www.icr.org/article/language-creation-inner-man/

44. http://en.wikipedia.org/wiki/Liberal_Christianity

45. http://en.wikipedia.org/wiki/Menes

46. http://creation.com/biologos-evolutionary-syncretism

47. http://en.wikipedia.org/wiki/Discovery_Institute

48. http://en.wikipedia.org/wiki/American_Scientific_Affiliation

49. http://en.wikipedia.org/wiki/Beringia

50. http://www.biologos.org/

51. http://www.icr.org/aaf/ The Theological Costs of Old-Earth Thinking Oct. 2010 Acts and Facts

52. http://www.answersingenesis.org/get-answers/topic creation-compromises A Critique of the Framework Interpretation of the Creation Account (Part 1 of 2)
    A Critique of the Framework Interpretation of the Creation Account (Part 2 of 2)
    A critique of the literary framework view of the days of Creation, by Andrew Kulikovsky)

53. http://www.answersingenesis.org/creation/v18/i2/haeckel.asp

54. http://www.answersingenesis.org/articles/aid/v2/n1/junk-dna-part-1

55. http://www.answersingenesis.org/articles/aid/v4/n1/are-humans-chimps-related

56. http://www.answersingenesis.org/articles/aid/v4/n1/why-did-god-make-viruses

57. http://www.icr.org/article/earths-magnetic-field-young/

58. http://www.answersingenesis.org/creation/v22/i4/niagara_falls.asp

59. http://en.wikipedia.org/wikiCreation_and_evolution_in_public_education

60. http://en.wikipedia.org/wiki/Time_dilation

61. http://www.answersingenesis.org/creation/v18/i2/haeckel.asp

62. http://www.answersingenesis.org/e-mail/archive answersupdate/2005/0108.asp
63. http://www.icr.org/article/recent-rapid-uplift-todays-mountains/
64. http://www.answersingenesis.org/creation/v22/i4/niagara_falls.asp
65. http://www.niagarafallsinfo.com/history-item.php?entry_id=1268&current_category_id=152
66. http://www.niagaraparks.com/media/geology-facts-figures.html
67. http://www.answersingenesis.org/creation/v13/i2/pig.asp, http://www.answersingenesis.org/articles/arj/v2/n1/controversy-in-anthropology
68. http://creation.com/general-and-special-revelation
69. http://www.reasons.org/siteSearchnode/?keys=humphreys&x=6&y=17
70. http://www.answersingenesis.org/creation/v21/i2/jericho.asp
71. http://www.answersingenesis.org/docs2002/1112animals.asp
72. http://en.wikipedia.org/wiki/Number of_species
73. http://en.wikipedia.org/wiki/Jubilees, http://en.wikipedia.org/wiki/Book_of_Enoch
74. http://www.ancientworldfoundation.org/tombofnoah.htm
75. http://en.wikipedia.org/wiki/Mountains_of_Ararat
76. http://www.icr.org/article/speciation-animals-ark/
77. http://www.answersingenesis.org/articles/nab/does-archaeology-support-the-bible
78. http://www.nationmaster.com/graph/cri_mur_percap-crime-murders-per-capita
79. http://en.wikipedia.org/wiki/Francis_Schaeffer
80. http://www.theomatics.com/theomatics/books.html#Anchor-49575 Del Washburn http://www.theomatics.com/theomatics/proof.html
81. http://en.wikipedia.org/wiki/Kabbalah
82. http://en.wikipedia.org/wiki/William_James
83. http://creationwiki.org/Biblical_chronology
84. http://www.answersingenesis.org/articles/ee/origin-of-humans
85. http://creationapologetics.net
86. http://en.wikipedia.org/wiki/Y-chromosomal_Adam
87. http://creation.com/origin-of-language by Charles Taylor
88. http://www.trueorigin.org/mitochondrialeve01.asp

89. http://en.wikipedia.org/wiki/Neanderthal
90. http://cienciaespiritualidade.com/blog/wp-content/uploads/2009/05/cjp_review_article_1-4-08.doc http://pb.rcpsych.org/cgi/content/full/34/2/63
91. http://creation.com/review-musicophilia-by-oliver-sacks
92. http://creation.com/age-of-the-earth
93. http://creationwiki.org/Biblicalchronology_dispute,http://creationwiki.org/Old_Testament
94. http://en.wikipedia.org/wiki/Noam_Chomsky on Language
95. http://en.wikipedia.org/wiki/Carbon_dating
96. http://en.wikipedia.org/wiki/Plate_tectonics
97. http://en.wikipedia.org/wiki/Instinct
98. http://plato.stanford.edu/entries/innate-acquired/
99. http://www.icr.org/article/finding-evolutionists-god
100. http://en.wikipedia.org/wiki/SETI
101. http://en.wikipedia.org/wiki/Lex_rex
102. http://www.sdss.org/includes/sideimages/sdss_pie2.html
103. http://www.google.com/search?q=big+bang+model&hl=en&biw=1003&bih=460&prmd=ivns&tbm=isch&tbo=u&source=univ&sa=X&ei=O1jmTdekC-jZ0QGJ7p3zCg&sqi=2&ved=0CC0QsAQ
104. http://www.aish.com/ci/sam/48951136.html
105. Whiddon, Andy Essay on Genesis: http://www.aboutgenesis.com/id2.html
106. http://www.aoi.com.au/bcw/neanderbasque.htm **Noel, David *How the Neanderthals became the Basques***

Appendix 1—Faith and Reason

Kreeft Chap. 2: Faith and Reason: Distinguish between the object of faith and the act of faith. "The object of faith means all things believed." For protestant Christians this means everything God has revealed in the Bible and God himself. The act of **faith has 3 aspects**:

1. Emotional faith—trust of and confidence in a person—Christ
2. Intellectual faith—belief, it can be stronger and more lasting than emotional faith. "The act of the intellect, prompted by the will, by which we believe everything God has revealed on the grounds of the authority of the One who revealed it" (p.30)
3. Volitional faith—an act of the will, a commitment.

Reason: Again distinguish the object from the act of reason. The act of reason can include subjective person's acts on one's mind. The object of reason means all that we can know. In Aristotelian logic this is all truths that can be **1. understood by reason, 2. discovered by reason, or 3. proved by logic.**(without faith} p.32-3 Kreeft set up a table classification of different **truths we can know in 3 classes:** (p.33-36)

1. Those by reason alone—Rationalism: Anselm, Hegel
2. Those by faith and by reason—Pascal argued that trusting our reason was an act of faith.
3. Those by faith alone—Fideism*

***Fideism** is an epistemological theory which maintains that faith is independent of reason, or that reason and faith are hostile to each other and faith is superior at arriving at particular truths (see natural theology). The word *fideism* comes from *fides*, the Latin word for faith, and literally means "faith-ism." From Wikipedia

Dualism: some believe in divorcing faith and reason as two separate fields. Kreeft stated that most believe there is some overlap of truths that can be argued from both faith and reason as in 2. above and this is the basis of some apologetic arguments(p.37). He also maintained as **Aquinas** did, that **Christian faith and reason cannot contradict each other**(p.38). Every argument against the main Christian doctrines has some error that can be disproved by reason. Also see 1 Cor. 1:20-25 "Where is the wise one?—God's foolishness is wiser that human wisdom" Kreeft discusses objections of Christian knowledge p. 40-43. In summary, he states that Christianity is reasonable but not obvious nor completely provable by reason. However there are good rational arguments for God's existence and for the Christian definition of God. Thus God becomes very probable by reason. It is also difficult to disprove God. One can be a good scientist or philosopher and be a Christian, as there have been many great ones before. "Brilliant minds reject Christianity because they don't want it to be true, because it is no longer fashionable or because it commands obedience, repentance and humility"(p.42). Believing in evolution and materialism has benefits for a reputable scientist and many do believe and exert peer pressure. (See the movie "No Intelligence Allowed")

Appendix 2 Logic and the *Ultimate Proof of Creation*—Lisle(2009) & Tofflemire 2009a

The Ultimate Standard in a World View

Lisle returned to the previous argument that supporting facts will not resolve the debate and world views must be brought out into the open and debated. A chain of beliefs will ultimately lead to a world view or ultimate standard. "A good world view must be logically consistent. If a world view has internal contradictions, then it cannot be correct, since the contradictions cannot be true."(p.37). Moreover some world views lead to the consequence that it is impossible to know anything. As an example, consider the philosophy of relativism. Relativists believe that truth is relative—that it varies from person to person and that there are no absolutes. But the proposition that there are no absolutes is itself an absolute proposition. This is a self-defeating philosophy that is inconsistent. Empiricists believe that all knowledge is gained through observation. Creationists also believe that some knowledge is gained through observation but not all. When the empiricist is asked the ultimate standard and how he knows that all knowledge is gained through observation there is no good answer. Knowledge cannot be seen; it is abstract. If empiricism is proved by some method other than by observation it then refutes itself. If a person's ultimate standard is uncertain, then all his other beliefs which are based on the standard are called into question. This calls into question the philosophy of empiricism and of knowing things (p.37-38). Scott, an evolutionist, affirms a quote of science by Montagu "The scientist believes in proof without certainty, the bigot in certainty without proof" (p.5). Lisle would add that one who believes in a view or theory without basic logic or internal consistency is a fool, and the Bible points this out (Prov. 26:4)

Introducing the Preconditions of Intelligibility

In addition to the world view being consistent it must account for the preconditions of intelligibility. These are conditions which must be accepted before we can truly know anything. The reliability of our mind and memory is one example; the reliability of human senses is another. If our mind, memory and senses were unreliable we could not know anything. Without these being true it would be almost impossible to conduct any scientific experiments. The laws of logic are also important to conduct valid reasoning and valid arguments and are another precondition of intelligibility. Both creationist and evolutionists must assume these preconditions in order to know anything. Lisle lists two other important preconditions, general uniformity in nature and morality and states that the Bible supports all of these preconditions, but most other world views supporting evolution do not (p.39). "Proverbs 1:7 indicates that knowledge begins with respectful submission to the biblical God and that rejection of wisdom and biblical instructions inevitably to irrationality—to foolishness" (Lisle, p.40).

Details of the Preconditions of Intelligibility

Several important preconditions of intelligibility include general uniformity in nature, the laws of logic and morality. The Bible gives a basis for morality. The Bible teaches that God is the creator of all things (Gen. 1:1; John 1:3). All things belong to God (Ps. 24:1), and God has the right to make the rules (p.48). We have the moral laws of the Ten Commandments (Ex. 20:3-17). God made us in His image (Gen. 1:26) with the ability to reason and understand the universe. "In the evolution world view, right and wrong is nothing more than chemical reactions in the brain,—the result of chance." The evolutionist might say man can create his own moral code without God and there is no absolute code. This has the weakness that whatever man decides is the code and it can change with time. It then becomes arbitrary. Hitler's government established a code to kill Jews and eliminate the insane. A remote tribe could decide to kill whomever they wish for whatever reason. This code has no consistency, and no personal responsibility and no ultimate theoretical basis. Without God, right and wrong are reduced to mere personal preferences. Some evolutionists might argue that right theoretical basis is what brings the most happiness to the most people. One might ask why should that standard be selected? If people are simply chemical accidents why should we care about happiness at all? (Lisle p.49-52)

The laws of logic and the law on non-contradiction have a biblical basis. The law of non-contradiction states that A cannot equal—A or not A. God made us in His image (Gen1:26) and therefore we are to follow His example (Eph. 5:1). God has a self-consistent nature and cannot deny himself (2 Tim.2:13). All truth is in God (John 14:6; Col.2:3). Since God is an un-changing, sovereign, immaterial being His thoughts would necessarily be abstract, universal, invariant entities. The evolutionist has difficulty accounting for the laws of logic. The evolutionist might respond, "Laws of logic are chemical reactions in the brain that have been preserved because they have survival value." There are several problems with this response. First, survival value does not equate to truth. Second, if they are just chemical reactions, they may not be universal and the same in all persons. Another response could be that the laws of logic are just conventions made up by human beings. However, if they are just conventions, different conventions could be made up by different cultures and they would not be consistent or universal (p.53). One might argue that the laws of logic are a description of how the universe behaves. But the laws of logic are abstract and conceptual and they describe the correct chain of reasoning from premises to conclusions. They do not really describe the physical universe. The laws of logic and one set of morals are also a problem for those believing in polytheistic gods. If there is more than one God, how can there be a single set of universal laws and morals?

A third precondition for science is the uniformity of nature and its laws. We assume the universe is logical and orderly and that it obeys mathematical laws that are consistent over time and space. Without uniformity of nature, predictions would be impossible about the seasons and rotation of the planets. To conduct scientific experiments scientists depend on uniformity of laws and conditions or they could not conduct a repeatable experiment. The creationist expects uniformity and order because God made all things (Gen. 1:1; John 1:3) and He upholds all things by His power (Heb. 1:3). God is consistent (1Sam. 15:29; Nub. 23:19; and omnipresent (Ps.138:7-8). He upholds the seasons, and the diurnal cycle (Gen.8:22; Jer. 33:20-21). Again the evolutionist has little or no basis for this uniformity(p.58-9). If the universe were created by random processes, it should not show much order or uniformity with time.

How would an evolutionist respond to the question of why the future will be like the past? A common response that Dr. Lisle gets is that "It always has and I expect it always will." However this is circular reasoning and does not provide an ultimate valid reason for uniformity. It makes the assumption the future will be like the past. The evolutionist may also say the nature of matter is such that it behaves in a regular fashion. This may be an aspect of the universe, but the question is again why. He can say that in the past that there seems to have been some uniformity. However, many things in the universe change; so how do we know that the laws of nature will not change?(p.60) Dr. Lisle asserts that ultimately the atheistic evolutionist has no good answer for these questions of uniformity, laws of nature, and basis of morality. As such the atheist is often inconsistent and irrational and his common arguments that one should not do this or think this have no rational consistent basis (Lisle p.62-3). 'Shoulds' are often tied to some moral basis or law of logic and become inconsistent in the evolutionary world view arguments.

A fourth condition concerns the conscious mind and is taken from Strobel 2004. He noted (p.247-272) that the some of the top neurologists state that the attributes of the mind can fully be accounted for by evolved chemical reactions and nerve transmissions. Consciousness involves thoughts, feelings, hopes, a point of view, self awareness, introspection, dreams, and rationality. Electrodes placed in the brain can stimulate certain muscles to move. However the patient states that it is not himself that is moving the muscles and can even restrain the muscles. Experimenters can observe that a patient is dreaming and having rapid eye movement and brain waves, but cannot interpret the thoughts. Thus they reason that the mind is something more than just a biological computer, in order to account for free will and self awareness. There are also the thoughts and feelings of love and empathy. As the philosopher Rene Descartes stated, "I think, therefore I am."(p.247).

People Choose to Ignore God even with some Knowledge of Him

The Bible states that the problem is not that people are unaware of God. The problem is that they suppress the truth by their wickedness (Rom. 1:8)(Lisle 69). Erickson states that people naturally knowing of God's existence is the theological doctrine of General Revelation (Erickson p.85). Rom. 1:19-23 states: "Since what may be known about God is plain to them. For since the creation of the world God's invisible qualities—his eternal power and divine nature—have been clearly seen being understood from what has been made, so men are without excuse. For although they knew God, they neither glorified him nor gave thanks to him, but their thinking became futile and their foolish hearts were darkened. Although they claimed to be wise, they became fools, and exchanged the glory of the immortal God for images made to look like mortal man and birds and animals and reptiles." This appears to be a prophecy relating to the future theory of evolution in the Bible (Lisle p.69-70).

Fools and how to Argue with a Fool

Proverbs 26:4-5 also gave instruction on how to answer a fool. This is a two step process of don't answer, and answer in which you reflect back the foolishness of his extended argument to him. For example consider this argument of a relativist. "I don't believe in absolutes. We can talk about the Bible if you like, but you can't use any absolute statements." We should respond as follows: "I don't accept your claim that there are no absolutes. But for the sake of argument, if there were no absolutes, you couldn't even say that there are no absolutes, since that is an absolute statement. Your standard is self refuting."(Lisle p.71-74). Everyone believes in a series of presuppositions which together make up his world view. Belief in the laws of logic and the uniformity of nature are common presuppositions that both creationists and evolutionists believe in. Often the evolutionist is not aware of his presuppositions and the reasoning for them.

Example Arguments

An example of the Proverbs 26 technique can be applied to scientific arguments. They'll say "All the scientific evidence shows that life evolved over billion of years. And besides, science would be impossible if God were constantly interfering with the laws of nature." One could respond as follows: "I don't accept your claim that scientific evidence supports evolution. In fact, there are many evidences that challenge evolutionary notions. For example DNA and information science, irreducible complexity, and carbon 14 dating all confirm biblical creation. Nor do I believe that God constantly interferes with the laws of nature. In my view, the laws of nature are a description of the consistent way God upholds the universe." But for the sake of argument, apart from biblical creation, why would the world have so many uniform laws of nature if it was a random accident and why would there be an underlying uniformity in a constantly evolving universe? In particular why would we presume the laws of nature will work in the future like thy have in the past? "The evolutionist might respond that the laws of nature have been constant in the past, so I expect they will be in the future too." Then we say that is a circular argument and a fallacy in logical reasoning. We can't assume things in the future will always be like the past; things in nature change, and according to evolutionary theory the universe is evolving. "It would be silly for me to argue that I'm never going to die, After all I've never died in the past, so I assume I will never die in the future."(Lisle p.68-78)

Another example can be made about Bible reliability. The critic may say "You can't trust the Bible. It's full of contradictions." One can answer as follows: "I don't accept your claim that the Bible is full of contradictions. But for the sake of argument, if it did, why in your world view would that be wrong? As a Christian, I believe that contradictions cannot be true because all truth is in God and God is self-consistent. But what is your basis for the law of non-contradiction, or for that matter any of the laws of logic? (p.79). In summary Lisle recommended that we use the two fold argument in all apologetics (1) Affirm the biblical world view as internally consistent and (2) do an internal critique of the unbelieving evolutionary world view, showing that it is internally inconsistent and leads to absurdity.

The Structure of and Weakness in Logical Arguments

A check list is now given from Lisle on how to refute illogical arguments based on an inconsistent world view. He recommends we first mentally critique the argument the evolutionist is making. Often the unskilled opponent will make simple errors that can be easily refuted. He gives the Arbitrary, Inconsistent, and Preconditions of Intelligibility (AIP) checklist details (p.87-95).

Arbitrariness:
(1) Mere opinion (Asserting beliefs with no reasons)
(2) Relativism (Asserting there are no absolutes and truth is relative)

(3) Prejudicial Conjectures (Substituting arbitrary conjecture for researched knowledge)

(4) Un-argued philosophical bias "Evolution must be true, because it is the only naturalistic way that life could come about" Refutation: "But sir, I do not accept naturalism. In fact If naturalism were true, it would be impossible to prove anything since there would be no laws of logic."

Inconsistency:

(1) Logical Fallacies
(2) *Reductio Ad Absurdum* (reducing to absurdity)
(3) Behavioral Inconsistency (A professor teaches that life is just a meaningless sequence of accidents, and we are evolved animals. Then he goes home and kisses his wife and cares for his kids and discusses helpful social projects)
(4) Presuppositional Tensions (The evolutionist will assert Christian-based ideas like morality, right and wrong, but then argue for naturalism)

Preconditions:

(1) Laws of logic and rationality
(2) Uniformity of nature
(3) Absolute morality (ethics)
(4) Reliability of the senses
(5) Reliability of memory
(6) Personal dignity and freedom

There are two kinds of logic: inductive and deductive. Inductive arguments deal with likeliness of truth, so are classified as strong or weak. Deductive arguments have a conclusion that is definitely true if the premises are also true. They are classified as either valid or invalid. Formal logic can be put into symbolic equations as follows: "(1) if p then q, (2) p, (3) therefore q." An example is (1) All mammals have kidneys, (2) All dogs are mammals, (3) therefore, all dogs have kidneys. This is a valid formal argument. A formal argument can be wrong if the premises are not true. Formal deductive logic can be further divided into two types: Categorical logic using words like **all, some, no**, and **not**; and Propositional logic using words like **if then, and, or** and **not** (Lisle p.128). An additional type of logic is informal logic which does not use symbols: it uses ordinary language and therefore is very intuitive and easy to use. The possible fallacies in informal (ordinary language) arguments follow:(p.109-125)

Fallacies of Ambiguity

(1) Fallacy of equivocation (the meaning of a word is shifted)
(2) Fallacy of rectification (personal attributes are given to an abstract idea)

Fallacies of Presumption (has one or more unproven or unfounded assumptions)

(1) A hasty generalization
(2) A sweeping generalization
(3) Fallacy of bifurcation (2 propositions are presented as if they were mutually exclusive)
(4) Begging the question and circular reasoning

Example: "Miracles are impossible because they cannot happen. They are in the Bible so it can't be true." The conclusion is simply a restatement of the premise. Rebuttal: "You have simply assumed what you are trying to prove. This is arbitrary. Do you have a reason for your conclusion?"

(5) A question begging epithet (imports biased and emotional language)
(6) A complex question (it contains an unproved assumption and also begs the question)
(7) A no-true-Scotsman fallacy (this also begs the question and assumes something to be true)
(8) A false analogy and fallacy of false cause
(9) A slippery slope fallacy (chain reaction argument that overlooks limiting factors)

Fallacies of Relevance (the conclusion is not strongly related to the premise)

(1) Genetic fallacy (based on source origin of data not on logic—a tabloid newspaper)
(2) Ad hominem fallacy (against a person rather than his position)
(3) Fallacy of faulty appeal (to fear, to pity, to mob, appeal to authority)
(4) Appeal to ignorance (no one has proved it false, so it may be true)
(5) Fallacy of irrelevant thesis (proving a conclusion that is not an issue & a straw man)

Example: "Why is the universe ideally suited for life? Because, otherwise we wouldn't be here to observe it." The response doesn't really answer the question. Rebuttal: "True perhaps, but irrelevant."(Lisle p.109-125).

Summary of the Need for an Ultimate Standard

Lisle (p.142) noted the importance of an ultimate standard. We all have presuppositions like the laws of logic, being consistent and non-arbitrary, rational, truthful and relying on our memory. These are descriptions of God in the Bible and we are to imitate Him (Eph. 5:1). We can't get started with any learning or argument without them. For any belief a person can always ask "How do you know that is true?" This will form a long chain (**p,q,r,s,t**) until it gets to the ultimate standard. If a chain goes on forever, it cannot be completed. An incomplete argument does not prove anything. If **t** is the ultimate standard it cannot refer back to **r,** and if **t** is false it calls into question **p,q,r, s**. However, in relation to the ultimate standard some circular and self attesting reasoning is necessary. A way to show that a particular presupposition must be true is to show that even to argue against it one would have to use its component presuppositions to argue against it. This would be true for the laws of logic. This is also true for God and His book the Bible. Proverbs 1:7 states "The fear of the Lord is the beginning of knowledge, but fools despise wisdom and discipline." Lisle states the Bible must be the Word of God because it says it is and if you reject this claim you are reduced to foolishness in your ultimate standard. Empiricism, materialism and naturalism are not self-attesting and do not explain the laws of logic, rationality, uniformity, morality etc (p.144-148). Lisle goes on to ask what is the place of faith in apologetics and its relation to reason? Faith is not contrary to reason and is not the opposite of reason. The laws of logic cannot be perceived with the senses. So some faith is involved if we trust the laws of logic. We must have some presuppositions we trust to even begin to reason. Some beliefs in the value of love and eternal life and that we have a soul or spirit are difficult to prove and are taken on faith. Lisle maintains that we should use the Bible first as our ultimate standard of truth and logic. It is acceptable to use scientific and historical evidence to support creation (p.156,162).

Appendix 3—Search for Extra-Terrestrial Intelligence (SETI)

Because this relates to information theory and **UDI** some internet research on the topic is noted below. Main article: Fermi paradox (web100). **Search for Extra-Terrestrial Intelligence (SETI)** is the collective name for a number of activities people undertake to search for extraterrestrial life. SETI projects use scientific methods to search for electromagnetic transmissions from civilizations on distant planets. The United States government contributed to earlier SETI projects, but recent work has been primarily funded by private sources.

Italian physicist Enrico Fermi suggested in the 1950s that if technologically advanced civilizations are common in the universe, then they should be detectable in one way or another. (According to those who were there, Fermi either asked "**Where are they**?" or "Where is everybody?")

The **Fermi paradox** can be stated more completely as follows:

The size and age of the universe incline us to believe that many technologically advanced civilizations must exist. However, this belief seems logically inconsistent with our lack of observational evidence to support it. Either (1) **the initial assumption is incorrect** and technologically advanced intelligent life is much rarer than we believe, or (2) our current observations are incomplete and we simply have not detected them yet, or (3) our search methodologies are flawed and we are not searching for the correct indicators.

National Aeronautics and Space Administration
NASA History Office
SETI: The Search for ExtraTerrestrial Intelligence

Since the beginning of civilization, people have wondered if we are alone in the universe or whether there is intelligent life somewhere else. In the late twentieth century, scientists converged upon the basic idea of scanning the sky and "listening" for non-random patterns of electromagnetic emissions such as radio or television waves in order to detect another possible civilization somewhere else in the universe. In late 1959 and early 1960, the modern SETI era began when Frank Drake conducted the first such SETI search at approximately the same time that Giuseppe Cocconi and Philip Morrison published a key journal article suggesting this approach.

NASA joined in SETI efforts at a low-level in the late 1960s and early 1970s. Some of these SETI-related efforts included Project Orion, the Microwave Observing Project, the High Resolution Microwave Survey, and Toward Other Planetary Systems. On Columbus Day in 1992, NASA initiated a formal, more intensive, SETI program. Less than a year later, however, Congress canceled the program.

For more background on SETI history and the cancellation of NASA's SETI program, you may want to read an article from the Journal of the British Interplanetary Society. Part of the canceled program was picked up by the private, non-profit SETI Institute, and a smaller part by the non-profit, grassroots SETI League. NASA is still very much interested in astrobiology and the question of whether or not we are alone has been adopted by the NASA Origins program. For a comprehensive look at current SETI issues, *Sky & Telescope* magazine's SETI Section contains regularly updated articles and resources. The fictional movie *Contact* is about SETI using mathematical signals(g p138). CMI provided a commentary on ufology as a religion: http://creation.com/ufology-scientific-religion. Rana2004 (Chap.14,16) pointed out the improbability of distant space travel with life.

We also have several related full-length books now on-line. You may want to view the full text and images of *The Search for Extraterrestrial Intelligence* (NASA SP-419, 1977), which was edited by Philip Morrison, John Billingham, and John Wolfe. The Web version of *Project Orion: A Design Study of a System for Detecting Extrasolar Planets* (NASA SP-436, 1980) is now available on-line. A third SETI-related volume that is now on-line is *Life in the Universe* (NASA CP-2156, 1981).

CETI (Communication with Extraterrestrial Intelligence) is a branch of SETI research that focuses on composing and deciphering messages that could theoretically be understood by another technological civilization. The best-known CETI experiment was the 1974 Arecibo message composed by Frank Drake and Carl Sagan.

CETI research has focused on four broad areas: **mathematical languages, pictorial systems** such as the Arecibo message, algorithmic communication systems (ACETI) and computational approaches to detecting and deciphering 'natural' language communication. http://en.wikipedia.org/wiki/Communication_with_Extraterrestrial_Intelligence

Note by Tofflemire: This CETI communication represents **UDI**(universal definition of information) as defined previously. The above sites indicate, to my knowledge, that no extraterrestrial intelligence has been found. **The Fermi paradox remains**. It would seem however, **that the truth of UDI, and mathematics extends throughout the universe, because the top scientists are using it that way to search for other life.** It would seem that if good evidence for other intelligent life were found that it would be widely cited by atheists and evolutionists that there must be no God. Morris (p.52) stated that the mathematical odds of finding a planet like ours that will support life are extremely remote. Morris, H. M. *Exploring the Evidence for Creation*, ICR, Dallas, Tx. 2009. Heeren, Fred *Show Me God* provides 12 arguments why life on other planets is very unlikely (p.57-63) and a summary in pages 74-77. Scriptures:(p.88) Is. 40:26; Ps 19:1-2,4; Rom. 1:19-20. Andrews song "Nothing comes from nothing and nothing ever could." After 37 yrs. of searching and $60 million spent, no evidence of radio signal feed back has been found (Heeren p.74,245)

Appendix 4—Instinct and Innate Characteristics

Wikipedia stated **"Instinct** is the inborn complex behavior of a living organism that is not learned. Since 1910, most scientific journals consider the term outdated although it remains popular among the general public and a number of scientists. Instincts are thought to occur as fixed action patterns. These fixed action patterns are unlearned and inherited. Problems occurred when it was discovered that stimuli can be variable due to imprinting in a sensitive period. An example of this are baby ducks following a man as if he were their mother who later, when they grew up, showed interest in mating with the man.

Speculated examples of instinctual fixed action patterns can be observed in the behavior of animals, which perform various activities (sometimes complex) that are believed not to be based upon prior experience, such as reproduction, and feeding among insects. For example, sea turtles hatched on a beach automatically move toward the ocean and honeybees communicate the direction of a food source by dancing, all without formal instruction. Other examples include animal fighting, animal courtship behavior, internal escape functions, and building of nests. Another term for the same concept is innate behavior." (web 97)

The Distinction Between Innate and Acquired Characteristics from the SEP (web98)

"The idea that some characteristics of an organism are explained by the organism's intrinsic nature, whilst others reflect the influence of the environment is an ancient one. It has even been argued that this distinction is itself part of the evolved psychology of the human species. The distinction played an important role in the history of philosophy as the locus of the dispute between Rationalism and Empiricism discussed in another entry in this encyclopedia. This entry, however, focuses on twentieth-century accounts of the innate/acquired distinction. These accounts have for the most part been inspired by the sciences of mind and behavior.

Innateness must be clearly distinguished from heritability, at least in the scientific sense of that term. The idea that heritability scores measure the degree to which a characteristic is innate is a vulgar fallacy. Heritability is a statistical measure of the sources of individual differences in a population. While heritability itself is well understood, its relationship to the innate/ acquired distinction remains highly controversial.

The belief that a trait is innate is today commonly expressed by saying 'it is in the genes.' But genes play an essential role in the production of every trait. Consequently, it will not do to say simply that innate traits are 'caused by genes' whilst acquired traits are 'caused by the environment'. Any relationship between genetic causation and the innate/acquired distinction will be far more complex than this."

Appendix 5 A Brief summary of *The Genesis Question* by H. Ross2001

Dr. Ross is the founder of Reasons to Believe and a Christian scientist. To give alternate views, a brief summary outline of this book is given along with some commentary. Ross's views are unique in that he favors a historical genesis but gives different interpretations to certain scriptures. His works are highly referenced with sources.

Chap. 2 Reasons for resistance: Pride, bitterness from hurt, lust, and being illiterate-can't identify 4 books of the Bible, 4 apostles, or the 10 commandments. Some secular professors teach that the Bible records a flat earth or geocentrism; Academy of Science statement: science and religion are separate and mutually exclusive realms; people rejecting blind faith(p.11-16).

Chap. 3 Creation and the Cosmos: Hebrew Bara = created means bringing into existence something new that did not exist before(p.18). Heavens and earth, Hebrew Shamayin and erets have varied meanings heavens =the abode of the stars and galaxies; Frame of Ref shift on Gen. 1:2 to earth, initial conditions, see scientific method(p. 20). **Thus Ross maintains as in Gen.1:1 the heavens, including the sun and stars, were created and then the earth**. This is a general statement. As in Gen. 1:2 the Earth was dark and covered with water; also see Ps. 104:6 **Ross says the whole story is written from the perspective of a viewer on earth**. The Gap theory as taught by Scofield has earth 'became' rather than 'was' empty and void (correct) and has Satan destroying the creation. For 'formless and empty' Ross implies the earth underwent natural planet formation by dust disc accretion(p. 24). Land masses then arise by volcanism due to heat of isotope decay, and plate tectonics(p.25). **He says the earliest earth was covered by water. It initially had an opaque atmosphere due to debris.** Earth formed at 4.59 billion yrs.(p.29) Density differences or globe rotation may drive plate tectonics according to Wikipedia(web95): "Regarding the driving mechanism of the plates various models co-exist: Tectonic plates are able to move because the Earth's lithosphere has a higher strength and lower density than the underlying asthenosphere. Lateral density variations in the mantle result in convection. Their movement is thought to be driven by a combination of the motion of seafloor away from the spreading ridge (due to variations in topography and density of the crust that result in differences in gravitational forces) and drag, downward suction, at the subduction zones. A different explanation lies in different forces generated by the rotation of the Globe and tidal forces of the Sun and the Moon. The relative importance of each of these factors is unclear. Plate tectonics is basically a kinematic phenomenon: Earth scientists agree upon the observation and deduction that the plates have moved one with respect to the other, and debate and find agreements on how and when. But still a major question remains on what the motor behind this movement is; the geodynamic mechanism, and here science diverges in different theories."

Chap. 4 Days 1 and 2: p.27 He maintains that the earliest life was unicellular marine organism identified in marine sediments. They relied on photosynthesis at 3.5-8 billion yrs(Gya) due to C 13-12 ratios. The oxygen for photosynthesis appeared 4.0-1 Gya. ago(p.27). He states there is a lack of any specific information on dinosaurs in the Bible(p.28). **Day one light comes from the Sun to earth after clearing of the earth's atmosphere enough to be translucent.** The moon formed at 4.25 Gya as a planet collided with earth and knocked off a portion to form the moon. He asserted that samples show the moon and earth are chemically different and did not form together. The moon also blasted off the earth's atmosphere which had to reform(p.30). The sun shines about 35% more brightly today than it did during the first life forms(p.33). Comets of all sizes rained down on the earth's atmosphere and contributed water that helped the earth's atmosphere (p.34).

Chap. 5 Days 3, 4:p.35 Land appears Ps. 104:6-9 29%land 71% water present. Plants appear Day 3. The Hebrew dasha or produce means abound in vegetation. Ross implies this took some time; but large trees date very early in the fossil record(p.37): Archaeopteris 370 million yrs; Flowering plants, also 290 million yrs.(p.38). Evidence exists for kerogen tars and carbonaceous molecules from C 12-13 ratios 3.5-8 million yrs. ago(p.38).

Recent amino acids are left handed for life and nucleotide sugars right handed(p.39). Life is not likely to survive cosmic transport(p.40). Radio decay sets up release of oxygen from the oceans. No life can occur with oxygen or without, due to Ozone shield effect(p.41). No plant species radically different from current ones has been observed to arise. Rapid extinction of plants has been observed. This implies many new plants don't come into being. The **Atmosphere went from translucent to transparent on day 4 and CO^2 dropped. On this day the sun, moon and stars became clearly visible from earth**. Earth's rotation slowed and this gave slower winds and less cloud cover (less sea spray). Plate Tectonics and volcanism driven by radio decay occurred. The advanced species show low tolerance for these prior events(p.42). Ross says the Hebrew asa verb does not require current creation of the sun, as it could have been prior(p.43). The moon could have been made on day 1. A problem with the 4th day creation of the sun is more than light(God could have provided his light), also gravity problem for planets and orbits(p.44). Ozone was balanced carefully for life(p.45).

Creation Days 5, 6: Day 5 Water has living creatures and birds fly, large sea creatures and everyone that swarms and crawls in water. Dinosaurs lived 65-250 million yrs. ago (p.48). A Behemoth, a hippopotamus, and dinosaurs don't breathe fire. Nephesh soulish creatures, can form relationships and emotional bonds with humans and be trained(p.49). Pakicetus, Nalacetus, Ambulocetus and Indocetus are fossils of sea mammals about 50 million yrs. ago. Freshwater to sea water adaptation requires different internal organs(p.50). Whales change slowly due to their large size and slow reproduction and numbers(p.51-2). Only species with a quadrillion population and generation times of less than 3 mo. can evolve(p.52). Also horses slow to change. He theorized multiple extinction and repopulation of whales by God. Ps. 104:27-30[27] All creatures look to you to give them their food at the proper time. When you give it to them, they gather it up; when you open your hand, they are satisfied with good things. When you hide your face, they are terrified; when you take away their breath, they die and return to the dust. [30] When you send your Spirit, they are created, and you renew the face of the ground.

Mathew Henry and John Gills commentaries do not agree with Ross's view that this means full recreation of species, but more preservation of a few favored ones who multiplied.

Day 6: land mammals and livestock, long legged and short legged quadrupeds from 3 Hebrew words. Man has **5 spirit traits:1**. Aware of Moral code in conscience.**2** concerns about death and life after, **3.** tendency to worship and communicate with higher being (have temples and altars), **4.** consciousness of self, **5.** drive to discover and capacity to recognize truth and absolutes.(p.55). Due to the Hebrew words ab and ben (father and son) meaning several generations, genealogies could be 7000 to 60000 yrs. to now. 1Chron., Matt 1, Luke 3, and Gen. 11 There are religious relics for 8000-24,000 yrs.(p.56). Most anthropologists insist that bipedal primates were human, mainly Neanderthal; but this link of them to humans is now in question(p.57). The sun brightens about 8% per billion yrs, and the earth's rotation rate lengthens about 4hr/day per billion yrs. Coal, oil and gas deposits formed over millions of yrs with vegetation(p.57).

Chap. 7 Other stories of creation and myths are not realistic like the Bible literal story.

Chap. 8 Day 7: Ross says the 7th day rest continues into the present and he implies the other days may have been longer as well(p.64). He pointed out that the 6-24hr. days creation is a stumbling block for many scientists and those that follow them. It was good and it was so is stated many times(p.67).

Chap. 9 Gen. 2 the spiritual whys of creation: Gen. 1 the physical creation. Vegetarianism fits with long lives and healthy diet(p.71). 4500 Birds and animals named by Adam would take a yr with 30-60 min per animal and 8 hr days. Eve may have come from tissue and not a rib. She was an ally not just a helper(p.75-6). Eden was located in Iraq near Babylon(p.78).

Chap. 10 Modern Criticism History: Jean Astruc in 1753 criticized the two accounts of Genesis 1, 2 as being contradictory(p.81). Soon the Germans added that Gen. also violated science and some concluded that the Bible was unreliable(p.83). Fundamental Protestants clung to solo Scriptura and the Bible is true in history and science. Some in the liberal or modernist camp claim that the Bible is only true in doctrines and guide to human practice and not in history and science(p.83-4). Some go as far as to deny many miracles. Many scientists either joined with the higher critics or liberals or left the church. Ross states although some theologians say Gen. is poetic or even mythical, this is not true; **Genesis is best classified as a historical narrative** or prose and not poetry. It does not have the style of poetry as does Ps. 104, which describes creation in a poetic style(p.86). Also see Prov. 8:22-31 "The LORD brought me forth as the first of his works, before his deeds of old; 23 I was appointed from eternity, from the beginning, before the world began. 24 When there were no oceans, I was given birth, when there were no springs abounding with water; 25 before the mountains were settled in place, before the hills, I was given birth, 26 before he made the earth or its fields or any of the dust of the world. 27 I was there when he set the heavens in place, when he marked out the horizon on the face of the deep, 28 when he established the clouds above and fixed securely the fountains of the deep, 29 when he gave the sea its boundary so the waters would not overstep his command, and when he marked out the foundations of the earth. 30 Then I was the craftsman at his side. I was filled with delight day after day, rejoicing always in his presence, 31 rejoicing in his whole world and delighting in mankind. Mathew Henry's commentary indicated that God's son Jesus is being referred to here as an example of high wisdom. Metaphors are used. Ross noted there have been some excellent reviews of the higher critics that have pointed out flaws in their arguments(p.86).

Chap. 11 Creation Science Develops: p.87 Price, G.W. wrote *The New Geology* in 1923; this insisted on the global flood. Ramm, B. wrote *The Christian View of Science and Scripture* in 1955 as a rebuttal to Price. In 1961 H. Morris wrote *The Genesis Flood*; which was a scholarly work. John Whitcomb, a theologian, also supported it. They formed the Creation Research Society in 1963(p.89-90). This splint in 1970 and ICR was re-founded by Morris in 1972. This book has a young earth and global flood view. Ross challenges that all animals were formed as vegetarians with man; that sufficient animals could get on the ark(30,000 pairs), and that animals could repopulate to so many species after the flood to form all the fossils(1/2 billion specics) and the species that presently exist(5 million species). Ross maintains that animals do not diversify that fast into all the species(p.92).

Chap. 12 How far the Fall. Ross maintains that the 2nd law or thermo was in effect from the beginning of creation and when Adam ate food, bacteria digested it and some died. The livers and teeth of ancient sharks are designed for eating animal matter, as are T-Rex's limbs and teeth. With the fall, pain and work were increased, not started. Adam did some work tending the garden(p.95-6). Carnivores perform a beneficial function of eating the weak and sick herbivores animals and keeping their population in check. Herbivores also have precise defense mechanisms to avoid carnivores like camouflage, speed, smell, spines (skunk and porcupine). (p.98). There is a balance of nature through plants, herbivores and carnivores. Some evil and sin may have existed before Adam as in the fall of the angels and Satan. These are good points.

Chap. 13 Cain's wife and City: Critics have questioned God allowing Cain's murder, Cain's wife after he was banished and his city. God asks Cain questions to draw his conscious, but allows free will(p.101-2). Adam and Eve had other children and Cain could have married a sister or a niece. There could have been a huge population growth with the long life ages. Murder may have reduced this some(p.103). Josephus noted that the early population became very wicked and thus God judged it(p.104). In Lev. 18:6-18 God rules out marrying close relatives; This was due to gene degradation. Today war and murder are the leading cause of death in the world: 1/1000 (p.106)(web78).

Chap. 14 Dating the origin of Humanity From early Bible genealogies to be about 4000 BC; Chinese history dates it slightly earlier, others(American Indians 9000 BC, Australian aborigines and Europeans 25,000-30,000BC)(p.108). Gaps in genealogies were pointed out from Ab and Ben for father and son(p.109). Religious relics up to 24,000 yrs; Art with spiritual content 5000 yrs.(p.110). Biochemical dates: Mitochondrial DNA from mothers—few 1000's to 10000's. y chromosome for men-35000-47000BC(p. 111-2). Neanderthals were dated 30,000-100,000 yrs ago.(Riddle challenges these dates in his *Origin of Humans*). Earlier studies concluded that Neanderthals were humans. However the latest studies showed enlarged nasal cavities and no tear ducts, and major differences in DNA from humans. It has been concluded that they are a different DNA track than humans(p.114-5). Ross states that there is no evidence of their spiritual activity like temples and altars.

Some animals like bower birds, elephants, chimpanzees, gorillas, and zebra finches engage in music, tool use, art and even burials(p.110). Also see web 86.

Chap.15 Long Life Spans: p.117 The early long life spans appear real. Long life spans could have contributed to knowledge and to evil. After the flood, life spans were shortened, Gen. 6:3. Ross lists factors shortening life(p.120). Cosmic radiation and telomerase enzyme activity are discussed further. A supernova, Vela occurred 6000 to 30,000 yrs ago and contributed considerable radiation. Telomere area causes chromosomes to shorten and cells to die. Stimulating telomerase can increase cancers. It is possible that in the pre flood time radiation was low and telomerase could be high and lengthen life. The vegetarian diet also helped(p.123-5).

Chap. 17 The Boundaries of God's Wrath:(p.130) Sin's damage is real; sins to body may be worse than those outside it. Reprobation is described in Rom. 1:18-32 and 2Pet.2:14-19 Continuing to sin and drawing others in. Defilement spreads in this order: 1. to the sinner, 2 to his progeny, 3. to his soulish animals, 4. to his material goods, and 5. to his land (p.140). Ross gives examples from the Bible on how God at times directed only males to be killed, at times all people, and at times also livestock(p.143). There is no need to destroy insects, ants or bacteria that are not soulish. To this day Sodom and Gomorrah is laid waste with no crops. The required extent of the global flood would be to humans and their livestock.

Chap. 18 The Flood Global or Local: p.145 Ross makes the point that the Bible phrases "the mountains under the entire heavens and over the whole world" could mean the world from the viewpoint of Noah's sight and view and the human inhabited world(p.146). Gen. 41:56; 1Kings 10:24 are cited as examples where over the whole world is stated but not intended. He says the flood was limited to the Mesopotamian valley which could be flooded with 400-500 ft of water. He notes that Gen. 8:5 says the tops of the mountains became visible in the 10th month, which implies visible mountains are being referred to(p.150). Also in Gen. 8:1 the wind aided in removing the water, which would help in a local flood. In Gen. 8:4 it says the ark landed in the mountains of Ararat, where mountains is plural and covers a large area. Also Olive trees do not grow at high mountain elevations. Ross challenges the plausibility of plate tectonics and volcanism occurring in one yr. during the global flood to cause the mountains and valleys. He states such large plate movements would have caused waves to destroy the ark, and the ashes from the volcanoes would have shut down photosynthesis for yrs.(My note: one point not noted in Ross's critique of rapid plate tectonics and volcanism is that some plate movement and volcanism could have continued for up to 140 yrs more until the dispersion at the tower of Babel. God could have protected the ark from high waves. The ice age that comes out of this model goes on for several hundred yrs. with more volcanism causing the polar ice caps.) Ross noted Noah began farming after the flood(p.154). Ross also questions how all the animal species we see today could have evolved so quickly into millions of species after the flood, into all the horse, and cat kinds from one pair of each. Ross states the carrying capacity of the earth is about 50 million species but there are ½ billion species in the fossils. He also questioned how the huge amount of biodeposits like coal, oil, gas, and kerogen could have formed from the flood. One covering of the earth with vegetation is not enough to form this amount(p.158). He noted that Mt. Everest has marine fossils near its peak and states that it was uplifted by plate tectonics slowly(p.159). He says there are several large alluvial deposits in the Mesopotamian plain. My notes: the 10 points from Snelling(p.73), my p. 64 in the Geology section, are not well refuted. Questions that people ask about the feasibility of the ark are answered in the Woodmorappe book *Noah's Ark a Feasibility Study*. If every assumption about the details of creation is naturalistic, there is less need for God and miracles.

Chap. 19 The Ark and its passengers: Ross states the ark was larger than any known wooden ship. Noah had time, 100 yrs. to build it. The animals taken were mainly birds and mammals(p.167). Ross hints that the ark may have landed 50mi north of Nineveh at an elevation of several hundred feet. It then would have been raided for its valuable wood. The numerous flood legends are noted.

Chap. 20 The origin of nations and races: God commands several times that mankind should multiply and fill the earth (Gen. 1:28; 9:7). Ross points out the dangers of large centralized governments. They can spread evil, just as one corporation monopoly can result in poor goods. About 50 million of the Russian people were killed by the government(p. 174). He points out that the early peoples from Adam to Noah lived in the

Mesopotamian valley and did not spread out as God instructed. Nimrod built 8 cities there after the flood. This problem came to a head at the tower of Babel where God confused the languages to get people to spread out. Ross says Noah and sons lived 20,000-30,000 yrs ago, and the scattering of peoples at Babel occurred about 11,000 yrs. ago(p.187). A study showed that the Bering Strait land bridge appeared 40,000-11,000 yrs. ago(p.178). Population migration may have occurred at 11,000 yrs ago, after which the land bridge was flooded, isolating the peoples(p.188). Ross proposed that God may have changed the genes of the separating peoples slightly along with the languages. Sun sensitivity does not completely explain the dark and light skins. The Bible contrasts the dark color of the Nubian and Ethiopians vs. the light complexions of the Egyptians, Jews and Mesopotamians(p.181-2). Wheat gene spread has been tracked from southern Turkey 9000BC to Egypt and Russia in 5000-6000BC(p.185). Also domesticated goats spread from Iraq and Iran areas 10,000 yrs ago to other countries(p.186).

Appendix 6 Some Speculations and Discussion from other Books

Ross2004 in *A Matter of Days* has some excellent points not in his other books, so these will be briefly summarized: My 7 page book summary is available on the web site, so only a few points are noted below: Ross has made a strong case for an old universe.

Chap. 12 Faith, Morality and Long Creation Days or Old Earth Creation:OEC: p. 131-7 YEC have attributed belief in OEC to be un-Christian and likely to promote poor morals. He stated that both Morris and Ham have made such statements, but the poor moral correlation is false. Neither Satan nor early humans knew of evolution, yet sinned over pride and self-exultation. Some distinguished OEC include theologians and apologists like Charles Hodge, Ben Warfield, Gleason Archer, Norman Geisler, and Walter Kaiser. Dallas Willard stated that the level of animosity among Christians on the issue blunts evangelism and sets a poor example of brotherly love. Ross provided an example of a talk he gave at Oak Ridge Nat. Lab. where he spoke to physicists there, convincing them of Gods creation. A group of YEC made a 4 hr. trip to cause difficult questions during the question period, somewhat disrupting the flow of the meeting. This may have lessened the winning of Christian believers intended. God calls Christians to treat each other with love as Acts 15:1-35; 18:24-8; 1 and Cor. 6:9-11 suggest.

Chap. 15 Challenges to an Old Cosmos p.161-174 Ross refutes many challenges here. A common one is God that could have created light waves already in transit. This appearance of age would provide us with false information. Triangulation has shown the vast distances to be true. Changing in the velocity of light is also unlikely and would also affect $E=MC^2$. Ross challenged the mathematics of Humphries in *Starlight and Time* as being incorrect, invalidating the time dilation values where clocks in the distant universe ran at faster rates. The two light yr. ball of water would have undergone nuclear fusion before it could assemble, and the black and white hole would take billions of yrs. to form(p.167). Ross also challenged the Hartnett model of earth, based clocks once running slower than the distant universe until day 4, after which the clock rates equalized. This goes against Jer. 33:25 that says the laws of the heavens and earth are fixed. Ross questions how a time discontinuity between the sun and earth can occur as they are gravitationally connected. Ross also challenged the earth at the center of the universe claim. The redshifts of the most recent surveys do not show the clustered redshift values that Humphries noted(p.170).

Chap. 17. The Case for a Young Cosmos—Refuted.p.185-206 **Lunar dust accumulates too quickly to allow for an old earth**: Ross noted recent dust estimates are lower and this invalidates the argument. Morris07(p.91) largely agreed. **Computer models of galaxy structures show that spirals tend to collapse after 2-3 rotations, so galaxies must be relatively young.** Ross noted that Prendergast found that continued star formation will stabilize the spiral. Also embedding of the spiral in a halo or in a dense central bulge will preserve the spiral. If these assertions are correct, the argument is negated. **A comets life span is limited to thousand of yrs. and the supply of new comments is limited, so the solar system must be young**. Again if Ross's detailed assertions are correct, the argument is refuted. Ross also noted that the lack of confirmed supernova remnants was more due to observational problems rather than a true lack of them.

Chap. 18 Physical Reality breaks through: p. 207-14 Many young earth creationists (YEC), have declared the apparent findings of science are not correct and must be interpreted and viewed through their biblical viewpoint like wearing biblical glasses. This has caused some to dismiss YEC as wearing blinders and not being open minded to evidence. For example a geologist Ian Plimer wrote a book *Telling Lies for God,* in which he charges YEC of deception. At one time, the Catholic Church persecuted Galileo for his finding that the earth revolved about the sun. More recently YEC bars OEC from speaking at their meetings or at evangelical churches and colleges. Paul taught in Romans and Galatians brothers should be welcomed and there should not be a spiritual caste system of Jew and gentiles for example.

My comments relating to Chap.12 and 18: These views raise the question of what should be our priorities in belief? It is submitted that **God, Jesus and the guidance of the HS should be our first priority**. Should our belief be formed and held to the tenants of any organization or church denomination? For example AIG has tenants that one must believe in six literal days of creation. The principle of the protestant reformation was **Sola Scriptura** or the scriptures are primary and trump any denomination view. As a practical consideration, it is recognized that one representing an organization or a denomination must subscribe to their policy and beliefs. Where do open mindedness and the value of reason come in? It is submitted that if one is to be a thoughtful Christian they **must adopt some view of inerrancy of the scriptures**. Once one adopts a view like full inerrancy, as defined by Erickson, or any well defined view, it somewhat sets your course. From there on one can fit in a view of science and reason. The full inerrancy view fits with the ICBI view, that science is secondary to the scriptures and not of equal standing as with its article 8. This is not to say one should not be open-minded or ignore the weight of evidence, however. **Where there is overwhelming evidence it must be acknowledged**. Where something from science appears to disagree with scripture, we could also say that we acknowledge the science, but do not fully know the answer or resolution with scripture. Some areas like the Trinity are somewhat mystical and by never be fully understood by man. The minute details of creation are complex and also may not be fully understood by man. **It appears that most authors have some bias, and tend to support their organization view**, regardless of all the facts. This gives me a slight advantage, in that I am not strongly tied to any organization. Job 38 is quoted: "⁴Where wast thou when I laid the foundations of the earth? Declare, if thou hast understanding. ⁷When the morning stars sang together,— ³³**Knowest thou the ordinances of the heavens? Canst thou establish the dominion thereof in the earth?** Because these topics can be divisive some discussion of Christian unity appears appropriate.

Scholes and Clinton 1991 in their paper on **Levels of Belief**, suggest that Christ desires unity and a brotherhood of believers. John 17:21 gives Jesus prayer—that all believers may be one with him in the Father. 1 Peter 3: also says to be of one mind and brethren. They point out that Paul's theology implied that there are three levels of firmness or strength on beliefs: **Strong convictions, persuasions, and matters of preference** or desire (Rom.14, 4:21, 1Cor. 7: 7, 14: 5). Examples of matters of preference or perhaps persuasions include holidays, days of worship, circumcision, whether you remarry or not, and what foods we eat. Paul counseled us not to judge our brothers in Christ, over these persuasions (Rom.14:10-13). The movie "Empires: Peter and Paul" delves into Christian history on this topic. This was a huge issue for Paul as he had started many churches of new gentile Christians, while the followers of James, who were Jews in Jerusalem, admonished Paul and the gentile believers for eating un-kosher food. They also did not think an uncircumcised gentile could be a true Christian. Most would say Paul was right, as history shows that the majority of Christians today descended from the many new gentile churches and not from the lesser Jewish congregation in Jerusalem. Peter was also counseled by God in a dream to fellowship and eat with new gentile believers(Acts 10,11). The paper raises the question of what beliefs are essential to be saved and what differing beliefs justify separating from a church or denomination of believers. The paper suggests that firm convictions are now in the early church creeds, and in some church written doctrines. The paper also suggests that beliefs that could cause one to loose there salvation are of major importance (1991).

Chap. 19 Narrow Window of Time p. 215-220 **Ross** noted that the universe is finely tuned for life on earth after 14 billion yrs. The ages of the universe, sun and of the earth are just right for life. The sun's energy stabilized and the moon stabilizes the earth's tilt and rotation. The earth is unique in its size and location for life, and it in not likely active life will be found on other planets. Extending the reasoning here, **if the whole universe was fined tuned for man, then why wouldn't man be placed at the center of it to observe it?**

Chap. 21 A Clear Day Interpretation p.227-38 **Ross** noted that creation of the universe after the earth on day four doesn't make good sense. In Gen. 1:1 God created the heavens and the earth: This is an overview verse. In Gen. 1:2-5 there was day 1, light and the earth which was formless and void. **My notes**: Light is related to matter by $E=MC^2$. Perhaps what was formless and void was the first matter including the earth's matter. Heb.11:3 "By faith we understand that the universe was created by the word of God, so that what is seen has been made **from things that are not visible.**" On day 2, the expanse was created and separated. This would fit with the stretching of the heavens. See pg 89(Humphreys p.34). **Ross** noted it would make sense that matter, space, time and energy were all created initially. **As how could one have the earth before <u>space</u>, time, matter and energy?** It would also make sense that the laws of physics, heat and gravity were created early on and the earth would be subject to them. The earth's orbital features are controlled by laws requiring the sun and moon. It would not make logical sense(but God can do anything) that one could just pop the sun and moon in on day 4 with the earth floating in space and rotating, unless most of the laws of physics were suspended previously. Wouldn't the earth need gravity if it was rotating for days 1-4 and there was morning and evening? My notes: Some YEC say one can have day and night by rotating the earth and God providing a light on one side. Ross gave the explanation that on day 4, the atmosphere of earth cleared enough so that from earth, the sun and stars could now be seen. He noted that the Hebrew verb asa for made in verse 16 denoted a completed action—as the sun and moon and stars were already there and could now be seen from earth. Perhaps time as we know it on earth wasn't fixed until day 4 with the sun and moon. The Hebrew word "mayim" typically means water, as in Gen. 1:2. But Maimonides and Dr. Schroeder said that in the original statements of creation, the word "mayim" may also mean the building blocks of the universe(web 104).

Ross commented on the fossil record and the order of creation(p.234). The lack of insects until day 6 is a problem. He noted that the word 'creeping things' in Gen.1:25-6 of day 6 could mean rodents, rabbits and lizards, not insects. **My notes**: Insects are needed for pollination of plants on day 3 and for bird and fish food on day 5. Too many insects would be a problem, but the birds and bats from day 5 kept them in balance. As noted previously, not every detail of creation is stated in the Bible and insects could have been created in the days 3-5 sequence. God may have fine tuned the creation as he went, as ecology requires that cycles be in balance and many creatures and plants are interactive and interdependent. Worms and bacteria also play an important roll in preparing the topsoil. **Ross** asserted that bipedal primates were created before humans as there is some evidence in the fossil record. He noted that about ½ of the species of birds and mammals in the fossils are now extinct. He suggested that God knew that man (post fall) would be more destructive of these than would the bipedal primates. Thus the primates were created before man to allow the birds and mammals adapt to being hunted and develop defenses for man's advanced hunting. Wise asserted that primates dispersed and multiplied more rapidly than humans. Humans may have remained concentrated in the Mesopotamian valley and their dead bodies lost in the flood. This could explain the primate fossils in Africa earlier than man.

Although the straight forward reading of scripture indicates a young creation of the earth, some puzzling questions remain. Ross noted that it would be difficult for Adam to **name** all the **animals** after they had previously been created on that day, recognize and miss his mate and then fall asleep, wake up and observe Eve and name her in the same day. It is agreed that it would be proper for Adam to observe the animals, their sounds, smell, and a little behavior before naming them. AIG allows 5 sec. each for this for 2400 kinds, taking 3.3 hrs.(web71). In 5 sec. the animals could walk by without stopping. Extending the time to 15 sec. would take 10 hrs. Using the 16,000 total animals estimated on the ark would push the task into a 2nd or 3rd day. Naming the animals in a rapid programmed fashion would not make sense, with God being curious as to what Adam would name them. The ark total may be inappropriate as only animals and birds that relate to man may have been named.

Ross also questioned how the huge amount of biodeposits like coal, oil, gas, and kerogen could have formed from the flood. One covering of the earth is with vegetation is not enough to form this amount(p.158). Snelling (p.962) noted the pre-flood earth may have had more land area and vegetation and could account for all the coal. Present earth has 30% land, 70% ocean, while the Pre-flood may have been 50/50 and had floating mats of vegetation. Ross maintains the mass of vegetation would still be inadequate to form all the kerogen. Wikipedia notes "**Kerogen** is a mixture of organic chemical compounds that make up a portion of the organic matter in sedimentary rocks. It is insoluble in normal organic solvents because of the huge molecular weight (upwards of 1,000 Daltons) of its component compounds. The soluble portion is known as bitumen. At the demise of living matter, such as diatoms, planktons, spores and pollens for example, the organic matter begins to undergo decomposition or degradation. In this *break-down* process, (which is basically the reverse of photosynthesis), large biopolymers from proteins and carbohydrates begin to partially or completely dismantle."

Ross also questioned how all the animal species we see today could have evolved so quickly into millions of species after the flood, into all the horse, and cat kinds from one pair of each. Ross states the carrying capacity of the earth is about 50 million species but there are ½ billion species in the fossils(Ross 2001 p.154). Wikipedia (web72) notes there are currently about 1.6 million species not including bacteria, insects and fungi. Ross argues that evolution of new species does not happen fast enough to produce all the species with the young earth and flood dates. YEC by arguing for rapid evolution in kind, are arguing for general evolution.

Ross in *Beyond the Cosmos* notes that more than three dimensions plus time is hard to conceive of. Physicists have been working on unified field theories to mathematically unite the four forces of physics(p.32). Einstein added the 4th dimension of time to unify his theory. The weak nuclear force and the electromagnetic force have been unified and six quarks found in the 1990's(p.35). String theory with 10 dimensions had been proposed to unify all the forces. Strings are like rotating vibrating elastic bands that behave like points, because of their small size. Ross gave 6 evidences for strings in his appendix(p.38,227). It is theorized that the forming cosmos at 10^{-43} sec., split its 10 dimensions into 6 and 4 (l,w,h, and time). The four continued to expand while the six are curled up and dispersed in the universe(p.40). Deut. 29:29 "The secret things belong to the Lord our God, but the things revealed belong to us and to our children forever"(p.50). Extra dimensions or going before time can allow other possibilities as God operated then with some causes. The extra dimensions can possibly explain how God can be near and in heaven.

Wikipedia is quoted "The **Book of Jubilees** sometimes called the **Lesser Genesis (Leptogenesis)**, is an ancient Jewish religious work, considered one of the Pseudepigrapha by most Roman Catholic, Eastern Orthodox and Protestant Christians. It is considered canonical for the Ethiopian Orthodox Church, where it is known as the *Book of Division* (Ge'ez: *Mets'hafe Kufale*). In the modern scholarly view, it reworks material found in the biblical books of *Genesis* and *Exodus* in the light of concerns of some 2nd century BC Jews."

"The ***Book of Enoch*** (also **1 Enoch**) is an ancient Jewish religious work, ascribed to Enoch, the great-grandfather of Noah. It is not currently regarded as part of the Canon of Scripture as used by Jews, apart from the Beta Israel canon; nor by any Christian group, apart from the Ethiopian Orthodox Church and Eritrean Orthodox Church canon. Western scholars currently assert that its older sections (mainly in the *Book of the*

Watchers) date from about 300 BC and the latest part (*Book of Parables*) probably was composed at the end of the 1st century BC."

Some excerpts from the **Book of Jubilees** (Schodde 2005) will be given as it contains some alleged facts not in protestant canonical scripture: The book is alleged to be written before 70 AD by Jews and divides history into 49 yr. Jubilee periods (p.4-5). **Chap.1**. "And it happened on the 1st yr of the exodus, 3rd month, the Lord spoke to Moses and said ascend to me here on the mountain, and I will give to thee the two stone tablets of the law and commandments, as I have written them. Moses was there on the mountain 40 days and 40 nights and the Lord instructed him to what was past and what would be. And He said to him, incline thine heart to every word which I shall speak to thee and write them in a book."(p.9). **Chap. 2** "And the angel of the face spoke to Moses by the command of the Lord saying write all the words of creation, how in six days the Lord God finished all the works which he created, and rested on the 7th day and sanctified it" (p.12). "And on the 6th day he made all the animals of the earth and all the beasts and everything that moves over the earth. And after all this he made mankind, a single one; male and female he created them"(p.13). **Chap. 3** "And on the 6th day of the **2nd Sabbath we brought**, by the command of the Lord, to Adam **all the animals** and all the beasts and all the birds and everything that moves on the earth and everything that moves in the water, each according to their kind, and each according to their similarity: on the first day the animals; the beasts on the 2nd day; the birds on the 3rd day; and everything that moves on the earth on the 4th day; whatever moves in the water on the 5th day. And Adam gave unto each its name.—And in the 1st seventh was Adam created, and his wife in his side, and in the 2nd seventh he showed her to him. Text Footnote: She was created at the same time with Adam, but within him, and it was only in the 2nd week that she became a separate creature"(p.15). I will extrapolate a possible order here: On day 8 man is placed in garden(as in Gen 2:15) but he can go in and out of garden; woman was not revealed to man until day 13, next Sat.; **Adam possibly named the animals on days 8,9,10,11,12** perhaps outside of garden. Sabiers noted a pattern of 7's in Genesis using numerics where each Hebrew letter is reduced to a number. An attempt to resolve or expand the days of creation using numerics is presented in my paper on the web site.

The **Jubilees** talks of a **long time in garden** (7 yrs) learning to care for the garden before the fall(p.16). The book is unique in that it gives names of many of Adam and Eve's sons and daughters. It **also says that Noah's ark landed** on a lesser mountain of Ararat—**Mt. Lubar** where he was buried(p.22). A (web 74) quote follows: "A veteran explorer to the region and a neuropsychiatrist by trade, Willis has led four expeditions up Mt. Ararat, the traditional site of the landing of Noah's Ark. Yet, the results of his investigation on that mountain, as well as years of research into historical sources, suggested to him that Ararat is not the mountain of Noah or the Ark. Furthermore, Willis does not believe the Ark is even intact. Noting the great time period since the event, the harsh topography, geology and meteorology of the region, and the Ark being a natural source of building material for generations, Willis does not expect to find any major portions still intact. Furthermore, despite all the reports of sightings, none have been substantiated by later exploration/investigation. "Those who continue to look for the Ark on Ararat are looking in the wrong place for the wrong thing," Willis said. His research suggests the mountain known today as **Mt. Cudi** is the best candidate for the Ark landing and the subsequent settlement of Noah and his family. Here, too, he believes Noah died and was buried. Called by different names over the years, including Mt. Ararat, Mt. Judi, Mt. Nisir, Mt. Nipir and Mt. Lubar, it is neither as high as Ararat nor as snow covered and treacherous most of the year. It was on this mountain's Ark plateau in 1953, a few miles from the site Willis believes is Noah's tomb, the German professor Friedrich Bender discovered pieces of wood he believed came from Noah's Ark. The samples carbon dated to 4500 B.C. The Ark is not the real focus of Willis' exploration. Evidence of Noah and his family in their post-Flood community is where Willis is concentrating. The structure he is looking for is the tomb of Father Noah, as Willis likes to refer to the ancient mariner. "After all," Willis said, "the whole human race comes from Noah by way of his three sons—so is the Father of us all." Modern local tradition places the grave of Noah on the southern slope of Mt. Cudi. In 1911, British explorer Gertrude Bell recorded the location of Noah's tomb on the mountain. She wrote "I ought to have completed the pilgrimage by visiting his (Noah's) grave, but it lay far down upon the southern slopes of Judi Dagh." In addition, the ancient "BOOK OF JUBILEES" states "Noah slept with his fathers and was buried on Mt. Lubar in the Land of Ararat" (10:13-17). One of the region's major cities lies just north of the mountain, **Sirnak**. "Sirnak," Willis noted, comes from Sehr-i-Nuh or "city of Noah." His recent trip to Mt. Cudi included traveling alone, staying in a local village and befriending its chief, sleeping under armed guards and carrying an AK-47, a gift from the village chief, for protection. From his accommodations in the village, Willis could see the ruins of Heshton ("Village Of The Eight"?) site of the first Noahic village according to local tradition. The site identified as Noah's tomb is in a solitary location on a gentle slope of the mountain's south side. It is overgrown and undisturbed. Cut out of solid rock as a horizontal cave, it has a facade of built stone. Inside the tomb, Willis believes he may find texts from the early post-Flood period. But his real hope is to find some antediluvian written material. "I know that most scholars do not believe that man wrote that early, but there are ancient references to pre-**Flood texts**," he said. "It seems reasonable Noah would have taken into the Ark any pre-Flood archives available to him. That would be the real find from Noah's Ark." Wikipedia(web 75)noted many mountains are alleged for the ark landing. "**Şırnak** is a town in southeastern Turkey. It is the capital of Şırnak Province, a new province that split from the Hakkari province. The Habur border gate with Iraq which is one of Turkey's main links to Middle Eastern countries is also on Şırnak. It is the mountain on which Noah's Ark is believed to have landed. One of its peaks, at over 2000 meters, is "Noah's Visit" (some Islamic scholars argue that Noah landed on Cudi mountain)."

Jubilees also noted **that Noah wrote down records and gave them to** his beloved son, **Seth** before he was buried on Mr. Lubar(p.32). The tower of Babel is also noted and God sent a wind to blow down the tower and confused the languages(p.33). About 350 yrs. is noted from the flood to the tower destruction. Let's briefly explore the book of **Enoch** (2004). This appears to be simplistic and allegorical. It is also not chorological and skips to different topics as it goes. It does have a brief section on the luminaries of heaven (p.92-107). "I saw 6 doors in which the sun rises and 6 doors in which the sun sets (12)."—There were also many windows to the right and left of these doors." The sun is like a sphere of heaven, and is quite filled with illuminating and heating fire(p. 92). In the sphere of the sun there are 7 portions of lights which are added to it-."(p.106). Perhaps this relates in some way to the 6 extra dimensions Ross notes in *Beyond the Cosmos*. "At the ends of the earth I saw 12 doors open to all quarters of heaven, from which the winds go out and blow over the earth"(p.102). "I saw 7 great islands in the sea and in the mainland, 2 in the mainland and 5 in the great sea"(p.105).

The **large biomass** of Kerogen that Ross questions will be considered. On day 3 plants were created. There are ways using numerics to stretch the days into longer periods. One might also assume a logarithmic time scale with each day from day 1 to 6 decreasing by a factor of 10. However when one does this the order and symmetry and scriptural truth of days 1-7 or 1-13 is lost. If one stretches the time of diatoms and algae grew in the ocean along with sea weeds and assumes a warm climate, biomass can be created. Once you have pollinating plants, the method of pollination by insects and birds is needed, although 10% of plants are pollinated by the wind. If very long times are allowed for these plants, bio-cycles would be messed up unless one has relatively short creation time periods that overlap. One could have vegetation growing in the ocean for up to 1650 yrs by the time of the flood when it was buried and compressed to create kerogen. It also possible as Snelling notes(p.470-75) that a warmer pre-flood climate existed and grew vegetation mats in the ocean at more rapid rates. Snelling also provides considerable evidence that coal, one form of kerogen, can be formed rapidly, when buried vegetation is heated and compressed(Chap. 70,120).

The question of how animals could form many different species after the flood will be explored using **Criswell** (web 76). Geographical and ecological isolation can cause speciation. This could have occurred after the flood as animals spread out. Criswell is quoted "However, it is not correct to assume that a few thousand species would have produced the millions of species extant (alive) today. There are fewer than 30,000 extant species of mammals, birds, reptiles, and possibly land-reproducing amphibians (many salamanders) that were represented on the Ark. The millions of other species are the invertebrates (>95 percent of all animal species), fish, and a few aquatic mammals and reptiles that survived in the water during the Flood. The processes of speciation discussed above need to only double the number of animal species from 15,000 to 30,000. This is certainly a feasible process based on observable science."

Some assertions in **Satinover**'s book on the Bible code will be briefly given because it relates to the view of Judaism and the age of the earth. He asserted (p.70) that many Jews believe in a layered meaning to Genesis, with children being taught the 6-24 hr day creation view. Jewish Rabbis studied the Torah and founded the Zohar and Kabbalah which give deeper and more mystical meanings of the Torah including four layers of meaning(web81). These Jews also appear to believe in a historical Genesis and Torah. He stated(p. 83, 275) that some calculations of noted rabbis gave and age of the earth of 15.3 billion yrs. These appear to use speculative ELS codes based on the 42 lettered name of God. These findings were written long before scientists discovered their more precise estimates of the age of the universe. Teachings about the Jewish Sephirot talks of 10 dimensions of light energy being reduced to 3-4 which fits with string theory.

Ross's book *More than a Theory* summarizes the arguments from science for an old earth and for man's creation about 50,000 yrs. ago(Ross p.59,181). This also argues that Neanderthals and other hominids, although old, are genetically much different that humans (p.185). Also see Rana's book *Who Was Adam* which is briefly noted at the end of the biology section. Legal cases have ruled against YEC and ID because it lacked scientific integrity and proof for a young earth(p.39, 219). Models and predictions must be detailed, distinctive and comprehensive to be of any use. Their RTB model is compared with 3 other models including YEC. RTB has created an ongoing electronic appendix for model updating and comparing of new findings and predictions. Concordists accept the record of nature and science as a second book of God's revelation. In this, findings of science appear primary and change our interpretation of the Bible, so both science and the Bible fit(p.32). The RTB model thus scores highest, when judged by findings of conventional science(p.231). However, sometimes conventional scientists start with a naturalistic and old earth viewpoint and thus end up there. When most details in creation are made to fit current science, there are fewer miracles for God to do.

A few points from **Schaeffer**'s book *Genesis in Space and Time* will be noted:

Chap. 1 p.13-31 He noted **Ps. 136 ties history of Creation**, the exodus and crossing Red sea to present times and meeting our needs. This means Genesis as historical as is the record of Abraham. There are evidences of God's planning before the creation: John 17:24; John 17:5 and Titus 1:2. A rhetorical question is raised: When does one stop discounting the miracles and history of Genesis? At Gen. Chap. 3 after the creation and fall; or at 6-9 with the Flood, or at 11 with the tower of Babylon, or in 18 where Sarah has a child beyond child birthing age, in 19 where angels appear on earth and Sodom is destroyed, in 30 where Jacob's flocks are multiplied, in 40 where Joseph interprets the King's dreams. 2 Peter 3:5-7 Has the flow of history from creation to the end as does Ps. 33:6,9; 148:5.

Chap. 2 p.33-52 Gen 1, 2 are complimentary; Adam and Eve are historical; Jesus refers to them as does Paul, Mathew and Luke. 1Tim. 2:13-4 For

Adam was first and then Eve. John refers to Cain and Hebrews to Abel. Man was created in the image of God and that differentiates him as in Gen. 1:27; 5:1-2. It is not that we are strong or have powerful brains; we are to have a relationship with God. Machines do not love. Man is to have dominion over the earth, but not of heaven. Gen. 1:16; 2:19-20; Ps.5:8; 115:16 The fallen man is separated from God but he is still in his image: **Chap. 3** p.55-66 God's creation was originally good. Many creatures and organisms were created in unity and order. They were not all aware of their purpose but did fulfill it. Adam and Eve not likely created on the same day and a day may be longer than 24 hrs. Creation was at peace with itself and vegetarian as in Gen.1: 29-30; Not until Gen.9:2 did animals fear man. **Satan's rebellion may have played a part** in the fear and earth changes as in Is. 14:12-17. History is going somewhere: Rom. 8:21-3 Creation groans, but will be delivered. Is. 11:6-9 tells of the wolf and lamb. Man is flawed as is nature now, and not at peace.

Chap. 4 Point of decision: p.69-83. We are to love God. Mat. 22:36-8; Deut.6:4-6. Loving also means obeying. Man is given freedom to obey or not. That is why disobeying was a problem for Adam and Eve, who had been warned of the consequences. Satan is a liar and back of many lies. Eventually proud humanism combines with Satan**.** Eve was tempted by Satan and her eyes. Coveting was part of it. Adam was only tempted by Eve. Marriage brings the union of man with woman. The point is made that the Bible is not exhaustive in truth on many topics as in John 21:25.

Chap. 5 The Fall: p.85-101 This results in the fall of the whole human race. Rom.5:12-19; Jer. 17:9; Is 53:6 We are now under the law, but can't keep it. Christ is our only hope. In the garden there was open communication with God. **After the fall** this was broken and **God made some changes**; the earth was cursed and brought fourth thorns and thistles. Schaeffer says the world was changed and became abnormal. There was perhaps a gene change in plants or a new creation here. Man was to eat by work from the sweat of his brow. Before this there was work in the garden, but it was easier. **Separations occurred**: Man from God, man from man as in the killing of Abel; Man from himself in psychological problems; man from nature in having less respect and care for it.

Chap. 6 The 2 humanities: Thy seed and her seed from Gen. 3:15 The serpent's seed and Eve's seed. Heb. 2:13-14; Rom.16:20. Christ is seed of woman in Gen. 3:15 and the second Adam and the founder of a new race of believers as in Rom. 5:12-21. Adam and Eve were given a new suit of clothes from an animal sacrifice, a covering from God. Christ was a solution to the separations. In Gen 4:4 Able makes an animal sacrifice to the Lord. However the Bible does not fully explain the need and reasons for sacrifices at this time. God may have communicated to the early believers beyond what is in the scriptures. Also for Noah taking clean animals in Gen. 7:2 and for his sacrifice in 8:20, the Bible does not yet define clean animals, but Noah knew.

Chap.7 Noah and the Flood: p.121-40 He also argues as in Gen 6:1-2, that the sons of God taking the daughters of men, means angels married earthly women and this resulted in the giants. He cites Jude 6-7 and Job 1:6 A number of scriptures warn against intermarriage of Godly and ungodly lines as in 1Cor. 7:39. There is a pattern of Godly men disappearing and following judgments as in Gen. 6:5. **"These are the generations of" appears many times in Gen. 5 uniting it as one whole.** Mat.24:26-7 makes a parallel of the times of Noah and the 2nd coming as does 2Peter 3:3-7 Watch and be ready. The flood was universal over the whole earth. In Gen. 6:4 there were giants on the earth from improper intermarriage. My speculation is that it is also possible that evil angels fostered mating of large creatures or apes with humans which would be an abomination to God.

Chap. 8.:p.143-60 Ark lands in Armenia. The Holman Bible says Turkey or Armenia. Gen. 11:4 "Lets make a name for ourselves" is a declaration on Humanism. Babel means confusion or we are at the gate of God.

A brief summary of the book by Ward on Rare Earth is given on the web site along with another article on time: see http://creatinoapologetics. net Ward's book is naturalistic but noted the high improbability of advanced life on other planets. The time article noted that God is in complete control of time using it for his own purposes. His reckoning of time on days 1,2,3 and in general may be different than ours. Also, Whiddon(125) tracked the us of the words 'God Created' vs. 'let there be' in Gen. Chap. 1 and pointed out that God Created is only used on days 1, 5 and 6. He infers that 'let there be' would allow the interpretation that the sun and stars could have been created earlier in day 1 and just became visible on day 4, where 'let there be' is used.

Some of **my own speculations and integrations** will now be given. For most of the book summary arguments from references and have been given presenting the original author's views. In a few cases some integration of several differing references was given with suggested resolution. My view of the 'how of creation' is still evolving and I try to be open to new evidences and revelations. Some key views were stated in the summary and will not be repeated here. This section is called speculation, as these views which could change with new information. Many other authors have stated their views well. There are many authors who I have not yet read. There is not great importance of arguing that the sun and earth are young, if it will trip up a new believer, with a science background. Although there are augments for a young sun and earth(Humphreys and Hartnett) they are not well accepted by most scientists. The augments that God created everything are enough. The old earth creationists believe God fined tuned the universe and the big bang. Some scientists have changed from atheists to dedicated Christians by believing in a fine tuned big bang, as in Heeren's book. There are the alternate views of the gap theory as in Gen.1:1 where the heavens (sun and stars) and the earth were created early on. These views are outlined by Ross in Appendix 5, Chap. 3-5. His view was that on day 4 the moon and sun and stars became visible from earth as the atmosphere became transparent and clear. Whiddon also supports this view. A straight forward reading of Gen. 1:14-19 does not appear to support this view, but it is possible. If one clips out this view plus the gap theory, then the sun and earth can be old without upsetting the remaining 24 hr. days of creation much. Then the animals and man can be all young (less than 10,000 yrs) and all soulish animal death can be after the fall. Many authors have made the point that the Bible is not exhaustive in truth on many topics. The Bible was not intended to be a precise scientific handbook nor exhaustive in truth (Schaeffer 1976-p.76). Some details are not stated. In this vein, it is then possible that God created cyanobacteria, other bacteria, algae, worms and insects early on and did not mention them. This could have formed some biodeposits and created higher oxygen in the atmosphere, and made the earth and soil more habitable. This would then also allow the documented bacterial fossils to be old in the oldest known rocks. Snelling appears more of an expert on geology than Ross. Snelling's explanations including the world wide flood in the days of Noah and the Baumgardner model of rapid plate tectonics during the flood, followed by the ice age seem to fit the puzzle more reasonably. Back tracking a bit, it appears more logical to me that Adam had an extra week, as in book of Jubilees Appendix 6, to name the animals and meet Eve. A very rapid naming of the animals and meeting of Eve in a few hours, does not seem correct. The early hominid fossils noted by Ross in *Who Was Adam* presents questions for study, as they are well documented. Nevertheless, I am reluctant to discard the genealogies in the Bible and in Cooper which appear true and thus agree with a young age for man of less than 10,000 yrs. Nevertheless, the days of creation and universe age could be viewed as a topic open for discussion and more understanding. The creation of the universe with the appearance of age is also possible as Bergman suggested at the end of the section on miracles. I pray that Christian scientists and theologians can remain open to new understandings and revelations, rather than entrenched in their stated positions. It is also my hope that some of this material in this book and on the web site will be useful in sowing seeds and in witnessing.

Appendix 7 Some Questions one can ask to expose WorldViews

Questions are often better than giving a lecture and aid in opening discussions. The purpose is to help the individual discover the truth. Many have not thought through their world view completely, and logical holes will be found. Lisle and Meister state that theism is the most logically sound world view. There are also holes or weaknesses in various progressive creation and theistic evolution views. Remember to do this with love and empathy for the person. Some may have not explored their world view before. Some may have explored it, but decided for personal pleasure or life style reasons, to reject God.

Questions for Atheists and Agnostics, Skeptics, Naturalists, Empiricists:

See pg.3-4 on logic and witnessing dialog and Appendix 2.

Ask if they think truth is knowable. If they say no, note that this is a self-defeating claim. Keep asking how do you know that is true? Try to get to the ultimate standard. Look for contradictions. Do you agree that things that begin have a cause? What started the universe?

A simple question to start: What do you believe happens when people die? Follow with how do you know that is true? Also ask what if you are wrong? (This relates to Pascal's wager). Does man have a purpose or meaning in life? He may say you can choose whatever purpose you want. Then if I choose a purpose to be cruel, and hurt as many people as I can without getting caught by the law, is that is OK then? How do you explain man's conscience, rational mind, reliable memory, language, instincts, retrospective analysis & planning and asking why questions about himself and the universe? Why are some rational men very cruel and others kind with bad thoughts at times? Are our feelings of guilt all irrational? Do you think man has free will and is responsible for his decisions? What do the courts and the majority of people think? Several statistical studies study found a higher incidence of depression and suicide among those with no religion (web 90). Are you a good person? Relative to the 10 commandments, have you ever lied, stole, had lustful thoughts, viewed pornography, called other persons bad names or bullied? Do you believe in naturalism and empiricism then? How do you explain instincts? For example a Monarch butterfly can fly to an exact destination over 1000 miles away and it has never been there before. It also dissolves itself from a pupa into a liquid and then reassembles itself into a butterfly. Do you agree with a number of scientists that say DNA is an information code? How do you explain the origin of life and the first bacterial cell? (See Chap. 10-12 of Rana The origin of Life p.79). The simplest bacteria has 1500 genes, which are composed of DNA and RNA which are composed of proteins, that are composed of amino acids. The probability of the 1500 genes forming is one in 10^{112500}

Questions for Moral Relativists: Do you think morals are objectively true? What is your basis of deciding right and wrong? Is it wrong then to torture babies as Hitler's agents did or burn wives at their husband's funerals as is done in some parts of India? If we evolved from random molecules and chimps why would that be true? Are we obliged to be kind and loving to other people? So if morals are just social constructs(we can make them up), can they change with time and culture? At one time slavery was legal in the US and in Europe. Why does slavery go against the idea of survival of the fittest? At one time the King or dictator was the law but he didn't have to follow general law. Why is that wrong? What is the basis for individual human rights? Point out that there is no basis, that we are aware of, for individual rights in humanism, Marxism and socialism, only rights for the masses. The dignity and value of the individual is based on being made in God's image.

Questions for Christians who do not hold to a Literal-Historical Genesis:

How do you view the inerrancy and truth of scriptures?

Are you aware that the books of the Bible are classified in groups as historical narratives, as poetical books, as prophetic books and as letters? Did you know that Genesis is often classed as a historical narrative just like the gospels and the book of Acts?

Do you think Genesis is full of myths and poetic allegory, or is it a book of history?

Why do you think the first 2-4 chapters are poetic and symbolic and the rest of the book is not?

What is your view of miracles and history in the Bible, is that true?

At what point in Genesis would you say the book changes and the miracles and history are now true, but they were not true before? There are history and miracles throughout most of Genesis and also in Exodus. Who do you think wrote most of the first 5 books of the Bible?

In John 5:46-47 Jesus said "<u>Moses</u>—because <u>he wrote</u> about me. But if you don't believe <u>his writings</u>,"—) John 7:19 "Didn't Moses give you the law?" So if Jesus says Moses had writings and gave us the law, wouldn't this be the 1st five books of the Bible? If not, why not?

How do you view the Fall of Man in Gen. 3? Is this true as the basis of all man's sin? If it is not true, why do we all need Christ as savior for our sin?

Do you think we evolved from chimps over millions of yrs and then God implanted his spirit in Adam and Eve? Aren't we physically and mentally also quite different from chimps?

Questions for Old Earth Evolutionists and Day-Age proponents: How do you explain Ex. 20:9-11 that states "for in six days the Lord made the heavens and the earth and sea and all that is in them, and rested on the seventh day." This was written by God's own finger in the context of keeping the Sabbath and a 7 day week. Mark 10:6 <u>Jesus said</u> "But from the beginning of the creation, God made them male and female." Would you agree this implies the Adam and Eve were created near the beginning of creation, not millions of yrs later? Also see Mark 13:19 and Luke 11:50-51. How do you explain the many uses of morning and evening in days 1-6?

Questions for those who do not hold to a world wide flood:

See Snelling in the Geology section, p. 92,94,97 Why would a huge ark be needed if the flood was local? Couldn't Noah, his family and the animals just have migrated to a different area, as he had a 100+ yr advance notice?

Do you know that continuous sedimentary layers with marine fossils are very broad in extent, some extending thousands of miles? Doesn't that argue for large flood/s not small ones?

How do you explain many layers of marine fossils being a mile high in the Grand Canyon and 5 miles high in the Himalayas? A very large flood from the ocean would explain one layer deposition. They could have been uplifted due to volcanism or mountain building from tectonic plate movement. How would you explain their repeated sinking and re-flooding millions of yrs later? Plate movements are generally reported as only few cm/yr. I am not aware of any mechanisms for sinking of the same mountains 7-9 different times are you?

Questions for 6-24hr creation, especially for days 1,2,3:

How do you explain having the earth before space, matter and energy? $E=MC^2$ Einstein said space was like a stretched fabric and thus the earth would be placed in it. How do you explain the bacteria and algae appearing before plants? Answer: This is a mystery I do not understand; one explanation is the big bang. The Bible doesn't note bacteria's or algae's creation. It doesn't note worm's creation either but they aid the soil. God views time differently than we do and left some mysteries.

Appendix 8 Power Point Presentations and Papers

Some of the talks below are brief (6-10 min) and a few are longer.

PowerPointPresentations	Audience	Papers
Arguments from Logic and Philosophy	Adult or College Nonbelievers	3
Creation Evangelism	Adult Church Group	1
Biblical Basis of Young Creation	Adult Church Group	1
Earth History, DNA, Races	Adult or College Nonbelievers	1
7 C's of Creation &A is for Adam	Grade School Church Group	
Dinosaurs and Odd Creatures	Grade School Church Group	1
Deception and Biases in Evolution	Adult or College Nonbelievers	1
World Views and Evolution	Adult or College Nonbelievers	1
Values of our Founding Fathers	Adult or College Nonbelievers	1

Apologetics for Kids	Church Youth Group
Are we losing our Youth to Naturalism?	Adult church Group

Creation Science and Apologetics Web site: http://creationapologetics.net, http://www.youtube.com/watch?v=Dhdy_LvnQoM

About The Author

Dr. Jim Tofflemire was an engineer and research scientist for over 40 yrs. He has a Dr. of Engr. in Environmental Engr. and Masters in Christian Ministry with Campus Crusade for Christ. He has written over 50 publications in various media and technical journals and is a Distinguished Toastmaster, DTM. He is available to do talks on creation science or apologetics for youth and adults. A reference list of books and DVD's available for borrowing or download of book summaries is posted on the web site above